GRAHAM LOVELUCK-EDWARDS

HISTORIC PUBS OF
WALES

Dedicated to my very patient and understanding wife for both indulging me, and for sharing in my passions.

I said I was only popping out for three and I'd be home by ten.
But I always get those two mixed up.
Graham Loveluck-Edwards

CONTENTS

FOREWORD

You could be forgiven for thinking that what you have here is just a book about old pubs. If I am honest, that is what I set out to write. I am one of those people who cannot pass by an old and decrepit-looking pub without popping in for a pint and asking the landlord, 'What's the story behind this place then?' This book is the fruit of a good thirty years of such conversations.

But as I started to string all those stories together, I realised that the sum of all those parts added up to something quite different – a history of Wales. I realise how grand that sounds, but it should not really come as a surprise. Pubs, inns and taverns have long played a central role in British society, ever since the Romans first came and introduced us to the concept of the *taverna*. They have always been socially inclusive, places where your station in life is left at the door, where everyone can talk to anyone. They are at the heart of our communities, fostering a culture of comradeship and fellowship between neighbours and colleagues.

And half-cut bonhomie is not the full extent of their influence on our modern world. Various religious movements used pubs as meeting places in their early days, some of which you will read about in these pages. Karl Marx and Frederick Engels, the godfathers of communism, famously bonded on a pub crawl along London's Tottenham Court Road. Many uprisings, revolutions, revolts, demonstrations and rebellions can be traced back to a meeting in (or in the room above) a pub. And a top tip to any politician whose expensive education might alienate them from the electorate: nothing says 'man of the people' louder than posing in your local boozer with a smile on your face and a pint in your hand.

As Samuel Johnson once mused, 'There is nothing which has yet been contrived by man, by which so much happiness is produced as a good tavern or inn.'

But things have not always gone smoothly for the local boozer.

They were the object of protest and derision at the hands of the temperance movement and the clean-living non-conformists and Methodists. During the Crimean War, they were blamed for the poor productivity of industrial workers supporting the war effort, which saw the introduction of the most bizarre set of licensing laws and opening hours anywhere in the world, and lead to Oscar Wilde famously quipping, 'Work is the curse of the drinking classes.'

But despite all the fluctuations in our artistic, political and economic climates, pubs have somehow managed to stand fast in our communities throughout the centuries. Not without compromise or change but, somehow, always managing to adapt and find their place.

Until now.

In the last twenty years, across the UK, pubs have been closing at a startling rate. For a long time I considered this largely trimming of the fat. That the places that were closing were mainly flat-roofed monstrosities on industrial estates, with nothing especially distinct to offer their clientele. However, in the last ten years things have clearly gone beyond that, and the ranks of truly great pubs that have been lost have only been swelled further by the COVID 19 pandemic.

Legislation to restrict the spread of the virus meant that many pubs had to be closed for over a year. Yes, there was some financial support, but after having their doors closed for so long, it is miraculous there are any pubs left at all.

It was this thought that made me realise the urgent need to capture the rich and distinctive contributions many of these establishments have made to our nation's history and culture. Before we lose many of them forever.

This book sets out to celebrate some of the most interesting buildings, with some of the most fascinating histories, in the land. For me these old pubs are as significant in their beauty and in their gravitas as any castle, stately home, palace or cathedral — it is only because they are, by definition, 'of the people' that they get nothing like the same degree of recognition or celebration.

Having said that, I have to confess a caveat. Comparatively little of what you will read in this book comes with much in the way of verifiable historical evidence behind it. In fact, I imagine there is something in pretty much every paragraph to make a serious historian tut, roll their eyes or shake their head in disbelief. Some real whoppers.

So why have I written them up? First of all, because they are great stories. I doubt if the brothers Grimm stopped what they were doing because they couldn't find a primary source to verify the location of Little Red Riding Hood's cottage. Many of the stories associated with these old pubs are so spectacular they will make your hair stand on end. So please do not get hung up on such trivial constraints as evidence or likelihood.

The reason why there are so many wild tales of folklore associated with our pubs comes, ironically, from a piece of legitimate, verifiable history. In the eighteenth century it was very fashionable for the young bucks of aristocratic families to broaden their horizons and go on what they rather nobly called 'the Grand Tour'. This involved travelling across Europe to visit what were then the great cultural capitals of the world, ostensibly to take in the majesty of their architecture, be moved by the allurement of their artworks, and seduced by the vibrancy of their cultures and populous. In reality it was just a very posh Club 18-30 holiday. The number of honourable young men who returned home having lost their estates and fortunes at gaming tables, or riddled with syphilis, betray what really went on. Then, in the nineteenth century, that cheeky upstart Napoleon Bonaparte decided to wage war on most of Europe, and our young aristocrats had to find somewhere closer to home to let their hair down. This led to a boom in what we would today call 'staycations', and places like the Wye Valley, Snowdonia, the Cotswolds, the Fens and the Lake District rocketed in popularity.

Back then there was no way for inns to advertise themselves. They had to rely on word of mouth. Places with legitimate, historical or aesthetic credentials were cleaning up, so the landlords of the other inns started to concoct wild and creative claims in order to compete. Perhaps their clearly seventeenth-century building had in fact been frequented by William the Conqueror's grandfather; maybe King Canute had popped by for a pint after failing to turn back the tide.

Then towards the end of the nineteenth century there was a huge gothic revival, and everyone became obsessed by the occult and the supernatural. It was no longer enough to claim that your pub was ancient; now you needed a gory incident or a resident ghost too.

This brings us to today, when it is quite hard to distinguish fact from ludicrous fiction. But if you secretly don't really mind which is which, then this is the book for you. It is our chance to give these stories, and the pubs they are set in, where the flag stone floors, oak beams and log fires creak under the weight of stories, legends, folklore, hauntings, history and various famous patrons, the recognition they deserve.

You may be wondering what qualifies me to write this account. Well first off: I love pubs. Probably more than most people would consider healthy. You know how happy your dog gets when you throw a ball for him? That's me in a pub. I just *really* love them.

Secondly, this book started to write itself. Let me explain how.

After I published my first book *Legends and Folklore of Bridgend and the Vale* (still available in all good outlets) people who had read it started emailing or coming up to me in the street, with stories of local folklore that I might be interested in. And without exception, they all took place in, or revolved around, a pub.

Here's an example. A very old friend of mine told me how, in the 1990s, she used to be in a relationship with a publican, and that they lived in a flat above the pub they ran together. I knew the pub she was talking about and had been there myself. It was in a coastal village in South Wales, and it was an establishment where people had been pulling pints for the best part of 300 years. The pub had a turbulent history. The stretch of coast near the village where it was situated was notoriously dangerous to navigate, littered with rocks that had ripped open the belly of many a passing ship. The bodies of sailors unfortunate enough to founder upon them would be carried up to this pub and stored on its tables, until they could be buried or disposed of. The landlord at the time, known to be an unscrupulous man of low moral fibre, would charge villagers and passing travellers six pence to come and view the bodies.

In the depths of many dark, stormy nights, long after the last customer had wound their unsteady way home, my friend and her partner would hear strange sounds over the wind and rain lashing against their bedroom window. The sound of wailing and agonised screams would emanate from the pub downstairs, but when they went down to investigate, there would be no one there. There were also cold spots in the pub where no degree of heating could get the temperature to a comfortable level.

Now, I hear you ask, why have you put that story in the introduction rather than write about the pub in more detail? The truth is, where this all took place is no longer a pub, it is someone's family home – and I would rather not scare the bejezzus out of them, if they are currently living there in perfect tranquillity.

This edition covers the pubs of my homeland: the ancient inns and taverns of Wales. From the rugged, mountainous north, through the rolling pastures of mid Wales, to the shores of the Bristol Channel in the south. And from east to west, we meander from the ancient monument of Offa's Dyke, which borders our neighbours in England, to the dramatic clifftops stuck in an eternal faceoff with the Irish Sea.

V

It is a journey, an adventure and a delight to share these amazing places with you, and the stories associated with them.

For clarity, I should point out that this book does not set out to be a good food or good ale guide. Pubs earn their place in this book by virtue of being ancient or interesting, their beauty and/or the stories and legends associated with them. However, where it is applicable, there is mention of particularly good home cooked food or fine ale. While I am visiting these fine hostelries, it would be rude not to. Not to mention, I couldn't otherwise justify claiming back all those receipts!

MONMOUTHSHIRE AND THE ANCIENT KINGDOM OF GWENT

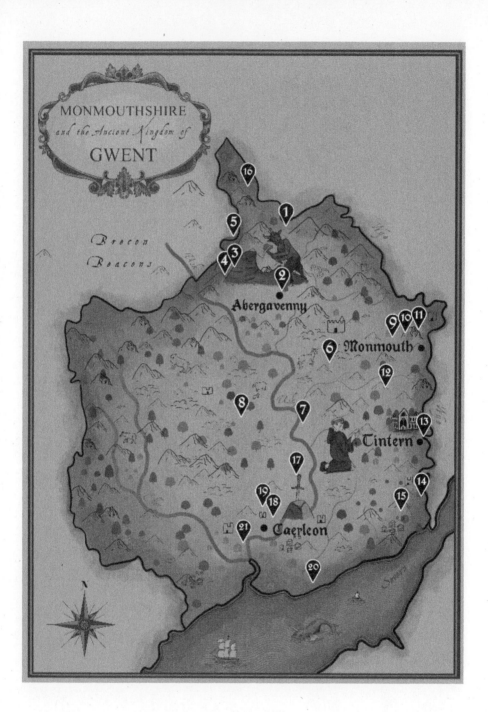

M onmouthshire, like all border counties, has a character and culture unique to itself. It is a beautiful, historic county, rich with conundrums and contradictions.

For many years, right up to 1974, it was not considered to be part of Wales at all, owing to its omission from Henry VIII's Act of Union in 1536. The first 'Welcome to Wales' sign you would encounter driving east to west was at St Mellons, just east of Cardiff. Even now there is a small political movement that manages to garner a few votes in elections, pledging to make the county part of England again.

As such, you may be forgiven for thinking that Monmouthshire is not a particularly *Welsh* part of Wales. However, I remember once walking into a pub in Monmouth one Saturday afternoon, when Wales were playing in a Six Nations rugby international. Everywhere you looked was awash with red, every man and woman in the establishment bursting with Celtic pride. When Shane Williams scored a glorious try, there could be no doubt what country you were in.

The landscape of the county is dominated by the courses of its great rivers: the Severn, the Wye and the Usk. It is good, fertile farming country and for the most part very lush and green, with soft, rolling pastures. It has a very flat southern flank which brushes against the lapping waves of the Severn Estuary, an area largely below sea level, drained initially by the Romans and more latterly by the monks of Goldcliffe to form the Gwent Levels. To the east the landscape is at its most dramatic along the border with England, where sheer cliffs and steep valley walls tower over the banks of the Wye between Chepstow and Monmouth.

It has a very rich history dating back to before the Roman invasion. Caerwent, which still boasts some very well-preserved Roman remains, was the capital of Silurian South Wales. The Silures were a loose affiliation of local tribes led by the charismatic, ancient Welsh chieftain Caradog. The Silures managed to repel Roman invasion for over a decade, but once they had been defeated, the Romans colonised the area, most notably at Caerwent and the Roman fort of Isca Augusta, in what is now Caerleon on the banks of the Usk.

After the Norman invasion of South Wales in the eleventh century, the castles at Abergavenny, Monmouth and Usk were all, at one point or another, royal households, and the county produced one of England's all time most celebrated monarchs, Henry V. Henry's fame rests on managing to defeat the French, occupying much of the country, then having the good fortune to die before the French summarily kicked the English back out again, thus immortalising him in British history forever.

During the Industrial Revolution, Monmouthshire became the tinderbox for a popular uprising, as the Chartists famously marched across the county into Newport to demand votes and fair treatment before the law for every man. By modern sensibilities, hardly the most radical of demands, but enough to get them massacred by the establishment of the day, just like their counterparts in Petersfield, Manchester.

Like I said, a rich history littered with conundrums and contradictions. Perfect territory in which to find some amazing old pubs.

1.1

THE SKIRRID MOUNTAIN INN, LLANVIHANGEL CRUCORNEY

T he Skirrid Inn is one of the most famous pubs in Wales, and the first of several we shall encounter that lay claim to be the oldest. Apparently, records of it date back to 1110. History and folklore drips from every stone of this pub, making it a great one to kick off this book.

As its name suggests, the Skirrid stands in the shadow of the Skirrid Mountain, a plateau that rises like a monolith out of the ground to the north of the historic market town of Abergavenny. It is well worth a ramble to the top, as on a clear day you have amazing views across five counties, uninterrupted in any direction. The climb to the top is relatively easy going, with a clear path and, in places, ancient stone stairways to help you on your way.

The reason for the stone stairs is that, in the Middle Ages, this was considered a place of pilgrimage to visit en route to the relics at Llanthony Abbey.

Looked at from below, the mountain peak has a castellated look, due to the collapse of a section of the plateau. There are several local legends about this event. One says that the rift between the two peaks was caused by the devil sitting on the mountain. As with most Welsh legends featuring the devil, this tale more than likely dates back to pagan Celtic history, with the perpetrator originally a beast rather than the devil himself.

The other legend is that the plateau was intact until 2,000 years ago, but in the hours following Christ's crucifixion, the mountain shivered violently until the rift collapsed away, forming the shape we see today. The bigger plateau thus became known as the Great Shiver, *Ysgyryd Fawr*, and the smaller one, the Little Shiver, *Ysgyryd Fach*. The name Skirrid is just an Anglicised pronunciation of *ysgyryd*, which is Welsh for 'shiver'. It was this legend that led to the site being declared a place of pilgrimage.

There is an intrinsic relationship between many old pubs and the church in Wales. You will see plenty more examples as we romp through this book. In this instance it is clear that a twelfth-century pub in this location would have owed a lot of its trade to pilgrims passing through.

Not all of the history of the Skirrid Inn is so godly, however. There are far more sinister stories attached to it. In addition to being a pub, from the twelfth to the seventeenth century the building was also used as a courthouse, as well as a gaol and a place of execution.

I mentioned earlier that it has long been claimed that the Skirrid Inn has been in existence since at least 1110. This claim relates to a record of a trial which took place at an inn in the village at the time. This was not especially unusual. In many rural villages across the UK, the only secular public building big enough to use as a court would have been the inn. For the same reason, they were also frequently used as temporary morgues. In this particular case, the trial was of two local men, one by the name of John Crowther, who had been charged with stealing a sheep; and his brother, who was charged with robbery and violence. They were convicted, and John was hanged until dead from a beam at the inn itself, while his brother was sent away to prison.

There are also stories that Owain Glyndŵr, the fifteenth-century Welsh nobleman who led a revolt to rid Wales of its tyrannical English King Henry IV, using the inn as a rallying point, to marshal his troops before marching on Pontrilas. There is a mounting stone in the inn's cobbled courtyard that he is believed to have used to climb onto his horse before leading his men into battle. Many of his men, returning from battle, are said to have returned to the inn for refreshment, or in the case of the injured, to receive treatment for their wounds. Many of those are said not to have survived the night.

I mentioned that the pub owes a lot of its more positive history to religion. But religion's darkest hour in British history also touched the Skirrid. In its long history, there is one bloody episode that eclipses all others in terms of goriness and notoriety.

The man at its heart was known as Judge Jeffries, who earned himself the nickname 'the Hanging Judge'.

It was 1685 and the reformation and counter-reformation had been raging in Britain since Henry VIII had declared himself head of the English church over 100 years earlier. James II had been crowned king on the death of his elder brother, Charles II. But James was treated with a great deal of suspicion, even hatred by his nobles and councillors, as he was a Catholic and they were Protestants. A plot was hatched to try to usurp him as monarch and put in his place Charles II's illegitimate but unimpeachably Protestant son, James Scott, the First Duke of Monmouth. The uprising culminated in a huge and bloody battle on the plains of Somerset, near the Great Sedgemoor Drain.

The attempted coup failed dismally as most of the troops fighting for Monmouth were little more than farmers and country folk armed only with pitchforks, and what they faced was, by the standards of the day, a well-disciplined and well-equipped professional army.

Monmouth himself fled the battlefield but was captured and beheaded for treason under an Act of Parliament (meaning he did not need to stand trial). The other rebel leaders and their surviving cohorts were rounded up and tried for treason. James II wanted to send out a signal and arranged it so that those charged with plotting against him were to be tried by someone who would take no nonsense, and dispense tough justice without compunction. The man that was chosen for that job was Judge Jeffries, and the series of cases he presided over became known as 'the Bloody Assizes', due to the sheer number of people who faced summary trial and execution. He heard cases in

7

courts from Chester to the Solent.

Which brings us back to the Skirrid Inn, where the Hanging Judge is reputed to have presided over the cases of those local men who had found themselves on the wrong side of the battle. Legend has it that more than 180 men were hanged from the beam at the inn, where the scorch-marks the ropes made can still be seen to this day. All at the hands of the Hanging Judge Jeffries and his Bloody Assizes.

This bloody episode, with its rich tapestry of religion, terror, conspiracy, death and pain, has earned the Skirrid Inn the crown of the most haunted pub in Wales. It has featured on TV programmes such as *Extreme Ghost Stories* and *Most Haunted* with Yvette Fielding, and over the years, its savvy owners have held ghost hunt evenings for souls brave enough to stay the night there. In my research for this book, I read accounts of all the usual stuff: guests getting a distinctly sinister feeling of angst in bedroom one, or the corridor where the hangman's noose used to dangle from the main beam; doors slamming, shuffling footsteps and hushed voices whispering in corridors; glasses flying across the bar before smashing against walls; cold spots; the unembodied sound of cackling, witch-like laughter, etc., etc. Typical ghost story stuff. But there are also a few more distinctive ghost stories specific to the inn.

The first relates to room number two, where the ghost of a thirty-five-year-old woman by the name of Fanny Price is said to prowl. She is reputed to have worked at the inn and died of consumption in the eighteenth century – but her spirit remains. She is sometimes heard and sometimes seen entering and walking around the room.

And in the main bar area, from time to time the ghosts of Owain Glyndŵr's army are said to appear, returning in celebratory mood from battle, occasionally heralded by the sound of a lute.

There was also a former landlord who complained of mischief and breakages occurring through the night, which only abated when he took to leaving a tankard of ale on a small stone shelf above the great fireplace every night. The tankard was always empty when he collected it in the morning. One night he heard a sound downstairs that he thought might have been a guest at the inn helping himself to the beer. When he crept downstairs and peered through the door, he saw the true recipient of the ale. The Devil himself.

The majority of the building as you see it today is late seventeenth century, so claims of roots stretching back to 1110 might have you scratching your head. Some of the roof beams are also said to have been recycled from the masts of an Elizabethan war ship. There are plenty of mood hoovers around who will tell you that the building clearly dates from much later than the events from all these stories. Or that there is no documented evidence that Judge Jeffries came anywhere near the place. But where's the fun in that?

1.2

THE KING'S ARMS, ABERGAVENNY

A bergavenny can trace its history back thousands of years, to a Roman fort standing watch over the river Usk. Later, the Normans built a castle and a priory in the same location, and the town grew around those. But its heyday was in the Middle Ages, when it was a booming market town. It is in this period, sometime around the fourteenth century, that the building the King's Arms stands in today was built, next to the old west gate, just inside the town's ancient town walls.

Abergavenny's boom gradually fizzled out, only to be partially resurrected during the Georgian era, when most of the houses and buildings in the centre of the town were extensively modernised or rebuilt. However, by the end of the nineteenth century, many of its once fine medieval buildings in the outer corners had fallen into disrepair and ruin.

The King's Arms continued to trade throughout, while the street it stood in all but crumbled around it. The state of dilapidation of so many of these buildings, combined with the lack of people prepared to throw money at saving them, led to a lot of this mediaeval street, the old west gate and the narrow, twisting streets, alleys and passages around it, being demolished and cleared away to create room for modern highways and car parks and other similar vacuums of romance and interest. The end result is that the King's Head now stands in isolation, an island of antiquity in a sea of modernity.

Around the time this was happening, Monmouthshire was blessed to have a very passionate and enthusiastic local historian by the name of Fred Hando, who used to write articles and draw sketches for the Newport-based newspaper *the South Wales Argus*. He wrote from the turn of the twentieth century until the 1960s, and as such captured a lot of the changing fortunes of Abergavenny, including keeping records and hand-drawn sketches of the houses that were demolished in this time.

He is also, incidentally, responsible for keeping alive a lot of the old stories captured throughout this book.

While picking through the bones of demolished buildings in Tudor Street, Hando made many fascinating discoveries, not least a cellar revealed by the demolition of a house that had formerly stood next to the pub. It was clear from the construction of this cellar that at some point it had been a prison cell accessed from the gate tower next door, which, by this point, had already been demolished. In another nearby building, 'Gunter's House', he spotted that the demolition of a neighbouring property had disturbed a false wall in the attic, now visible from outside the house. That disturbance had revealed a religious painting on the other side of the wall, which had previously been hidden from sight since the Reformation. Clearly the inhabitants of this house had remained Catholic, and met in secret there to celebrate Mass. Fortunately, this building has survived and is now marked with a blue plaque, thanks mainly to Hando's determination to save it.

The King's Arms itself is a long, low whitewashed building with bowed walls, black painted sash windows and a cluster of red and yellow brick chimneys. It also boasts a striking coat of arms above the door, commemorating a royal connection. In 1625, Charles I, whilst on his flight from defeat at Naseby, is reputed to have stayed at the King's Arms, and in doing so gave it its name. He is also thought to have stayed there on a second visit, much later in his reign, during his flight from the Parliamentarians. In the nineteenth century, a sculptor was commissioned to carve a coat of arms to commemorate this royal patronage.

Inside, the ceilings boast some fine carved beams, and in the main bar the ceiling is bowed and very low. This room is the headquarters of the Royal Navy Association, and as such there are plenty of framed ships on the walls. In the nineteenth century, the pub had its own micro-brewery attached. It also has its own ghost. The figure of an old woman dressed in black has been seen many times descending what in the original house would have been the stairs.

1.3

THE BEAR HOTEL, CRICKHOWELL

Like all working, living buildings that have been in perpetual use across the centuries, the Bear, formerly, the White Bear has undergone substantial alterations and changes. As such, it stands today as a hodgepodge of styles, influences and ages. Its elegant Georgian façade is testimony to the seventeenth and eighteenth centuries, when it was a popular over-night stop for travellers making the five-day journey from London to Fishguard. Behind this, however, is a far older building, possibly dating from 1430. The vaulting in the cellar suggests another phase in the building's seventeenth-century regeneration.

The inn is notable for its cobbled courtyard and a stone archway leading through to the old stables. Above the entrance to the rear yard there is a sign saying 'Post Horses', marking where the coaches of the Royal Mail would stop. There are some steps in the yard positioned to ease alighting from the post coach. The stable and yard have been very well-preserved, and the frames of old coaching timetables and bell pulls for travellers to summon service still in place. At the end of this bell would have been the ostler, the servant assigned to look after the horses; 'boots', the servant who saw to the travellers' footwear; and the maid or waiter to bring some urgently needed refreshment.

Inside, the interior is large and spacious. Strange, therefore, that a well-known Georgian traveller, Sir Richard Colt-Hoare, wrote of it, 'There is not room for a large party.' Just how large were his parties?

The inn has a beautiful dark-beamed ceiling, and it is claimed that the timbers came from a yard in Newport, which specialised in recycling the masts of great ships. Now, you may recall me mentioning that the old landlord of the Skirrid Inn also claimed that *his* beams were made from the timbers of old ships. And not wishing to spoil the rest of the book, let me pre-warn you: it will crop up a few more times again!

If both these inns were on the coast or in major ports, then I probably would not even flag it up. But Crickhowell is the best part of twenty-five miles inland from Newport, and Llanvihangel Crucorney about the same. Given how bad roads were in the seventeenth century, when these ceilings were built, transportation of these timbers would have cost a fortune. Yet all around are abundant forests, where timber could have been cut, milled and transported cheaply and simply. And it's not as if the seventeenth century was a time when recycling was seen as a major priority. So, is this just another example of over creative publicans making up stories to make their pubs sound more interesting?

To give the benefit of the doubt, all these claims might originate in an innocent misunderstanding. In the seventeenth century, timber was used for pretty much everything. From building materials to household fuel. So, for ease, timber was graded. For example, if you needed firewood, you would buy the low-grade cheap stuff. If you were building a coach or a cart or a house, you might get a more premium grade. The very best timber you could buy was called 'ship's grade'. This was the stuff the Royal Navy made its ships out of, timber from hardwoods, cut from parts of the tree that didn't have any blemishes or faults, strong enough to withstand the pressures of the sea on a ship's hull or the power of a raging wind billowing the sails. It might just be that the claims of many pubs stem from a misunderstanding of the fact that a pub's roof beams are simply made from ship's grade timber. That's my theory, but who knows?

The Bear has its fair share of folklore. In 1485, men from the Crickhowell area, including Sir Richard Evans, met at the White Bear, as it was then known, to have a last drink before joining Henry Tudor's army marching east out of Pembroke. From here they marched on to Bosworth Field, where they met and defeated the army of King Richard III and the last Plantagenet king of England himself met his doom.

The Bear has always been known as a warm and welcoming place to stay. But on one evening a farmer and his daughter must have been particularly glad to arrive, after a very disturbing experience on the road from Brecon. They had been travelling all day in a horse-drawn trap with their trusty sheep dog, across the Black Mountains from Carmarthenshire, a route daunting at the best of times and especially trying in bad weather. Dusk had started to fall on the road between Brecon and Crickhowell, and as the two began their descent down the hillside towards the town, they saw in the twilight what looked like an elderly woman hobbling along the side of the road. They agreed to stop and offer her a lift into the town. But it soon became plain that something just wasn't right. Even though the two of them were in a horse-drawn vehicle, and the woman was on foot, they just did not appear to be catching up with her. The farmer flicked the reigns to encourage their horse to break into a trot, but it did nothing to increase their progress towards the old lady.

As the road began to level out, the woman turned off the road, over a stile and into a field. Out of curiosity, they pulled up at the stone stile and could see her standing some way into the field, further than it seemed likely that a woman of her advancing years could have progressed so quickly. She appeared to be in some distress, and she beckoned at the farmer and his daughter for assistance. But before either could react, their trusty sheepdog, who had been lying silently in the trap leapt to his feet, barking and snarling at the old woman. The farmer's daughter tried to calm the dog, who was upsetting the horse, when, out of the blue, the normally docile animal leapt from the trap and charged across the field, barking frantically as he went. They called and called to him to return, but although normally obedient to a fault, he ignored their calls, continuing his advance until within a couple of yards of the woman – when suddenly he foundered.

With a sharp yelp the animal found himself struggling in a deep, boggy marsh. He turned to make his way back to his master, but the ground was too soft to support him, and as he yelped and cried, it swallowed him up.

The old woman, who was known locally as 'the Gwyl', straightened her back and let out a terrifying witch-like cackle, which filled the valley air and echoed around the cwm. Then she vanished into a mist.

There is still a cheery welcome at the Bear, and it maintains many of the traditions of a coaching inn. Let us hope, for these poor two travellers' sakes, that there was a particularly warm reception that evening.

1.4
THE BRIDGE END INN, CRICKHOWELL

As the name might suggest, the Bridge End is located at the end of the ancient bridge, which crosses over the river Usk on the south side of Crickhowell. If, as you stroll across the bridge, you notice there is something quirky about the arches, you haven't lost your marbles. When the new road was built through the town, to cope with cars rather than horses, it was necessary to lengthen the bridge. But as the bridge is at an angle to the road, the end result is that it has twelve arches on one side and thirteen on the other.

The Bridge End Inn was also impacted by these changes to the road, and it now sits quite awkwardly in a fork in the road system. The part of the pub on the right as you approach it over the bridge (on the road leading up to the castle) is the oldest part. Facing the bridge, the hexagonal cottage now incorporated into the corner of the pub is an old toll house, dating back to that hated imposition on Welsh travellers, the turnpikes.

The turnpikes were billed as the solution to a very old problem. In the seventeenth century, the road network in Britain was sufficiently bad to attract the following comment:

'What am I to say of the roads in this country... mere rocky lanes full of hugeous stones as big as one's horses, and abominal holes... without either direction posts or milestones'.

Then, in Hertfordshire, in 1663, someone had an idea. All land back then was owned by one estate or another, even the roads. So if the owners were to make good the state of the roads which crossed their land, they should be allowed to charge travellers for using them, to offset the expense. To enforce these charges, these roads were run by associations known as Turnpike Trusts, which established a network of tollgates on country roads, where traffic had to stop to pay the toll. It sounded like a good idea, until some of the greedier landowners decided to charge whatever they liked.

The particular toll house now incorporated into the Bridge End Inn was built in the nineteenth century. In 1811 the annual rent for the Pontcumbeth and Crickhowell Bridge Gates, along with the Pontbrynhirt Side-Gate, was set at £416. By 1817 the rent had reduced to £370 but in 1826 the same gates commanded a rent of £665. This rollercoaster fluctuation of price hikes, without rationale or logic, is part of what made the turnpikes so hated.

In the nineteenth century, people were being taxed left, right and centre. And they were getting pretty sick of it. The turnpikes in West Wales became the subject of insurrection, in the Rebecca Riots, and there was similar unease in Crickhowell over fishing rights in the Usk. Wealthy, unscrupulous landowners were more than happy to exploit ordinary people with scandalously expensive fishing licenses. Raising the subject of fishing and tollgates in the Bridge End Inn round about 1900 would no doubt have been like debating the pros and cons of Brexit in 2016. You could easily start a riot.

But enough of nineteenth-century politics. We've all had a drink. Let's just enjoy our evening. And the Bridge End Inn is a very pleasant place to do just that. It boasts plenty of exposed stonework, aged timber beams and a beautiful fire in one of three lounges. And at the turn of the nineteenth and twentieth century, it had another big attraction. It's landlord, John Williams, had a reputation for being a bit of a healer.

In 1894 a newspaper article boasted that, by simply laying on his hands, he was able to heal conditions like rabies. It compared his track record with 'that of Monsieur Pasteur of Paris'.

And it seems he was not the only hero of the Bridge End Inn. In May 1915 the Revd. D Adams, minister at Gwernllwy Independent Chapel in Dowlais (near Merthyr Tydfil) had brought his Sunday School on an outing to Crickhowell. When walking along the bridge he spotted a child floating face down in the fast-flowing waters of the Usk. Without a moment's hesitation or thought to his own safety, he leaped onto the wall of the bridge with the agility of an Alpine Ibex, and without removing a stitch of clothing, leapt into the torrent below. He pulled the boy to the riverbank, and once assured of the child's safety, went to the landlady of the Bridge End Inn to ask for some dry clothes. This landlady was the widow of the late John Williams, and provided him with some of her departed husband's old clothes and no doubt a stiff drink too. Purely medicinal of course.

On the subject of diving into the Usk, about four miles upstream from the Bridge End Inn, there is a Neolithic standing stone called the Fish Stone. There is a legend dating back centuries, possibly millennia, that says on the night of the summer solstice, the Fish Stone comes to life and plunges into the Usk. It has a little swim about, and then leaps back into place.

1.5

NANTYFFIN CIDER MILL, TRETOWER

The Cider Mill stands on the edge of Tretower, a village that gets its name from a unique bit of Norman architecture that can still be observed to this day. A stone cylindrical tower within a square, stone keep. It is all that remains of an early twelfth-century castle that once stood surveying the strategically significant passage between the Black Mountains, into which the old Welsh tribesmen had been banished, and the lowlands of Monmouthshire, colonised by their Norman conquerors.

The castle was later besieged, first by Llewelyn ap Gruffydd, the last Welsh Prince of Wales, then by Owain Glyndŵr, who almost destroyed it completely. But this tower survived and later was incorporated into a very grand fourteenth-century manor house, which stands on the site to this day.

The Cider Mill itself was an old drover's inn. The building is listed, on account of its original stone-tiled roof. It started out as a farmhouse, built in the seventeenth century, with the cider mill itself added later. In the nineteenth century its reputation for excellent cider put it on the map of every local drover.

Droving is the act of herding livestock, usually cattle, from one place to another. It has been going on in these parts since pre-Roman times, and by the Middle Ages it was commonplace for Carmarthenshire drovers to drive herds up to 400 head, from farms in

West Wales to the markets of Smithfields in London. The drovers created their own roads, usually across ground unworkable by the people who owned it. The drovers made their road wide enough to herd cattle. Generally, this meant snaking across the mountaintops of Mid and South Wales on a route that was known as 'the ridgeway'; handily, it also meant that they avoided paying tolls when the turnpikes were introduced in later history.

The drovers themselves were a hardy bunch. They had to be. It was a very tough life. The value of their charges meant that they were targeted relentlessly by highwaymen and bandits. It was down to the drovers to defend themselves and their cattle. They would travel in groups of four or five men per herd, often consisting of fathers, brothers and sons. They would make the 200-mile journey to London on foot, usually supported by a couple of well-trained dogs. They would make the journey in all weathers, often sleeping rough under hedges and on windswept mountaintops. Staying at an inn would have been a special treat, so it is small wonder the Cider Mill was held in such high regard. For those used to such a spartan life, the opportunity of sleeping off some cider in a soft, warm bed, possibly with the company of a local girl, would have been irresistible.

Today the establishment is altogether more genteel, highly regarded for its excellent food, with a menu the owners go to great lengths to design around local produce.

1.6
THE SHIP INN, RAGLAN

The village of Raglan gave its name to its most celebrated inhabitant, Lord Raglan of Raglan Castle, the Marquis of Worcester, and more latterly the Duke of Beaufort. His castle stands on the outskirts of the village. It is no longer inhabited and is open to the public. When built, it was an architectural marvel, one of the first castles whose primary purpose was as a domicile with a military consideration, rather than the other way round. It was designed primarily to be decorative, impressive and comfortable rather than impenetrable.

Having said that, it did have some defensive features, the most impressive being its Great Tower, which stands surrounded by a water-filled moat. It's a good job too, as it was needed to hold out during one of the longest sieges of the English Civil War, which lasted from June to August 1646. That siege marked a sea change in the fortunes of Lord Raglan, and, as it would transpire, in the fortunes of the then owner of the Ship Inn too.

Raglan was a Royalist, and his loyalties caught up with him when Cromwell's troops rocked up outside his castle and started pounding it with cannon fire. This went on for the best part of three months. Raglan held out for as long as he could but in the end surrendered, giving himself up to the Parliamentarian soldiers of the New Model Army. The order was given to 'slight' the defences, and as a result the castle was smashed. Once the walls had been breached, its rooms were ransacked, initially by the troops, and then by local villagers.

Not wanting to miss out on the opportunity, the landlord of the Ship decided to take a wander around the breached castle to see what pickings remained. In the great hall he found an artifact both beautiful and valuable, but far too heavy for the opportunistic soldiers. It was a rather magnificent, engraved stone fireplace. He looked at it, smiled and said to himself, 'I'm having that.'

And to this day, it still stands in the lounge of the Ship Inn. If you look closely at the fire surround, you can see that the edges are decidedly rough-cut and jagged, especially in comparison with the rest of the carvings. The carvings are also clearly older than the rest of the Inn. The visible damage to the lintel is claimed to have been caused by cannon fire during the siege.

There is further local folklore that suggests the siege actually started at the inn. A contemporary wrote that the siege owed to a 'skirmish in the yard at the sheep dip', the Sheep Dip being an old nickname for the pub, originally called the Sheep Inn rather than the Ship Inn. This is because there used to be a sheep market held on the cobbled yard in front of the pub, now ostensibly used as a beer garden. Supposedly some Roundhead soldiers were encamped nearby at Clytha Hill and decided to go to the pub for a couple of pints. There they encountered troops from Raglan Castle, loyal to the King. After a few too many pints downed by both sides, the inevitable hostility all spilled over into a pub brawl.

The Roundhead soldiers, on returning to camp, had to give an explanation for their cuts and bruises, and supposedly, the day after they had reported to their superiors, Sir Thomas Fairfax rocked up with 3500 troops and six deadly mortars and surrounded the castle.

In later history, the Ship continued to play a pivotal role in the village. Notably, in August 1827, it hosted a feast thrown by the local druid's lodge, which claims to have entertained 4,000 people. Not sure how they pulled that off, but it was reported in *the Bristol Mercury* and can still be read about in their archive.

1.7

THE CROSS KEYS,
USK

This pretty little town on the river it takes its name from is another remnant of Roman Wales. There was a fortified Roman camp here for a brief period, even before there was one in Caerleon. Then Norman invaders settled in the same spot, building a castle on a hill above the river. It is one of the few castles in the UK that is still in private ownership and still inhabited. It was built by the De Clares, who also opened a leper's hospital here in the fourteenth century. A Benedictine priory was established in the twelfth century, making an income from ironworks.

When Owain Glyndŵr attacked Usk in 1405 he flattened it, but the castle was left intact, and in the ensuing counterattack, the English garrison that had been stationed there mercilessly routed the Welsh force. Over 300 Welsh prisoners were executed in the castle grounds.

In the centuries after that, for a long time Usk was the poor relation to Caerleon and Abergavenny, its neighbours on either side of the river. As late as 1799, Archdeacon Cox described it as rather shabby: 'many ancient houses are in ruins, and a considerable district is much dilapidated.'

Not so today, when it is full of pretty historical buildings, an old market square, great fishing on the river, with the original, medieval street plan of the town pretty much unchanged. Over the years, Usk has done very well in the annual Britain in Bloom competition, and it boasts not only a very interesting museum but maybe the most attractive prison I've ever seen. Now there's a thing you don't hear often. If I were ever to be convicted of something, this is where I hope they would send me. Although I'm not sure it works like that. It has medieval-looking walls (although it was built in the nineteenth century) and it stands behind the old priory building and the town square. Well-established wisteria flowers trail along its perimeter walls.

The Cross Keys stands on the road leading to the main entrance to the town, the Usk bridge, and its name is a reference to St Peter, who is claimed to hold the keys to the gates of heaven. It may not be as pretty as its near neighbour, the Three Salmons, which is a rather picturesque seventeenth-century coaching inn that serves as a hotel and restaurant just up the road; however, it is fairly photogenic in its own right, and it is the oldest of the town's pubs. The historian and author Paul Harris, who wrote a book on historic pubs, suggested that the building dated back to around 1600, but I have seen several other accounts that suggest the mid-fourteenth century, albeit with some later alterations. There are several visible clues to its antiquity even before you step through the door. The bowed outer walls; the low slate roof, which at one time would have been thatched; and the stumpy chimneys are all dead giveaways. The large mounting block at one of the corners of the building also harks back to an age where horses were the transport of choice.

The Cross Keys is another pub that claims that its ceiling timbers were sourced from the much-fabled yard in Newport – despite the fact that, between Newport and Usk there is a very large area of land known for obvious reasons as Wentwood Forest. But I suppose that the law of averages suggests this claim surely must be true somewhere.

Inside, there are two main rooms: a lounge and a dining area, with a bar between them occupying a space that once would have housed a huge, central fireplace (another suggestion of thirteenth- or fourteenth-century origins). At the back of the dining room, a passage leads to a low cellar reached by a flight of stone steps and lit only by a tiny, barred window, which many believe to be the remains of a

28

prison cell. If they are correct, this would have originally been part of the older building the pub has incorporated into its present structure.

This prison cell is not the only feature that seems out of kilter. The interior is full of multiple architectural features that seem to have been brought in from other properties. For example, there is an impressive Inglenook fireplace. The lintel above it is quite plain, as you would expect, but the oak mantelpiece above that is surprisingly ornately carved, quite incredible craftsmanship. Similar to the fireplace in the Ship Inn in nearby Raglan, this might suggest that at some point in history, this was nicked from a much grander building. There is also a decorative plaster ceiling in one of the upstairs rooms, again out of place in a building like this.

I have already mentioned that a lot of pubs claim to be haunted, but few have as much proof as the Cross Keys.

A haunting in a room on the first floor manifests itself through some odd goings-on with the bedroom door. 'No matter how firmly the latch is fastened,' a former landlord by the name of Mr Hoffman said, 'it still manages to raise itself.' A local newspaper got hold of the story and in 1958 sent a bunch of reporters to stay the night in the room, with cameras and recording equipment. At first, absolutely nothing happened. Then at 5am, the door unlatched itself, despite the fact that it had been deliberately stiffened. The door slowly swung open into the room. A cold blast of air swept into the room behind it, extinguishing a candle the reporters had been using for light. The candle was re-lit and the door firmly closed, care being taken to check that the latch was firmly down. Within half an hour, exactly the same thing happened again.

The paper ran with the story and it reached a group of spiritualists from Blackwood, who read the piece and asked Mr Hoffman to allow them to run a séance in the room. The reporters returned to monitor what unfolded.

While in a deep trance, a medium succeeded in communicating with the restless spirit. They discovered that it was the ghost of a seventeenth-century girl called Clair or Clara Bernhardt. She had been imprisoned in the room by her parents, who disapproved of a love affair she had with a boy who was not deemed suitable for a lady of her station. Desperate that she should be allowed to marry the man she loved, and not be forced to marry some brute twice her age, she picked berries and ivy leaves from the wall outside her window and ate them, deliberately poisoning herself. The medium pleaded with her to stop opening the door – thereby trying to find a physical way out of the room – and instead to 'pass into the light'. The group left the inn, confident that they had put the 300-year-old spirit to rest.

But the door still opens.

The current owners describe the Cross Keys as a 'proper pub'. No pretentiousness nor airs nor graces. Just a convivial atmosphere for the consumption of pints.

1.8
THE HORSE AND JOCKEY, PONTYMOEL

The Horse and Jockey is a beautiful seventeenth-century inn. It has a long, low thatched roof and whitewashed walls, and it stands opposite the church of St Michael. It is one of only a tiny number of pubs of this age in the industrialised region of northern Gwent. There is a pub from the Victorian Era on every street corner in places like Pontypool – or there used to be anyway – but there are only a tiny handful of pubs predating then. This is because until the industrial revolution, many of the towns of South Wales were remote and rural spots, without the population to support any great number of public establishments.

The very few surviving buildings that once did serve as pubs are nowadays mostly put to different use. For example, the Penllwyn Arms, which started out as a Tudor manor house, became a pub and is now a museum.

But Pontypool is a bit different from other industrial towns in the area; there were ironworks in Pontypool since the reign of Queen Elizabeth I. The Horse and Jockey would most likely have been a favourite haunt for workers from day one, a welcome break after a hard day's work in the foundry, before returning home to the village of Pontymoel.

A guaranteed footfall across the centuries meant that successive landlords never had any reason to make up stories to attract customers.

As such, the Horse and Jockey boasts no false claims of antiquity. They don't even claim that their ceiling timbers were recycled from the Mary Rose!

Amateurs!

But the pub did play a role in an important moment in history.

In the nineteenth century, there was a growing dissatisfaction among ordinary working people. As we have already mentioned in our chapter on the Bridge End Inn, they were being taxed from all sides: for fishing rights, for use of public roads, for the accommodation they rented. And yet in return they were seeing precious little back from the establishment. Their children were not being educated, opportunities for them to better themselves were non-existent, and they were treated with total contempt by the legal system when they sought redress against unscrupulous landlords or employers. They did not even have a vote.

Attempting to have their grievances aired, a strong contingent from the village and the Pontypool area took part in a protest march across Gwent to Newport. One of the three ringleaders was William Jones, a watchmaker from Pontypool, who would have been well known at the Horse and Jockey, where he often met with a group of local men to discuss the state of the nation.

Maybe even with the great orator Henry Vincent, who was at the vanguard of spreading the word about a working men's charter in Gwent and South Wales. After all, when he was imprisoned in Monmouth Gaol, it was for inciting crowds at outdoor rallies and spreading dissent among secret meetings in pubs.

Every now and then you come across an old pub with a tradition of its own. In the case of the Horse and Jockey, it's a famous jug. Bear with me on this.

It's another relic the record of which we have Fred Hando to thank for. He managed to sketch it before it was sadly – though perhaps inevitably – smashed. This jug was made in 1837 and was about two and a half feet high, holding approximately five pints. Every Christmas it was a tradition to pass it round the pub with a sovereign on offer for whoever could down it the quickest. In such a macho environment as an ironworker's pub you can imagine the atmosphere. You can of course equally appreciate the dented male pride the year the prize was won by a woman.

The pub has the obligatory ghost, called Martha, but the current owner is sceptical about her. She is believed to be the ghost of a very fastidious former landlady, whose grave can still be seen to this day in the churchyard next door. Cleaners at the Horse and Jockey have noticed that if they don't put furniture or ornaments back the way Martha likes them, she moves them to their proper place. I think we could all do with a Martha in our lives.

In the 1964 Tokyo Olympics, the Welsh athlete Lynn Davies (nicknamed Lynn the Leap) took gold in the long jump event after an astonishing eight-metre seven-centimetre jump. Later that year he was having a drink with friends at the Horse and Jockey, and the regulars were nagging after a display of his talents. Once he had the benefit of a few pints, he agreed and stepped outside, followed by everyone in the bar. As the thronging crowd eagerly awaited, he stretched out his muscles, started his run up, then just in front of the pub doors took a jump to rapturous cheers and applause. If you look in front of the pub today, you will see two yellow lines on the floor. One marks where his jump began, and the other where he landed. If you get your tape measure out, you will find that the gap between them is eight metres and ten centimetres. Three centimetres further than he had jumped in Tokyo.

Lynn then went on to smash the long jump world record by jumping eight metres twenty-three centimetres in Berne in June 1968 – to this day the fourth-longest long jump of all time.

If you visit the Horse and Jockey today you will find a beautifully restored pub full of old world charm. The beer garden appeared in *the Guardian* earlier this year, listed as one of the best in the UK, and the owners have recently added a horsebox converted into a bar to save outdoor revellers having to go inside for a top up.

1.9
THE ROBIN HOOD INN, MONMOUTH

Monmouth has played host to some distinguished people down the ages. King Henry V, that monarch William Shakespeare loved above all others, was born here, as was Charles Rolls of Rolls Royce fame, not to mention the Chartists John Frost, Zephaniah Williams and William Jones, who led the march on Newport and became the last men in Britain to be hung, drawn and quartered for treason. Then, of course, there's Geoffrey of Monmouth, the twelfth-century monk and scholar who wrote extensively about the legendary King Arthur and his knights of the roundtable at Camelot.

And that's just the A list, people who were actually born here. Once you get into people who spent time in Monmouth, you can add Horatio Lord Nelson and Lady Hamilton, the poets William Wordsworth and Samuel Coleridge, and the artist J.M.W. Turner. To say nothing of the rock royalty who recorded so many anthems in the nearby Rockfield recording studios: Queen's 'Bohemian Rhapsody' originates here, to say nothing of Black Sabbath and Oasis. 'Wonderwall' is supposedly about a wall on a farm in Monmouth where the Gallagher brothers would sit and compose songs.

At the start of these chapters I can usually summarise a town's history in a paragraph or two, but in the case of Monmouth I fear that I am very much out of my depth. The history of this town goes back millennia. There is evidence of boat building on the banks of the river

Monnow that dates back to the Bronze Age; the Romans had a fort and town here; and in the Middle Ages, when it grew and prospered, Monmouth was one of very few Welsh towns to be listed in the thirteenth-century Domesday Book. Its significance continued right up until the industrial revolution.

As you would expect with such a backdrop, there are a lot of ancient buildings in the town, and at the lower end of Monnow Street, where the road narrows to cross the magnificent fortified bridge over the Monnow (the only one of its kind surviving in Britain) stands the Robin Hood Inn.

The Robin Hood is claimed to be the oldest pub in the town, and the Tudor arched doorway built in dressed stone suggests that this claim is not without merit. Inside, like most buildings of this age, you can see bits that have been added or modernised, like the carved wooden beams and partitions, which seem to be late seventeenth century, or on the first floor, a room with a very impressive decorative plaster ceiling that probably dates from the same period. But besides these, the Robin Hood remains pretty true to its origins, which I would put at mid-fifteenth century.

The eagle-eyed traveller/boozer will notice that Welsh pubs built in this period are different from their English counterparts in a number of ways.

First of all, there aren't many of them about, even as a proportion of the buildings that have survived from that age generally. Why should that be? It surely wasn't that the pre-Tudor Welsh were less likely to drink beer than their English counterparts. We know that the consumption of beer in the Middle Ages was pretty universal. In fact, it was more widely consumed than water, its alcoholic content making it safer to drink, killing off a lot of the impurities, viruses and bacteria that were rife in water. Even children drank it, albeit what was known as 'small beer', which had a lower-than-average alcohol content. It is from this drink that we derive the term 'It's just small beer', meaning something trivial or insignificant.

No, it was not any lack of beer that kept pub numbers down in

Middle Ages Wales: it was the absence of towns and cities.

Ancient Welsh society was ordered quite differently to English society. People generally lived off the land in farmsteads scattered across the countryside, much like the crofters of Highland Scotland. Towns did not become part of the Welsh landscape until the Norman incursion into Wales in the eleventh and twelfth centuries, and the introduction of feudalism. This consolidated all land ownership under the Norman nobles, leading to the creation of villages and towns as places for labourers tied to the land to live, in proximity to their lord's castle. Without a town, with its captive audience of potential customers, there was no way a Middle Ages pub could ever have been commercially viable, at least not without some other revenue stream to compliment it. Hence the low numbers in Wales.

There are some other differences between the two countries' pubs, an obvious one being the choice of building materials and building methods. When you think of pre-Tudor pubs in England, places like Nottingham's Ye Olde Trype to Jerusalem, or the inaptly named New Inn in Gloucester, you envisage timber-framed buildings coated with whitewashed wattle and daube, girded by black-stained timbers. But in Wales, pubs of this period are more commonly constructed of stone, owing to it being a more abundant building material.

English pubs also often followed a different layout, consisting of numerous interlinked small rooms overlooking a rear courtyard with stables. The main reason is that English inns were often purpose-built hostelries, put up to accommodate travellers, more specifically pilgrims. Most pubs in Wales dating back that far were not originally intended to be pubs. They would have started their lives as houses, cottages, farms or shops, and only converted into pubs in later history, when there was more of a demand for them.

I mentioned two things in my introduction to this book that are about to be borne out in this chapter. The first is that there is an intrinsic link in Wales between pubs and the church. The second being that pubs have always been prominent in the country's storied history of rebels, outlaws and underdogs. Never was this truer than in the case of the Robin Hood, which acquits its namesake well, despite the man himself never coming within miles of Monmouth.

In the sixteenth century, Britain was wrestling with the ramifications of Henry VIII declaring himself head of the church in England. The Reformation may have started with academic theologians questioning the church's mandate for accumulating such vast wealth, but the involvement of the King and his court politicised the issue, giving a lot of opportunistic nobles an excuse for a land grab and to disenfranchise families reluctant to desert Rome. Being a practising Catholic therefore became a very risky business. It was viewed as seditious, and followers were persecuted.

Despite the great personal risk, the landlord of the Robin Hood allowed the upper room to be used as a safe space for Monmouthshire's Catholic community. There is even evidence that it was used to celebrate Mass in secret. Had he been caught he would have instantly been shut down and imprisoned, possibly executed. However, there is no doubt that these secret gatherings continued for more than 100 years, because by 1778 religious tensions had cooled sufficiently for parliament to pass the Catholic Relief Act, in which places of Catholic worship were given licenses to exist. It took the council in Monmouth fifteen years to act on this reform, but when they finally did, they granted the Robin Hood Inn a license to act as a 'Publick Catholic Chapel'. It was a condition of the license that the building could not be made to look like a place of worship and that worshippers could not enter from the main street. Once the restriction on Catholic worship was lifted, a lot more people felt comfortable turning up to Mass, and the upper room of the Robin Hood Inn quickly became inadequate to support their numbers. Instead, the landlord of the Robin Hood at the time, a man called Michael Watkins, financed the building of a purpose-built chapel.

In another chapter of our history, William Shakespeare was believed to have patronised this historic pub. As the historian Fred Hando wrote, 'Scorn my conjecture if you will, but in my mind the light relief in his *Henry V* savours of the Robin Hood taproom.' There are certainly plenty of references to Monmouth in the play, which I strongly recall from studying it for my English Lit O Level. I was at a school in England, and I took pride in these references and reminders of home. Coupled with the belief that the character of Puck in *Midsummer Night's Dream* is based on the Monmouthshire legend of a sprite called Pwcca, it is more than likely that the Bard did indeed visit the town.

Another pub on Monnow Street worth popping into is the Vine Tree. It can boast nothing like the depth of history as the Robin Hood, but when you enter this seemingly Victorian pub, it comes as a surprise that its bar has a genuine timber-frame wall dating from the 1600s, as well as a lovely dressed-stone fireplace in the dining room. Obviously, this is a structure that, like so many others with origins from the Middle Ages, was revamped beyond recognition to keep up with Victorian fashion.

1.10
THE QUEEN'S HEAD,
MONMOUTH

The old town of Monmouth used to have a curtain of fortified walls running around its perimeter. Most of them have long gone now, although two round towers remain. They date from 1297, and they used to be part of the defence network. Now they have been incorporated into the walls of the Old Nags Head pub on James Street, a pub this book would otherwise have skipped over altogether, as the rest of it is thoroughly modern. Lower down the same street, on the corner of Weybridge Street, is a pub with proper vintage credentials, and which also has incorporated part of the old town wall into its structure: the Queen's Head.

It is a vast timber-frame building dating back to 1630. It suffered a similar fate to many ancient buildings on the outskirts of towns like Monmouth, places wealthy in the Middle Ages but seeing a decline in later history, wealth moving to the new industrial hubs like nearby Newport. The Queen's Head was, at the start of the twentieth century, in rather a sorry state. But it was thrown a lifeline when extensive renovations were done in 1922. Most of the exterior you can see now, including the timbers, date from this renovation, although great care was taken to follow the plan of what had been there previously. A lot of original features survived on the inside, most especially a beautiful post and panel partition in the lobby, made from wood so ancient you feel that a strong gust of wind might send the panels toppling like dominoes. There is also a large and attractive inglenook fireplace in the bar.

The pub was a favourite of Lord Nelson. He stayed a while at the Kymin, a folly on the hillside on the English side of the Wye, owned by the Admiralty and made available to senior officers for respite after battle duties. It overlooked the town, and with a pleasant walk through the woods leading to the doors of the Queen's Head, it's no surprise that Nelson made good use of it.

Stepping a little further back in time, the inn was also a favourite of Oliver Cromwell. During the English Civil War in 1642, Monmouthshire maintained a patchwork of allegiances, although most were Royalist. Historian of note JR Phillips has asserted that, in particular, the Catholics down at the Robin Hood Inn were said to be 'to a man, for the king', although I have more recently read a paper by Robert Matthews that casts some doubt on whether things were this black and white.

But given the undoubted strength of Royalist feeling in the area, it is not too surprising that when the great general was spotted taking food, drink and lodgings at the Queen's Head, designs against his life should be made. A man spotting Cromwell took the knowledge of his whereabouts to Edward Somerset, aka Lord Herbert, Earl of Glamorgan, Marquis of Worcester, Lord Raglan (who you may remember getting his fireplace nicked earlier in this book). There, a plot was hatched. One night, Oliver Cromwell was relaxing in his chamber at the inn after a hearty meal, blissfully unaware that downstairs a man had entered by a secret passage. It had been dug under the cellar, its exit hidden from view by a half-empty cask. The assassin climbed up from his hiding place and presented himself as a member of staff. At the opportune moment, he pulled back his cloak to reveal a pistol, taking aim at the Parliamentarian commander... But at the last second, a quick-thinking officer ran at him, knocking him to the ground. The thwarted killer gathered himself to his feet and ran, but the lodgings were so full of Roundhead soldiers, he didn't stand a chance. He was chased and shot in the back as he ran into the bar, falling to the floor by the fire.

To this day the ghost of the failed assassin is said to haunt the bar. His arrival is normally heralded by the bar door swinging open and a very cold draft sweeping into the room behind it, sometimes accompanied by his screams of agony as he is shot. Staff have also reported seeing a man dressed in seventeenth-century military uniform sitting by the fireside.

Hapless Royalist cutthroats aside, the pub has more than its fair share of spectral patrons. A lady dressed in white haunts the upstairs rooms and landing, and the ghost of a little girl, around four years old, has been glimpsed running through the premises. The landlord also told me about an incident not that long ago, when a couple he knows well were working at the bar late at night and saw an apparition that so terrified them they swore never to set foot in the place again.

I must admit I did snigger when I read an article that listed the Queen's Head as 'the third most haunted pub in Wales'. I am not sure what criteria is used to rank these places. It's a bit like when the charts started to include streaming services. Does one ghost appearing on rotation count more than multiple infrequent ghosts? How regularly are these leagues updated? And by whom? If the Queen's Head had a really busy year of apparitions, could they move up the table and take the top spot? Anyway, there you have it: third – good, but perhaps the resident spirits could try just that little bit harder.

With all this paranormal energy knocking about, it's unsurprising that when multiple sightings of a cloaked vampire were reported in the 1980s, a tide of fear gripped the town of Monmouth. Some years later, Dave Vanean of the gothic band the Damned suggested that it might have been him. The band had been working on a new album at the Rockfield recording studios and he used to de-stress by walking around the old streets of Monmouth late at night.

Another interesting Rockfield related story involves the Stone Roses, who had been at the famous recording studio for eighteen months, undergoing a slow (and presumably expensive) collapse. Rifts were deepening between the bandmates and their label, not to mention each other. At one point, after a heated exchange, Mani, the band's bass player, stormed out, and no one saw him for the rest of the night. After a couple of days passed, they began to get concerned. Where was he? The band were aware that he had been talking with a local girl down the pub, but no one knew who she was or where they could find her – until one night, quite by chance, they spotted the two of them working side by side in the local chip shop.

I have to confess, many years ago I came very close to buying the Queen's Head, but I got cold feet. Probably just as well; it would have been a sentimental purchase, rather than any recognition of a golden business opportunity. In 2005 it was saved from oblivion by a collective of local enthusiasts, who kept it running as a co-operative pub rather than let it fail. Something to be commended in my book – quite literally. The current owner was one of the collective, who ultimately bought out the others with a view to keeping live music alive in the town. Today the Queen's Head is very much a live music pub, focussing mainly on blues and jazz. It is run as a pub and B&B; they don't do food, but they do sell plenty of real ales, including Wye Valley Butty Bach.

1.11

THE KING'S HEAD HOTEL, MONMOUTH

W hen I was compiling this book, I had a real dilemma: whether or not to include places that started out as inns but which are now primarily hotels. There are some, like the Three Salmons Hotel in Usk, that are very old, very pretty, and welcome guests who only want to drink at the bar. However, I decided to be strict and took the line that, unless they had some great story attached, either by virtue of genuine history or the outlandish claims of previous owners, they should be excluded. But if a great story does qualify you, on this criterion, the King's Head in Monmouth, despite not strictly being a pub, qualifies for a chapter in its own right.

It is a classic seventeenth-century coaching and posting inn. It is Grade II listed and one of the most significant examples of such an establishment in Wales. And it comes packed with history.

It stands opposite the Shire Hall on Agincourt Square, the beating heart of ancient Monmouth. It incorporates several buildings: the original coaching inn, the country club and the Monmouth bank building. The old stables (now part of the hotel) were accessed from behind these fine buildings, so the postal and stagecoaches would have come up St Johns Street. The stables and yard on the St Johns Street entrance are a whole storey lower than the main buildings at the front, as they are built in what was once the defensive ditch around Monmouth Castle.

The inn first rose to greatness in 1645, when its owner and landlord Richard Ballard became both Monmouth's lord mayor and its postmaster. He was a passionate and vocal Royalist in the English Civil War, and his loyalty was rewarded when King Charles I himself came to his inn when visiting Raglan. Ballard was so impassioned by this patronage he began minting and issuing brass tokens bearing the King's head on one side and an inscription on the other: 'God preserve our gracious king'. This is where the name of the inn originates. Ballard also erected a plaster moulding of the King, which can still be seen hanging above the fireplace in the bar.

In the early eighteenth century, on the opposite side of the square, the Beaufort Arms opened, and the two establishments fought hammer and tongs over the coveted postal and stagecoach franchises. The pro-establishment politician the Duke of Beaufort is said to have made electioneering speeches from the balcony of the Beaufort Arms when he stood for parliament; meanwhile, over in the King's Head, William Corbett, the pamphleteer and pro-reformer, also gave political speeches.

By 1835 there were fifteen pubs and inns dotted around Agincourt Square. This prompted a satirical ditty to be written which went, 'A gin court here, a gin court there, no wonder they call it A-gin-court square.' And oh, how they all laughed.

These days, the King's Head is a Wetherspoons, so you know what to expect.

1.12
THE LION INN,
TRELLECH

H ere's an interesting claim: there is a group of archaeologists who believe that Trellech was one of the largest settlements in medieval Wales, even though these days it is nothing more than a pub, a church and a scattering of houses. The archaeological project they are working on is called 'the Lost City of Trellech' and their work was featured on the BBC TV programme *Hidden Wales* as well as written about in the national press.

It all started back in 2004, when retired tollbooth operator Stuart Wilson had a hunch that this picture-postcard village in the woods above the Wye Valley was the site of a forgotten metropolis. He sunk his life savings into buying a field at auction and ever since has been digging away at it with his trowel and brush. The digs have so far uncovered no end of treasures and evidence to support his claim, suggesting that Trellech was a town that thrived due to the contemporary demand for charcoal and iron. The powerful De Clares of Chepstow Castle bankrolled it, hungry to make an armoury of weapons to help them with their military campaigns against the indigenous Welsh. So far, Stuart and his team have uncovered a round stone tower, a fortified manor house and medieval pots and metalwork by the ton.

Here's the really big claim though: they reckon that, in its thirteenth-century heyday, the population of Trellech would have been around 10,000. Not only bigger than Cardiff, but at the time, a quarter of the population of London.

There is also evidence that hints enigmatically at Trellech's more ancient history, in the form of three megalithic standing stones just a couple of fields along from Stuart's dig. These are called Harold's Stones. They were carved from puddingstone and are thought to be late Neolithic. The tallest of them is four and a half metres high, but no one knows their origins or why they are there.

A walk along Llandogo Road and you will also discover the Virtuous Well, or St Anne's Well. This horseshoe-shaped well, where four springs meet, once welcomed pilgrims and travellers from all over ancient Britain, who came for its iron-rich healing waters. Though now the stones appear rather humble, in the eighteenth and nineteenth centuries people flocked to them to cure eye ailments. It is also said that ladies would drop pebbles into the well to find out when they would marry (each rising bubble symbolised another month to wait).

Supposedly, the monks at•Tintern Abbey•tapped into these precious 'holy' waters via a three-mile tunnel.

The Lion Inn does not date back quite as far as any of these artefacts, but it has a considerable age and history of its own. It was built by a retired ship's captain and completed in 1580. The structure as we see it now incorporates several formerly separate buildings: the original coaching inn, a farm and a brew house. Many of the features of the brewing cellar still remain, as do the pig sties from the former outhouses, which are now incorporated into a lettable room. It is Grade II listed.

There is a belief that a Reformation-era priest hole is hidden under the flagstones in front of the fireplace. Cost has stood in the way of excavating it, but there is certainly something down there that creates a sizable updraft, rather handily helping with the draw on the fire.

The pub today has a traditional bar menu that includes ingredients that have been foraged locally. They always have at least three ales on, including Butty Bach and an artisan cider. The owners are very proud to have won many awards, including Best Free House, Casque Mark accreditation and a CAMRA recommendation. They also run three beer and cider festivals each year, showcasing local independent breweries.

1.13
THE ANCHOR,
TINTERN

Most people will know Tintern on account of its famous abbey. It was the first house of the Cistercian order ever founded in Wales, by Walter De Clare of Chepstow Castle in 1131. After the Dissolution of the Monasteries in 1536, its treasures and valuables were handed over to the treasury of Henry VIII and the buildings to Henry Somerset, 2nd Duke of Worcester (also of Chepstow Castle). The duke had the lead from the roof stripped and sold off, with local villagers helping themselves to masonry, and so began the abbey's slow decay, which persisted until Cadw took over custody of the buildings in 1984.

The ruins are very elegant and dramatic, especially against the backdrop of the Wye valley. It was an aspect not lost on various artists down the years, who flocked to the area to be inspired by it. Masterpieces depicting the ruined remains of Tintern Abbey hang in museums and galleries all over the world, painted by such revered masters as Francis Towne, J.M.W. Turner, Thomas Gainsborough, Peter Van Lerberghe, Thomas Girtin, Thomas Creswick and Samuel Palmer. It also attracted poets like Mason, Grey, Wordsworth, Tupper, Coleridge and more.

In the Middle Ages, the abbey derived an income from many things. It had a lot of land, given to it by local nobility; some of it the monks farmed themselves, the rest they rented out to local farmers.

There is also ample evidence that the monks at Tintern were learned in metallurgy: only a few yards along the wall facing the beer garden of the Anchor Inn, there is a plaque commemorating the invention of the alloy brass at the abbey's lime kilns and foundry.

Some of the principal sources of incomes for abbeys and monasteries in the Middle Ages were donations and board from visiting pilgrims. In the Middle Ages, people tended not to travel much, but pilgrimages were the exception. It was deemed essential that Christians should travel to visit shrines, relics and places blessed by miracles. Such places had a point system attached to them; for example, two visits to the remains of St David at his cathedral in Pembrokeshire was worth the same as one visit to Rome. Tintern, meanwhile, owed a plentiful flow of visitors (and cash) to a statue of the Virgin Mary, which was said to have miraculous healing powers.

At many pilgrimage destinations, the monastery would often have their own inn, sometimes ran by the monks. After the Dissolution of the Monasteries, many of these old inns continued to trade as secular inns. That is the history of the Anchor – sort of. I say 'sort of' because it has not been in continuous use. As much as the bar area was originally the cider mill and granary of the twelfth-century abbey, it was only licensed as an inn in the nineteenth century, to meet the demands of wealthy tourists doing the Wye Tour.

A millwheel has been reconstructed in the bar area to reflect the original use of the building, but the Anchor has also incorporated other buildings too. The old stone-arched watergate and a slipway down to the river are now attached to the side, and the old boathouse and ferryman's cottage now form part of the restaurant. The pub has an extensive beer garden, with outstanding views of the remains of the abbey and the Wye. High up in the trees, on the opposite bank of the Wye (the Gloucestershire side) you can see a platform that is known locally as 'the Devil's Pulpit'. If you get a chance to climb up there, it is an excellent place to view the abbey from above. Legend has it that it got its name when the devil himself climbed up and stood on this vantage point to plead with the monks down below to give up their devotion to Christ. He promised them great riches if they were to leave the abbey and cross over the river to him, on the dark side. Or 'England' as it is otherwise known.

The devil may not have won out that day, but the pub does have its obligatory hauntings. A ghost blowing a tin whistle and the ghost of an anguished white lady searching for her lost son are both regulars.

1.14

THE BOAT INN, CHEPSTOW

C hepstow, like Monmouth, is the sort of town that has so much history, there is no way I could do it justice in a couple of paragraphs of preamble.

It has always been of strategic importance, as it stands on a crossing point of the Wye, overseeing the historic border between England and Wales. The castle guarding that crossing point is believed to be the oldest surviving stone-built castle in Britain. The town's other main defence was its old town walls, much of which are still intact today as well. Another throwback to Chepstow's Norman past are the remains of a Benedictine priory, now incorporated into the town's church.

Throughout the Middle Ages Chepstow thrived as a market town, but it was sacked in the English Civil War as a Royalist stronghold, becoming something of a backwater. Its fortunes rekindled in the seventeenth and eighteenth centuries, when the main skillset of the town's men, ship building, became in very high demand in the commercial ports springing up along both sides of the Bristol Channel.

The Boat Inn has a beautiful aspect. It stands on the banks of the river Wye in the shadow of Chepstow's awe-inspiring castle, with views up the cliff-edged valley taking in the old bridge and its ornate iron railings. The pub has an inscription that says it was built in 1789. It has plenty of character and original features, including low ceilings with timbers and flag stone floors and a split-level staircase up to the restaurant.

The Boat was built right at the heart of the industry that revived the town's fortunes. The street the pub stands in is called 'the Back', a word that once held the meaning 'quay' or 'harbour'. There was once a dry dock there used for repairing ships' hulls. It was an area nicknamed 'hell's acre' as it had a reputation for rowdiness, lewd behaviour, prostitution and bar brawls. There were, at one point, more than a dozen pubs in the area, as well as a customs house keeping a watchful eye on goods coming and going.

It was from this quayside that young men convicted of taking part in the Chartist 'riot' in Newport were deported to Australia on board a prison ship.

The Boat Inn was originally called the Chepstow Boat, and in 1880 four men, described as being from 'respectable positions' in the town community, were arrested and charged with hauling a fisherman called Thomas Scott from the Chepstow Boat and throwing him into the river on the evening of the Chepstow Boat Races. Their defence was that he had reneged on a bet. They were fined 30s each plus costs and told that they were lucky not to be charged with manslaughter.

For a period from the Second World War until the 1980s, the building ceased to be a licenced premises. In that time, it was both a private residence and also a tribunal chamber where inquests were heard to investigate, amongst other things, deaths on the river.

An area of the Boat Inn, just to the right of the entrance, is said to be haunted. There is a sign on the wall which reads, 'while sitting here you [may] experience a sudden shiver or catch a fleeting glimpse of a figure from past times.'

1.15
THE MOUNTON BROOK LODGE, PWLLMEYRIC

I f you come to Mounton Brook Lodge, formerly known as the New Inn, straight after a visit to the Skirrid Inn, you could be forgiven for thinking you have just driven round in a big circle. Both pubs are practically identical, built within a few years of each other, in the late seventeenth century, and, by all accounts, from exactly the same set of plans.

The building is Grade II listed, as it is quite unusual to find an inn of this age in South Wales with its stabling largely intact.

The inn was a popular stop over point when the principal route into South Wales ran along the course of the old Roman road that linked the forts at Gloucester, Caerwent, Caerleon, Cardiff and Neath – a route predominantly followed by the A48 today, on which the inn now stands.

In 1748 a seasoned traveller by the name of Viscount Torrington visited South Wales. He was not, it has to be said, overly impressed. However, one place he did write of approvingly was the New Inn. On a visit to Chepstow, which had to be cut short owing to inclement weather, he wrote, 'but e'er I had gone three miles, a violent shower drove me into a small public house, the New Inn at Poulmick for shelter.' He spoke warmly of the reception he received there, before going on to slag off pretty much everywhere else in the area.

From outside the New Inn you can see the outline of a blocked

Tudor arch, which at one time would have been the entrance. On the other side of the walled-up arch is a long corridor separating the hall and parlour rooms, which led to the rear stair turret. The partitions which once would have stood on either side of the passage have been taken down to create a more open plan bar and lounge with grand fireplaces at either end.

Legend has it that the inn was established by the Bishop of Llandaff as a place for pilgrims passing through to stop for refreshment. That is not as absurd as it sounds, because while Pwllmeyric is in the dioceses of Monmouth, rather than the dioceses of Llandaff, the bishopric did own a palace in the near-by village of Mathern.

These days, the Moulton Lodge promotes itself more as a wedding venue than a pub.

1.16
THE LLANTHONY PRIORY
HOTEL, LLANTHONY

I know it's a hotel so let's not get off on the wrong foot, but by the criteria of allowing visitors a drink at the bar, and boasting some interesting history, folklore or beauty, the Llanthony Priory scores high. Not to mention, across its history, it *was* at times an inn – and what a history it was.

Today, the Llanthony Priory is the only surviving building amongst the ruins of the old Augustinian priory, founded in 1118 by Hugh De Lacey.

Its location in the beautiful Black Mountains, just north of Abergavenny, may be a blessing now, but it was something of a curse when it was built. When the Normans invaded Wales, it was to places like this that the Welsh tribesmen were banished. This was something they did not take kindly to, and they would frequently mount reprisals and raids. The twelfth-century monk Gerald of Wales commented at the time that Llanthony Priory was 'fixed amongst barbarous people'. In 1135 it was completely flattened in a raid. Subsequently rebuilt, it is the remains of that second building that can be seen today. Its church was one of the great medieval buildings of Wales, with its cruciform layout and mix of Norman and Gothic arches.

Little remains of the cloisters that once stood here, and the house and farm buildings which have been incorporated into the hotel building were largely built in the thirteenth century.

As a priory, Llanthony's fortunes ebbed and flowed. It was destroyed again in the fifteenth century by Owain Glyndŵr, and after that went through sporadic pockets of revival, only to enjoy a heyday in the eighteenth and nineteenth centuries when tourists came in search of the ancient and the picturesque. The remains of the old priory provided both by the spade full, with the option to stay amongst them making them all the more special.

It will come as no surprises that a place like this has its fair share of ghost stories. There is a phantom monk occasionally to be spotted in the road between the monastery and the Skirrid, near the village of Capel-Y-Ffin. He is described as wearing the garb of a Benedictine monk, which is weird as Llanthony was Augustinian.

The ruins of the priory themselves are said to be haunted. People have reported sightings of the ghost of a monk allegedly murdered there during the time of the Reformation, as well the ghostly sound of coughing, and the sensation of an 'icy terror'.

1.17
THE WHITE HART, LLANGYBI

Llangybi lies on the road between Usk and Caerleon, a pretty little village clustered on a hill above the banks of the Usk. Right at the heart of the village is a small village green, and this beautiful sixteenth-century inn stands on one edge of it. There is a bench on the green itself, canopied by a great oak, where you can sit and take in its ancient, whitewashed walls, soaking up the atmosphere of this quaint, rural idyll – albeit one dominated by modern traffic.

There is a vast weight of amazing folklore associated with both this village and the pub itself. The village church is believed to have been established by Saint Cybi, a very early Welsh saint from the fifth century, who gave the village its name. There is a legend that the saint himself once planted his staff into the ground just north of the village, and from the point of impact a spring gushed forward with crystal clear drinking water. It flows through the village to this day and bares the saint's name.

Now I don't want to cast doubt on such a lovely story, but the more well-travelled reader of legends and folklore may at this stage be saying, 'Hang on, I thought that legend was about Anglesey!' To which I would have to concede, yes, the legend of St Cybi's staff is more generally attributed to a spring on Anglesey. Who knows, maybe it was his party piece?

Mind you, when talking about a man putting a stick in the ground and producing a spring, I'm not sure exactly *where* this happened is the main issue. If the people of Llangybi and Anglesey ever went to court over this, I'd be interested to see what evidence either side was able to produce.

There is a story that the church once formed part of a larger Cistercian monastery and that the building the inn now stands in was originally built to house the monks. The name 'the White Hart' is nothing to do with deer but is in fact a corruption of 'White Habit', describing the vestments monks of that order wear. There is also supposed to be a secret tunnel which runs between the church and the pub. A lot of old pubs have stories about secret tunnels, and we will discuss many in future chapters, but in the case of the White Hart you can actually see where it starts. Behind the unusually deep fireplace in the lounge, there is a low, dark passage with a small flight of stone steps leading to a small recess that could once have been an opening to a tunnel now blocked by the addition of a nineteenth-century stable block. There are conflicting claims about it, although the most probable explanation is that it was a priest hole.

After the Dissolution of the Monasteries, it is claimed that the pub, by virtue of its attachment to a monastery, was gifted to Jayne Seymour, third wife of Henry VIII, as a dowry. The family already owned extensive estates in Monmouthshire, including Penhow Castle.

In the eighteenth century, during the expansion of the pub, which saw it incorporate the buildings around it, a former courtyard was built over. This yard had previously been part of a path across which parishioners exercised a right of access to the cemetery. The local vicar was not happy at all about the proposed work. Even though he had no legal right to block the build, he had an equitable claim of 'easement' (or passage), as the route had been in constant use by his parishioners for a long time. As such, even after the yard had been built over, the church took steps to maintain this right, and for the best part of 100 years, every now and then it would exercise its right of easement, sending funeral corteges and accompanying mourners through the pub to the cemetery, ensuring their right of access would never be lost through disuse. For all I know, they still do this now.

Another tale is that the inn was built and run by the Knights Hospitallers of St John, to provide accommodation and respite for soldiers returning from the crusades. The inn certainly looks old enough for that to be true. Plain stone walls, sagging rooflines, low timber ceilings and windows, plus clustered, diagonal chimney stacks, all speak to its clear antiquity. However, the White Hart is far more likely to have been founded in the Elizabethan era, rather than the earlier heyday of the Knights Hospitallers. It is also clearly made up of several properties that were once independent of each other, before being absorbed into the one.

There are several indications of its re-decoration over the years. One of the more interesting is a plaster ceiling in the first-floor chamber, above the front part of the pub, which once would have been the grand house. It bears a variety of emblems including the Tudor rose, the fleur-de-lis, a horse's head and either a flower or a thistle. If it *is* a thistle (it is hard to tell), this would suggest the ceiling was decorated in the reign of James I.

This inn is another ancient Monmouthshire building that owes the survival of its historic integrity to the ineffable Fred Hando. In the 1950s he wrote in his regular column, 'Some years ago, a few of us saved the White Hart from desecration. A great beam from the fireplace had been removed in readiness for the introduction of a modern atrocity. Fortunately, some enlightened directors stepped in at the right moment and saved a 16th century relic.' If you ever see the beam he is referring to, I think you will be very impressed anybody ever managed to budge it. It is like a tree trunk.

An interesting quirk of the pub's history is that three blacksmiths used to work in its attic. That may sound odd, but at the time many old houses kept sleeping chambers for servants in the roof space. Once servants were not quite so commonplace, left behind were large spaces with access to the building's chimneys, and light streaming in through the roof lights – perfect for craftsmen such as blacksmiths.

As you would expect from a place with such a rich history, over the years the White Hart has played host to some very notable persons. Oliver Cromwell, seemingly never far from a Monmouthshire pub, is believed to have set up local headquarters at the White Hart, staying there many times. And none other than T.S. Eliot immortalised the pub in his writings. The poet, from St Louis, Missouri visited Monmouthshire on a tour and wrote a short poem entitled 'Usk', which begins 'Do not suddenly break the branch, or / Hope to find / The white hart behind the white well'.

1.18

THE HANBURY ARMS, CAERLEON

Ihave already mentioned the Roman remains at Caerleon in my introduction to this chapter. But they weren't the first. There are also the remains of an Iron Age hillfort on the edge of the town, and many other indications that suggest this was a significant settlement long before the Romans came, which is doubtless why they chose to colonise it themselves.

The remains of the Roman amphitheatre near the old fortified camp of Isca are quite spectacular by comparison with other Roman remains in Britain, though a bit disappointing if you are expecting something like the Colosseum, or the remains you find dotted around the Mediterranean. Alas our weather is not quite as forgiving as theirs, and that takes its toll after nearly 2000 years. It may be quite amusing for us today to note that the people of Caerleon, for many centuries, used to believe that this circular structure was in fact the remains of King Arthur's legendary round table. Why not remind a few locals of that while you are visiting? I am sure they will be abundantly amused.

To be fair to them, it was a belief not wholly born out of ignorance. It was more to do with some wild conjecture on the part of a twelfth-century monk and chronicler called Geoffrey of Monmouth. He had studied the town, its history and layout and was convinced that it all proved beyond doubt that the town was, in fact, the long-lost location of King Arthur's legendary court of Camelot. He wrote extensively on the subject in his book *City of Legions*. So if the people of Tintagel fancy bringing over that statue of theirs, the people of Caerleon would be most grateful.

The Hanbury Arms is an elegant sixteenth-century coaching inn on the banks of the river Usk. The main bar at the Hanbury is called the Court Room, a nod to the building's previous use as a courthouse. It also boasts a rather unique piece of kitchen hardware not commonly seen these days: a dog wheel. These were relatively common in the nineteenth century. It is a wheel suspended from the ceilings, connected to various gears, in which a small dog would have been placed. When walking, the dog would turn the wheel, which in turn would turn a spit, which itself would turn a joint of meat over a fire to cook.

But that is not the Hanbury's most unusual feature. Rather uniquely, it has a stone-built Norman tower attached to it, dating back to 1219. No one is altogether sure what the origins of the tower are. There are theories that at one time it had an identical twin on the opposite bank and a chain ran between the two of them, allowing a ferry to operate across the river. But there are no visible remains of such a structure, which casts some doubt on that. Another theory is that the old town walls at one time extended further than they do now, and that this tower was a part of that former structure. Or possibly that it was originally part of a fortification that has subsequently fallen down. One thing is known for sure: the tower, which today is an ancient monument and fascinating folly, once had an altogether more practical purpose: a useful space to hurl troublesome drunks into, to sleep off their excesses.

This old inn is situated just outside the ancient town walls of Caerleon. Pubs in the sixteenth century situated outside town walls were not bound by the same by-laws enforced on those within the town walls, prohibiting or limiting activities such as gambling and prostitution. As such, these establishments tended to be dens of iniquity. Given Caerleon's booming sixteenth- and seventeenth-century quayside, with its steady stream of newly paid sailors, the Hanbury would undoubtedly have been a very raucous place.

Its best feature for visitors today is its gorgeous, south-facing beer garden, which trails down to the banks of the river Usk below. It offers a place to catch the rays on a sunny day, but also affords wonderful views downriver to the old bridge, or upriver to the pretty countryside. Just to the south of the Norman tower, there are the remains of a quay wall and a slipway that are listed structures in their own right. What you see today is an early eighteenth-century structure, but there are many who believe that, underneath, there is a Roman construction that the legion based at the fort of Isca used as a dry dock. The remains of Isca and the amphitheatre annexed to it are no more than a few hundred yards away, so this is very possible.

The Hanbury's beautiful aspect as seen from the riverbank made it a favourite haunt of the celebrated poet Alfred, Lord Tennyson. In 1856 he began writing *Idylls of the King* while visiting the Hanbury, and a blue plaque commemorates this on the wall by his favourite seat. He drew on both the location and aspect of the Hanbury, as well as Caerleon's Arthurian connections, when noting of his time composing there: 'The Usk murmurs by the window as I sit like King Arthur in Caerleon.'

And he was not the only writer to enjoy a pint at the Hanbury. Arthur Machen, who lived locally, was also a regular. He was a writer of horror, supernatural and fantasy fiction, most prolifically at the turn of the twentieth century, and is credited with creating the legend of the Angel of Mons while writing as a reporter during the First World War. Stephen King famously described his novel *The Great God Pan* as 'maybe the best horror story in the English language'.

The river Usk at the point where it flows past Caerleon is wide, deep and fast, and the banks on either side are very flat and muddy. As such, it was always notoriously difficult to bridge. Before the building of the stone bridge we can see today, there used to be a rather rickety and perilous wooden bridge which spanned the river near the Hanbury. Any travellers approaching it would no doubt have balked at hearing a local tale. Supposedly, in the dead of night, a weary traveller from Chepstow crossed the bridge on a journey west along the old Roman road. He was heading right into the barrage of a tremendous storm. The wind blew the raindrops so hard against his face that they felt like a swarm of angry wasps. The sound of the river rushing beneath him echoed the deafening thunder overhead. Seeing the hospitable looking inn on the opposite bank, a hearty fire burning in the hearth, the traveller decided to stay the night. In the morning, he looked out of the windows of the inn, back across the path he had ridden on his horse the night before, only to see that the bridge had all but washed away. All that remained of it was a narrow string of brittle planks, which his horse had somehow navigated like a tight rope in the darkness the night before. He immediately collapsed from the shock of the sight of it. He died the same day.

1.19

THE OLD BULL INN, CAERLEON

The Old Bull Inn is in the centre of the old town, and it is believed by some that there was originally a taverna on the same site, as far back as the Roman occupation itself. Most of what you can see now dates back to the sixteenth century, but some of the masonry is substantially older. At the same time, a lot has been changed and modernised through the subsequent centuries.

Standing next to where the old market hall used to be, the Old Bull was originally a townhouse, home to the Morgan family of Machen. Edmund Morgan was a very ambitious social climber who married well (three times!) and accumulated a great deal of wealth and power. His children became high sheriffs and MPs. One of his descendants was Lord Tredegar of Tredegar House. Supposedly another descendant was an altogether less savoury character, the cutthroat pirate and privateer Henry Morgan; credible or no, anyone looking for an excuse to order a tipple of his namesake rum, Captain Morgan, in the Old Bull, there you have it.

There are several conflicting theories as to how the Old Bull Inn ended up with such an unusual name. One is that it is a mocking reference to Ann Boleyn, the beheaded queen of Henry VIII. Another theory is that the Morgan family (who lived at the property) were descended from the Welsh warrior king, Bledri ap Cydifr, whose head crest was a bull. Keeping up the Arthurian theme of this chapter, it is worth mentioning that Bledri ap Cydifr is also credited with having written some of the original stories about King Arthur and the Knights of the Round Table.

There are two really fascinating remnants of this building's Roman legacy that are still visible to this day. The first is in a first-floor room, where a carved stone head is embedded into a partitioning wall. It is a reworked piece of Roman masonry. The other is a low, arched recess in the cellar, which extends in the direction of the river, and is likely to be part of the old drainage system for the Roman baths situated next door. You can still visit their remains; the entrance to the museum is through the old stable yard behind the pub. It is believed that, before this conduit was walled up, it was used to smuggle contraband into the cellars; we will encounter many such claims throughout this book, but in this instance, I am inclined to believe that it is true.

There are further claims of other tunnels linking up with the old priory across the road. If true, these possibly served as escape routes in the time of the Reformation.

I mentioned the author Arthur Machen in my chapter about the Hanbury Arms. He also plays a part in the history of the Bull. Firstly, he used to drink there. Secondly, and more significantly, he wrote it into one of his story lines.

1.20
THE ROSE INN, REDWICK

R edwick is on the Gwent levels in southern Monmouthshire, near the Severn estuary between Newport and Caldicot. It is a tiny little village, no more than a handful of cottages and farms clustered together around a village green with a church on one side and a pub on the other, and the old Victorian schoolhouse somewhere in between.

If you visit Redwick, there are five things of interest around the old church that you should take a moment to survey. First of all, just below the top of the door of the outer porch there is a marker carved into the wall, more than six feet off the ground. This mark shows the extent of the flood water of the great flood of 1607, when a tsunami washed up the Bristol Channel and decimated huge areas of the Gwent and Somerset levels. Redwick was right in the epicentre of it, and a lot of life, property and livestock was lost as a result.

A recreation of an old wood carving, depicting the flood and the havoc it wrought, is our second object of interest, to be found above the church door.

If you then go inside the church (which is very pretty), in front of the chancel-side of the wall, between the chancel and the nave, on the left-hand side of the church by the organ, there is a grave on the floor marked only with a skull. The children of the village have always been brought up to believe that this is a pirate's grave. In reality, it is an example of a common enough phenomenon known as Memento Mori. These markings were very popular in the Middle Ages and in the Victorian era. They were intended to depict the transient nature of life. But I for one used to love to watch the delight in the eyes of my small children whenever I perpetuated the myth.

On leaving the church to find the fourth fascination, head out along a path beyond the church tower to the west, into a field behind the church. In a bed of overgrown brambles and hawthorns on your left-hand side, there is a car that was parked up in the field in the 1930s and has never been touched since.

And finally, as you leave the church by the main, east gate, to walk towards the Rose Inn, in front of you, there are some stocks and a display of artefacts built around an old cider press wheel.

There is an interesting legend attached to the church in Redwick. Over the years the people of the village yearned for a bell in their church tower. So between them, over time, they saved up enough money to buy one. It was cast by the finest craftsmen they could find, and as roads in those days were not very good, to bring it to the church it was mounted onto a raft and floated down the network of reens that criss-cross the levels. You may not be familiar with the word 'reen', as it is unique to folk living on the levels (on either side of the Severn). It is the name given to the man-made canals that run along the fields of the levels to drain the ground water off the land. They are emptied into the Bristol Channel at low tide, but are dammed at high tide to stop the sea from flooding back into the land, which mostly lies below sea level.

The idea of floating the bell down on a raft may have seemed good at the time, except that the villagers had seriously underestimated the immense weight of it. When the raft was set afloat, it pretty much instantly sank, taking with it the raft, the bell and all the people standing on it, all to be lost forever in the murky, muddy depths. All that remained were a few bubbles on the water's surface. It is said that, ever since that day, when the fields of the levels are in danger of being reclaimed by flooding, you can hear the bell toll from the depths of the reen, as an alert to the people of the village and the moors which surround it.

For centuries this area was owned by the various monasteries nearby. Testimony to this history can be found in the names of the two roads that lead to the village. One is called Blackwall and the other Whitewall. There is no wall on either route; that is just a corruption of 'walk'. The 'black walk' was the route taken to the village by the Benedictine monks of Goldcliff (who wore black robes) and the 'white walk' was the route taken by the Cistercian monks of Llantarnam Abbey (who wore white robes).

I had the privilege to live in this village for many years, and cynics might say that, had this not been the case, the Rose Inn would have escaped mention in this book. It is neither ancient nor especially interesting – especially when just three miles up the road, in the village of Magor, there is a proper, bonafide sixteenth-century coaching inn, the Golden Lion, which scarcely gets a mention. However, there is one thing the Rose has that the Golden Lion does not. A bit of folklore that is just too good to skip.

It relates to a man who was known locally as Tom the Lord. He was descended from nobility but was a brash drunkard, who lived alone in a once grand old manor house, which had since gone to wrack and ruin. He was well known in all the drinking holes on the levels, but he usually ended his revelry at Redwick. He had a reputation for drinking until he could no longer stand, at which point he would attempt to stagger home, usually assisted by one of the local farmers, only to begin the cycle all over again the next day. Frequently he did not make it home, only managing to stagger a few yards down the lane from the pub (back then the King's Arms, now a house) before collapsing into the hedge opposite Rose Cottage (now the Rose Inn). There, he would sleep off the drink until the morning. This happened so frequently that the hedge was perpetually disrupted at the point he tended to fall.

Then one day came when he was not seen in any of his usual haunts. When some of his acquaintances enquired after him at his home, his servants reported that he had not returned the evening before. There was nothing unusual about that, but if he wasn't at home, and he wasn't in the pub, where was he? Suspecting that he may have been robbed at the roadside by a bandit or highwayman, they set off along his last known route to see if they could track him down. After a few hours of searching, they came across his body floating in the still, green water of a reen. His blood-soaked arm was caught up in the branches of a bramble bush, lacerated from the struggle he must have made to free himself before drowning.

They carried his body back to the village, and he was buried in Redwick churchyard. 'He'll never trouble us more,' a villager was heard to comment on the day of the funeral. But scarcely a week had passed before reports of unusual mischief started to spread throughout the village. Farmer Thorn walked into his barn one morning to see that the taps on his cider barrels had all been opened and had been running all night. Then a maid at Rose Cottage saw the apparition of Tom the Lord, sitting in the hedge opposite, where he had so often spent the night in a drunken stupor. She screamed with fright at the sight of him.

To appease Tom the Lord, farmer Thorn took to leaving a tankard of cider out for him of an evening. As long as that routine persisted, the villagers were left in peace. But if ever a night passed where he forgot, the taps on the barrels would be left running and other mischief would ensue. Eventually a minister was sent for, to exorcise Tom the Lord's spirit and free the villagers from his mischief. Whether from lack of faith or insufficient experience it is not certain, but the pastor failed in his attempt to lay the ghost. Still the troubles increased, and at harvest time Tom was seen among the boughs of the apple trees, hurling fruit at the workers.

A full-scale attack was now staged. In the presence of all the men and women of Redwick, not one but twelve ministers 'laid' Tom the Lord with bell, book and candle. And that finally did the trick.

On the spot where he was 'laid', a bed of white violets has bloomed every springtime since, shaped like a coffin. And as for the bit of hedge opposite Rose Cottage, which he frequented so much in life as in death, it never grew back and eventually had to be replaced with the stone stile you see there today.

The Rose Inn usually has a selection of one or two ales. The landlord drinks Guinness, so that is always in good nick, and they serve wholesome, simple pub grub. The area around the village is great for walks along the sea wall, and as it is so flat, it is also good for cycling.

1.21

THE OLD MURENGER HOUSE, NEWPORT

'What is a Murenger?' you may well ask. It was the person in a medieval town responsible for the upkeep of the town's walls. More often than not, this was through the levying of taxes, rather than actually working on them personally. The office became extinct in 1324, when King Edward II granted the townsfolk a royal charter for the repair of their defences. So, it can be inferred from the presence of this pub that, at some point before this date, Newport had town walls. They surrounded the far smaller Norman settlement which grew around the castle and ancient port just south of where the main bridge now stands.

I am not sure how good these defences could have been, as there are records of raiders burning Newport to the ground in 1294, 1316, 1321 and 1402. There are historians who believe that the gate towers were the only part of the early structure that was built of stone. The rest was mainly timber.

It is very unlikely that this building dates back quite as far as that. In fact, I have to say that the poor Old Murenger House comes in for a bit of stick when it comes to claims of genuine antiquity. If you ever read its Wikipedia page, the words 'all fake' tend to stand out a bit. And it is a little bit unfair.

The building is genuinely very old. It is more than likely the oldest intact building in Newport today. Traditionally, experts put it at 1530, but even if that is not spot on, it is certainly Tudor dynasty. However, some of its features, like the jutting upper levels, were embellished in the Victorian era. In the twentieth century the building became very neglected, the frontage starting to crumble away, and by 1980 it was in real danger of collapsing completely. It could have been lost forever but for some swift conservation work, which, over the course of a year, saved the day. Of all the places in this book to be accused of falsehood, the Murenger is perhaps the least deserving!

As you approach it from the main street, the Murenger really stands out. It is all gleaming half timbers, leaning front, and whitewashed bowed walls at odd angles. As Paul R Davis put it, 'It would not look out of place in Ludlow or Chester.'

Having said that, it should be pointed out that it was never the house of an actual murenger. This was under the walls themselves and demolished in the nineteenth century. No, the Old Murenger House was more than likely the townhouse of the Herbert family, who were county sheriffs and lived at the time in St Julian's Manor. They became incredibly wealthy and powerful in the Tudor era and went on to live in greatly expanded living quarters in Cardiff Castle. The building the Murenger House stands in first became a pub in the seventeenth century and was originally called the Fleurs-de-Lys.

The exterior is by far the most impressive part. Jettied upper floors hang over the street, and on the ground floor is a broad bay window with a leaded panel depicting a coat of arms. But it has to be said that there is also a real treat on the upper floor: a plastered ceiling with decorative features including a Tudor rose and the pineapple badge of Catherine of Aragon – no doubt an acknowledgement of the marriage between her and Henry VIII from 1509-33.

The pub these days is owned by the Samuel Smith brewery chain. It has a few ghosts, but the only one worth mentioning is a lady who is frequently seen by a window on the upper floor.

GLAMORGAN AND THE ANCIENT KINGDOM OF GLYWYSING

Glywysing was an ancient kingdom in south east Wales, dating from the fifth century. It was latterly merged with Gwent to form the much bigger kingdom of Morgannwg, which itself was conquered by Robert Fitzhamon, first Duke of Gloucester, in the twelfth century, to create a single South Wales region closer to what we would recognise today. Its outline roughly corresponded to the old county of Glamorgan. It was made up of the coastal and inland areas stretching between the river Rhymney, with its estuary on the Wentloog Levels at its eastern boundary, to the Neath estuary in the west, and as far north as the foothills of the Brecon Beacons.

It incorporated Wales' capital city of Cardiff and a lot of what later became the country's industrial heartlands: the Taff, Cynon, Rhondda, Ogmore and Neath valleys. Interestingly, as much as these areas make up such a huge proportion of the national population today, for the most part of history, up until the nineteenth century there was very little going on there. Pretty much all this area was rural.

Even Cardiff itself is a relative newcomer as a settlement of note. On the Itinerarium Antonine (a very early list of settlements along the Roman roads of Britain) Cardiff is not listed as a settlement at all, only as a Roman fortified camp. Even by the year 1300 the now sprawling capital city of Wales only had a population of 2,200.

In fact, in the Middle Ages, there were only a handful of towns in the area at all. The first was Llandaff, a town in its own right back then, although these days it is a leafy suburb of Cardiff, agglomerated as the city expanded out to absorb surrounding villages and towns. The diocese of Llandaff used to pretty much exactly mirror the borders of the old kingdom of Glywysing, although it has subsequently been redrawn to more closely match those of Glamorgan.

The only other settlements of any note in the area were the monastic town of Neath and the commercial hubs at Cowbridge and Kenfig. The latter is now long lost, as we will elaborate upon later in this chapter. However, despite its rural isolation, Glywysing did boast a university – not only the first ever to exist in Britain, but its first ever school or educational institution of any kind. It was located in Llantwit

Major and was called the Cor. It was founded in the fifth century by St Illtyd and was still running until the Dissolution of the Monasteries in the sixteenth century.

In the seventeenth and eighteenth centuries, Llantwit Major and the coastline of the Vale of Glamorgan were caught up in less scholarly pursuits: they were a hot bed of pirates, ship wreckers and smugglers, and we will delve into the stories and folklore of this time throughout this chapter.

Until the discovery of coal, the main reason anyone might have had for visiting anywhere inland, north of Mynydd-y-Garth, was to pilgrimage to the grotto at Penrhys. There is a holy well here which was established by the monks of Llantarnam, after a vision of the Virgin Mary was seen in a tree. By which I mean that a likeness of her was seen within the fabric of the tree itself, as opposed to sitting in its branches; she left that to Tom the Lord.

2.1
THE RUMMER TAVERN, CITY CENTRE, CARDIFF

The Rummer Tavern is situated opposite the castle in the centre of Wales' capital city. It has long claimed to be the oldest pub in Cardiff, although this was maybe dubious before the Cow and Snuffers in Llandaff closed down (the latter being a favourite haunt of both David Lloyd George and Lord Nelson). But if you define 'Cardiff's oldest pub' as a still-trading establishment that has served the community for the longest continuous period, then the claim is *probably* true. People have been supping ale here since at least the eighteenth century. We know this for certain as a copy of its licence from that period hangs on the wall. Bear in mind that districts of the city like Llanishen and Whitchurch were originally villages in their own right and have only latterly been absorbed into the sprawling metropolis that is Cardiff today.

The building itself is believed to be built on the site of a medieval 'burgage' plot: a rectangle of land at right angles to the street. Having said that, the famous cartographer John Speed drew a map of Cardiff in 1610, and there is a noticeable gap where the Rummer Tavern should be.

Back in the late 1980s it was managed by a friend of mine. He was doing some work down in the cellar one day when he found a genuine iron ball and chain in the floor, a discovery indicating that not all of this pub's history is exactly wholesome. In the interest of historical reconstruction, I was made to wear it on my stag night as we went from pub to pub in the city, much to the amusement of all around.

The name of this famous old Cardiff pub may prompt you to ask an important question: what's the difference between a pub, an inn, a tavern and an ale house? Or are they all the same thing?

Well, originally they were quite distinct entities, but across the course of history the distinctions between them have been blurred and ultimately lost.

A public house once referred to any establishment that was a secular house open to the public to use as a meeting place, a court or even an administrative centre. Before the days of licensing laws, a public house could have been pretty much anything. The consumption of alcohol would have been incidental.

Inns were more specific in their definition. They were places where travellers could find accommodation for the night, a function now more associated with hotels and guesthouses. One big difference between inns, back in the day, and hotels now is that in an old inn you would be sharing your accommodation with others, rather than having a room to yourself. That is why even the biggest old inns only have a small number of rooms, and why walls between them often have modern partitions fixed to the roof beams. As a guest at an inn, you would usually expect to be provided with some food and drink, but that was a secondary rather than a primary function.

Taverns and ale houses were much more aligned to what we might think of as a pub today: places primarily for food and drink. The main difference between them was largely snobbery. The tavern, borrowing its name from the Latin *tavernae* was for the more discerning customer, a place for the well-heeled to indulge themselves. They were, perhaps, closer to what we would call a restaurant today, although that concept did not exist until after the French Revolution, when the former cooks of aristocratic households had to find a new way of making a living once their employers had fallen victim to the guillotine.

Most of our old village and town pubs these days follow the

tradition of alehouses, even though they tend to call themselves inns. Alehouses were places where any old soul could just rock up and buy a beer.

These distinctions were enshrined in law. In 1604 a parliamentary act on the subject declared that 'the ancient, true and proper use of inns, alehouses and victualling houses is for the receipt, relief and lodging of wayfarers... and not for the entertainment and harbouring of lewd and idle people.'

All well and good, you might say, but what exactly is a 'rummer'? Well, it was a sixteenth-century vessel used for drinking wine. It is derived from the German word *römer*, which is a cup usually used for toasting.

So there we are. I hope that's settled that. Let's talk a bit about the pub.

The Rummer Tavern, I am sorry to say, has never really been sure what it is trying to be. When you approach it for the first time, and see all the whitewash and black timbers, you could be mistaken for thinking that it is a typical Tudor pub. In reality, however, what you see are the fruits of a mock Tudor reconstruction of the twentieth century. To be fair, there's nothing unusual about that; as we have discussed, everyone was at it back in the day. The act of trying to imbue your establishment with a little bit of mystique is as old as the hills. The weird thing in this instance is that, in the twenty-first century, the current owners have decided to go completely the other way.

The interior has been modernised and turned into a sports bar, with the addition of vast, plasma screen TVs. If you have ever seen the Simon Pegg film *The World's End* you may be familiar with the line, 'Starbucking, man. It's happening everywhere.' 'Starbucking': corporately sanitised to within an inch of its existence, stripped of any discernible character or individuality. That is what has happened at the Rummer Tavern.

It's a difficult balance, isn't it? Which holds the moral high ground: the eighteenth-century inn claiming to have been established 300 years earlier, or the eighteenth-century tavern looking like every other pub in Cardiff? At the end of the day, pubs first and foremost are businesses. They live and die by the relentless laws of commerce. If an accountant somewhere can say that takings are up exponentially since the Rummer Tavern modernised, who am I to cry foul? Especially when so many old pubs are closing down every day. I would rather see ancient pubs preserved in any form than to see them lost forever, which more often than not is the choice we face.

There is one interesting thing about the Rummer. It has a ghost which hangs around in the toilets. This is never a good start. It is believed to be the ghost of a sailor who died of a broken heart soon after finding his wife in bed with another man. The significance of the toilets? Who knows.

According to local historian Dic Mortimer, who clearly found records I could not, Cardiff's other pubs with claims to have been established before 1800 are what is now Elevens, formerly Dempseys, and before that the Globe, which was established in 1720; the Owain Glyndŵr, which is not far from the Rummer Tavern, which he puts at 1731; the Model Inn at 1770; and the Sandringham at 1792. There are also a couple more which I have elaborated upon further in the next couple of chapters.

The pub is now owned by the Craft Union.

2.2

THE GOAT MAJOR, CITY CENTRE, CARDIFF

This charming little old pub opposite the castle gates has been a favourite of Cardiffians since 1813. The building it inhabits is much older than that though. It is only a few yards away from the Rummer Tavern, but perhaps tellingly it is included in Speed's 1610 map of the town.

The pub was originally called the Goat, then for a while the Bluebell. The pub's current name is a nod to its long, traditional association with Welsh infantry regiments that used to have their headquarters at the castle opposite – regiments such as the South Wales Borderers, which saw a lot of action in the desert campaign of the Second World War, and subsequently got disbanded and absorbed into the Royal Welch Fusiliers.

The RWF regimental mascot has been a white Kashmir billy goat since Queen Victoria presented them one in 1860. She also gave some to the Mostyn family in Llandudno. These are the ones that now roam free on the Great Orme above the town. It is normally one of their offspring that is chosen to be the regiment's mascot. Even though it was championed by none other than Queen Victoria, I am not convinced that the gifting of goats ever really caught on. I certainly can't remember the last time I gave anyone a goat.

Since 2006, there was further amalgamation with the Royal Regiment of Wales, and now the regiment is simply called the Royal

Welsh. Each Battalion of the Royal Welsh has its own traditions for the naming of their goats. Mascots chosen by the 1st Battalion are called Billy, goats chosen by the 2nd Battalion are called Taffy, and those chosen by the 3rd Battalion are called Shenkin. The latter is most commonly associated with his ceremonial duty of leading the regimental band out onto the pitch at the Principality Stadium, for them to perform the national anthems before international rugby matches.

The Goat Major is not actually the goat himself, but the title given to the soldier who is his appointed handler. Inside the pub there are lots of old photographs and memorabilia of the regiment and their famous mascot.

These days the pub is a typical example of the Brains chain: just general-purpose pie and pint stuff, nothing which regulars might describe as fancy.

It has one rather nice bit of folklore attached to it, albeit comparatively modern. As I have said, it was a pub traditionally associated with Welsh infantrymen. One night during the Second World War, a couple of off duty American GIs wandered in for a pint. There was naturally a bit of rivalry between the Welsh and American soldiers, and when one of the GIs struck up a conversation with some pretty local girls, tempers began to boil over. The oft chanted cry of 'over paid, over sexed and over 'ere' was levelled, and the inevitable brawl broke out – one that, as it turned out, was settled pretty quickly. One of the American soldiers was very useful with his fists. He is said to have sparked out anyone who came within a foot of him before dusting himself down, finishing his drink and heading back to base with his friends.

He turned out to be Rocky Marciano. As unlikely as this may sound, it is quite possibly true: he was known to have been stationed just up the road, in Swansea, during the Second World War.

2.3
THE CITY ARMS,
CITY CENTRE, CARDIFF

The City Arms stands, on the corner of Quay Street and Womanby Street, opposite the Principality Stadium, in a building built around the turn of the eighteenth century. At the time, and for over a century afterwards, this was a bit of a no go area in Cardiff. Back then the river Taff had its banks in what is now Westgate Street, and Quay Street, as the name would suggest, was the original Cardiff dock. The long and short of it is that the City Arms would have stood just outside the old town walls, and we all know what that means! (If not, see the chapter on the Hanbury Arms in Caerleon.)

The area continued to be a bit seedy even after Cardiff started to expand and grow in importance. Although today Womanby Street (the narrow street running between the pub and the castle) is now filled with plush, expensive office blocks and fashionable city bars, during the Industrial Revolution it was where the slums of the city stood. Poverty and deprivation were rampant, and diseases spread like wildfire as people struggled with very little money, no sanitation or ventilation, poor diets and cramped living conditions.

In 1830, a man called Dr William Henry Duncan wrote an account of slum dwellings in industrialised cities around the UK. In his view, roughly a third of the population lived in the cellars of back-to-back courthouses. He described them as having earth floors and no ventilation or sanitation, with as many as sixteen people living in just one room. These conditions were predisposed to the spread of epidemic disease, in particular cholera. Right up until the mid-twentieth century, this was not a place for the faint hearted, especially after dark.

It is very hard to say how long there has been a pub on this site. Dic Mortimer, in his book *An Autobiography of Cardiff*, puts its origins in 1793, which sounds plausible enough, though I am not sure what his source was. There are those who believe that there has been an establishment here ever since there was a commercial harbour, which would mean the fourteenth century. The chances are that there was some kind of hostelry to cater for the costermongers unloading the boats and the sailors passing through. The earliest records I could find were dated 1880, when it was a pub called the Cattle Market. It then became the Cardiff Boat, and in fact did not become the City Arms until 1955, when Cardiff saw off competition from Caernarvon to be named Wales' capital city.

These days, the City Arms is part of the Brains Brewery chain of pubs. If you don't find that concept scary enough, it is also reputed to be haunted by a mischievous poltergeist. He frequently knocks over ornaments and makes pictures drop off the walls. He even moves furniture around, no doubt trying to inject a bit of character and individuality back into the place. Heed his cries, Brains.

2.4
THE PRINCE OF WALES, CITY CENTRE, CARDIFF

I t has to be said that this is not an especially old or beautiful pub, but all the same it has quite an interesting history. When I was little, my mother used to hurry past it on days out in Cardiff. I subsequently learned that this was because in the 1970s it was a known hang out for the grubby mac brigade, a cinema that only showed blue movies to customers over eighteen.

It was originally built as a theatre in 1878. It was Cardiff's second Theatre Royal after the Crockherbtown Theatre Royal, which stood on Park Place but was destroyed in a fire. This place was also burned to the ground in 1899 but was subsequently rebuilt in its original style, and then had a big refit in the 1920s, creating some of the wall and ceiling features you can still see in there today.

Crockherbtown, by the way, was the name given to the town that grew up outside the town walls of Cardiff in the run up to the old east gate. It was a line of buildings built on either side of the old Roman road leading into the town, which is now about five feet under modern day Queen Street.

Historically, the most interesting thing about the Prince of Wales is on the outside wall on its south facing side – the side nearest the railway station. You can see in the masonry a clear brick outline of what is unmistakably a church building. That is because St Mary's church originally stood on this site. On Speed's map of 1610 the church is vast. I am not sure how accurate his scaling was, but it looks as if it would have dwarfed most cathedrals. To be fair, he may have had to use a bit of imagination with his map because, at the time he drew it, the original church had been destroyed by, of all things, a tsunami.

I mentioned in my chapter on the Rose Inn in Redwick that in 1607 a tsunami swept up the Bristol Channel, devastating buildings and settlements in South Wales and Somerset. Well, St Mary's Church was one of its victims. There were plans to rebuild it, but they were never executed. All we have as a reminder is the brickwork on the Prince of Wales, a tribute to its somewhat godlier forebearer.

The pub is now part of the Wetherspoons chain.

2.5
THE CHURCH INN, LLANISHEN, CARDIFF

There are plenty of people who will tell you that the *real* title holder of 'oldest pub in Cardiff' is in fact the Church Inn, in Llanishen. As always with these things, it totally depends on what criteria you set. Is it the pub located in the oldest building? Is it the pub that has traded as a pub continuously for the longest period? What if the name has changed?

Do you see? It is rife with permutations. Getting the correct answer depends entirely on the question you ask. It's a bit like Deep Thought in *the HitchHiker's Guide to the Galaxy*: it's hard enough to figure out the question, let alone to work out the answer. Which, incidentally, is forty-two.

The village of Llanishen itself was founded in the fifth century, by missionary monks from nearby Llandaff, who wanted to establish a new church in the lowlands in front of Caerphilly Mountain. Llanishen seemed an ideal siting, as it had a stream fed from a nearby spring called Nant Fawr, which had good drinking water. In the twelfth century, the Normans built the church that forms the foundations of the one which now stands opposite the Church Inn.

I have heard claims that the building housing the pub is fourteenth century. I am not totally convinced, but you never know. Possibly the cellar and foundations are the remnants of a former structure, but the building there today is clearly Georgian.

It was listed in 1975, and the listing describes it as an 'eighteenth century vernacular house with lobby entrance, formerly with kitchen, hall and inner room. The building subsequently became an inn, and a parallel range was added to the north, probably in the C19.'

It has had its brushes with celebrity. The seemingly ardent boozer Oliver Cromwell had a pint there, as he did in many villages north of Cardiff. His mother was born and brought up in Whitchurch, and as a boy, he is believed to have spent a lot of time with her family on their estate, in what was then a village, even though today it is just a leafy suburb of the city.

An altogether more verifiable claim, and a far better story, relates to that golden voiced Welsh politician David Lloyd George.

In 1881 the Welsh Sunday Closing Act had been passed, prohibiting, by law, the sale of alcohol in pubs in Wales on a Sunday. And in June 1895, David Lloyd George visited Cardiff on a fact-finding mission, to see how meticulously this new law was being implemented and enforced. He and two local dignitaries had decided that the best way to do this was to go on their rounds unannounced and incognito. They even wore disguises. A newspaper article which subsequently reported the matter in *the Western Mail* claimed that they had dressed in a 'totally disreputable manner' in order to avoid being recognised. So it was that, slumming it, off they went, on their tour of Cardiff pubs on that warm and sunny Sunday afternoon.

At first, it looked like things were going well and that they were going to return to London telling of a success story. Nothing seemed to be going on in the pubs in the centre of town and Canton, and at the Cow and Snuffers in Llandaff north, where all they were offered was a glass of lemonade. However, it is also known that David Lloyd George had visited this last pub many times previously, and it might just be that his disguise was not quite good enough to fool the landlord.

If the future prime minister had called it a day at the Cow and Snuffers, he would have returned to London with nothing but good news. However, he pushed his luck by instead going on to the Church Inn, in Llanishen.

I don't want to dilute what happened next by putting my slant on it. Here are the actual words of one of Lloyd George's companions, as quoted in the newspaper article in *the Western Mail* that broke this story:

'As we approached, we noticed, about 50 yards from the house, three men standing beside some inanimate object on the roadside. It was a man sleeping off the effects of drink.'

Not the best start then. They went inside. The companion continued:

'The door was wide open and business was brisk. There were not many people in the bar, but there was a good deal of beer carried to another room.'

Lloyd George himself said, 'I found a good deal of drinking taking place in those villages, more especially at Llanishen. There were people there drinking beer in the Church Inn. I saw one man swinishly drunk on the roadside.'

Despite everything he had seen, however, Lloyd George must have decided to let sleeping dogs lie. On his return to London, his summary of the visit was: 'Speaking generally, I did not see much drunkenness.'

2.6
THE TRAVELLER'S REST, THORNHILL, CARDIFF

This very pretty inn sits above Cardiff, on a sharp bend in the road that crosses Caerphilly Mountain. It was built in the early 1800s and granted its first license in 1864, and it oozes with antiquity and quaint cottagey features, from its thatched roof to its low ceilings in the main bar. If you look closely at the walls, you cannot help but notice some of the vast boulders that have been incorporated into the wall masonry. The stone for the building was exhumed from a quarry just a few yards behind it.

The Traveller's Rest is one of the few pubs that stayed open throughout the Second World War. Perhaps it was used to such strife. It is located on the historical boundary between the flat and fertile low land areas occupied by the Normans and the mountainous areas to which they banished the Welsh. The road over Caerphilly mountain was a gateway between both worlds. If you venture into the woods behind the pub, you will find the crumbling remains of Morgrair Castle. It's a really early Norman stone castle, built to defend Norman Wales' northern boundary, on the site of an earlier Iron Age hillfort. Most people, even locals, do not know it exists, but to be fair to them, no one at all knew about it until 1895. There are those who believe that construction may never have been finished, as there is no evidence that any of the buildings had a roof. It clearly became redundant after the De Clares built the seemingly indomitable fortress on the other side of the mountain, in Caerphilly itself. But more about that in our next chapter.

While the Traveller's Rest was built from stone quarried a few yards away, this castle was made from stone quarried near Ogmore-by-Sea in the Vale of Glamorgan.

The Traveller's Rest today is part of the Vintage Inns network.

2.7

THE COURT HOUSE, CAERPHILLY

aerphilly Castle is famous throughout the world and is the second largest castle in Britain after Windsor. When it was built by Gilbert De Clare in the thirteenth century, its design was revolutionary. Simply put, it was the most advanced instrument of war anywhere in Europe at the time. It has inner and outer baileys, is surrounded by lakes, moats and defensive ditches and split across two well defended islands in the middle of it all. The huge fortified outer walls have no windows or any ornamental features. Everything is designed purely to give strategic edge and to allow the Normans to subdue the Welsh.

One of its most recognisable features is its leaning tower, the effect of seventeenth-century cannon fire on the thirteenth-century masonry during a siege in the English Civil War.

And directly opposite the castle, in the town centre, is this lovely old pub. As the name would suggest, it was originally a court, a dispensary of medieval justice. Many of the maxims we associate with British law today originate from this period. Things like, 'innocent until proven guilty', 'the right to remain silent' and 'the right to be tried by a jury of our peers' were enshrined in the Magna Carta of 1215. Incidentally so was a clause that made the pint the official quantity in which to buy beer. But none of that really had anything to do with the sort of justice that was dispensed here. That only applied to knights and nobles. If you were just an ordinary peasant, you had an altogether more rudimentary process before the law.

There were trials by ordeal, which relied on the intervention of God to show if the accused was innocent or guilty. For example, the ordeal by fire, in which the accused had to hold a red-hot coal in their hands. Their burns would then be bandaged and they would be thrown into a cell for a week to give the wounds some time to heal. Once the bandage was removed, if your wounds had healed cleanly, then it was a sign that God had protected you as your heart was pure. If they blistered it was an indication of guilt. Harsh, I'm sure you will agree, but there is at least a semblance of logic to it, unlike the ordeal by water. In this, the accused was tied to a chair and submerged in the waters of the lake. If, when you were pulled back to the surface, you had not drowned, it was proof of your guilt, as it meant that the baptismal waters had repelled you. If, however, you *did* drown, it was proof that you were innocent of all charges. Figure that one out.

The court the pub now stands in was built on a burgage plot back in the fourteenth century and was part of the old south gate to the castle, the remains of which can be seen just behind the beer garden. And what a glorious beer garden it is, with outstanding views of the castle, moat and lake. The glass extension on the back of the building means that you can enjoy these views even when the weather is not conducive to sitting outside. Which, in South Wales, is of course quite often.

It is a Grade II listed building, and its listing describes it thus:

'Medieval with later additions. Built as a courthouse in the C14 on a burgage plot next to the south gate of Caerphilly Castle. The court was previously held inside the gatehouse.

'Repairs were undertaken to the roof by the Lord of Glamorgan in 1429. Originally two units and a single storey one with central passage and entrance to rear. Raised to two storeys, and wings added to each end: West wing is late C17, East wing C19.'

The building has had many uses down the years. It has been a medieval court, a doctor's surgery, and a private house, just to name a few. It was also an artisan dairy and cheesery, where they made the world-famous Caerphilly Cheese. Production these days is on a somewhat bigger scale, in a large factory on the outskirts of the town.

The Courthouse is now part of the Greene King chain offering simple food and ales.

2.8

THE KING'S ARMS, PENTYRCH

Have you seen the 1995 film *The Englishman Who Went Up a Hill but Came Down a Mountain*? It starred Hugh Grant and was about a surveyor who was sent to a small Welsh village to determine if its nearby peak qualified as a mountain or not. While he was there, he fell in love and some other stuff happened. You get the gist. Anyway, that story was about Pentyrch.

This pretty little village nestles on the slopes of the Garth, which is the highest point for miles around. The views from the top, over Cardiff and the Vale of Glamorgan and across the Bristol Channel, are stunning.

Without wanting to spoil the film for you, as high as it is, it still is not quite high enough to be officially called a mountain. Which is a pity, as it has been known as the Garth mountain (or in Welsh, Mynydd-Y-Garth) for centuries. It is quite hard to stop calling it that even though you may be aware of the facts. Or maybe that's just me? I still haven't got my head around calling Jif 'Cif'. I think the condition might be hereditary. As a small boy I remember my grandfather wandering into a room where my father was watching football on the TV. 'Who's playing?' my grandfather asked. 'Austria, Hungary,' came my father's reply. My grandfather raised an eyebrow. 'Versus whom?'

We digress.

Despite not being a mountain, the Garth was always a significant site. There are a series of Bronze Age burial mounds (rounded cairns to be precise) dotted along its summit, which date from 2000BC. In prehistoric times this high vantage point was a place of pagan worship, something that in their time the early Christians were keen to exploit in their mission. St Cadoc, a sixth-century saint who established churches and monasteries throughout the Vale of Glamorgan, founded the church here as part of a monastic colony. The church is still dedicated to him to this day, as is the well that traditionally gave the village its water supply. It was believed to have magical healing powers. As Cadoc is the patron saint of skin conditions and burns, one has to assume that these were the sorts of conditions its waters were most effective at healing. As a result, Pentyrch was an early place of Christian pilgrimage in Wales.

Even though the King's Arms was not trading as an inn during the medieval period, the building is contemporary with the sixteenth century. It would originally have been a 'long house', a traditional farm dwelling of the period, very common across Wales at the time. It would have consisted of, as the name suggests, one long and low stone-built building, with living accommodation for people at one end and livestock on the other, and a large inglenook in the middle to provide heat for both.

It became an inn in the seventeenth century and still has a lot of its original features, such as exposed masonry and timber beams and an open fire. It also is home to a rather unusual and inexplicable phenomenon. Every evening, at roughly 4-5pm, a draft blows across the bar, irrespective of whether there are any doors or windows open. It appears to blow up from under the floor. The floor was pulled up in front of the bar to see if there was some kind of conduit allowing this draft in. Not only did they not find anything, but they found that some previous owner had packed the space below the floorboards with a heavy bag, no doubt in an attempt to stop this draft. But to no avail. It continues to this day, as regular as clockwork.

Perhaps connected, the present owners have also encountered the obligatory pub ghost. In this case, they were having a drink after a busy night in their bar, after all the customers had gone home and the doors had been locked. They looked up to see a man clutching what looked like a bundle of paperwork, walking hurriedly across the room. He then walked into a wall and vanished from sight.

I started this chapter talking about the time the village played host to Hollywood glitz. As it turns out, the King's Arms is no stranger to this world of celebrity. As you might expect, Sir Tom Jones has been spotted in there from time to time. Probably more of a surprise is that one half of the pop group Bros, Luke Goss, has been known to pop in too. On one occasion he did so with his friend Keanu Reeves. Film nerds like me will remember that they were both in the epic film *Matrix Reloaded* together, so when Mr Reeves was filming in Wales, it was where they chose to go for a pint. If you are a sports fan, you can also expect to see Cardiff City players old and new, as the owner used to be the club's chef. There is no shortage of rugby royalty popping in for the occasional pint either.

If you pop in yourself, you will find that it serves a decent selection of real ales and good, hearty home-cooked food. It is also a very dog friendly pub, which suits all the walkers on the Garth who pop in for a pint on the way home.

2.9

THE BARON'S COURT, COGAN

I have to confess that I always assumed that this place was not really that old. I thought it was a Victorian gothic reconstruction made to look like an old castle. It was partly down to the size of the place, and partly down to the absence of anything else of particular antiquity anywhere around it.

Oh, how wrong I was. To my credit, the original building has been substantially extended, and it was in the Victorian era that these alterations were done. But the original parts of the building are in fact so old, no one is totally sure when they were built.

We do know that, when the antiquarian John Leland toured South Wales in 1540, it was already a substantial manor house, of an age sufficient for him to make a note of it in his writings. Various sources tell us that, in the Tudor period, it was the home of Sir George Herbert, a descendent of the family that used to live in the Murgenger House in Newport. His coat of arms still appears on the porch above the main entrance, and that is why, before it was called the Baron's Court, it was for many years known as Sir George's Hall.

There used to be a harbour just in front of it, on the banks of the river Ely, and the manor raised an income for its owner by charging ships to use it. We have an account from 1520 of a rather scandalous miscarriage of justice that shows just how unscrupulous the Herberts were when it came to claiming these dues. Walter Herbert (George's son) had seized a Portuguese ship and got its captain thrown into prison. His justification for doing so was a claim that the ship had attempted to berth and unload without paying for the privilege, and that the ship's captain and crew were felons on the run. The captain protested his innocence and accused both Herbert and the Sheriff of Cardiff of corruption and 'tyrannous behaviour'. The next thing he knew, he was being fitted up for the unsolved murder of a woman whose body had been found in a nearby wood.

The matter was brought before the court. There were only two witnesses who gave testimony: two members of the ship's crew who were unable to speak a word of English. Their entire testimony was given in Portuguese with a running interpretation provided to the court by a servant in the employ of Herbert himself. No one knows what they actually said, but the English version given to the court was enough to see their captain hanged and his ship, crew and cargo impounded by the Herberts.

As impressive as the original manor house was, the Herberts grew in wealth, status and power, until the mansion at Greyfriars in the centre of Cardiff seemed a more fitting place for them. The old manor at Cogan Pill was vacated and tenanted out to a family of farmers. It was neglected for about 200 years, until it was bought in 1851 by a local magistrate and agent to the second Marquis of Bute, by the name of JS Corbett. Let me put all that into some context.

I have already said that, during the Middle Ages, Cardiff was very insignificant. But by 1851 all that had changed. All the coal and steel from the booming South Wales valleys was distributed to the world from the docks in Cardiff. Those vast docks had to be built quickly to cope with the demand, and housing needed to go up to accommodate the labour force that worked there. It was all built on land which the first Marquis of Bute had acquired as part of a dowry when he married his wife, land which, when he acquired it, was pretty worthless. But by this point in history, the Cardiff Docks were the second biggest in the world – only New York could surpass them for volume of trade. As such, the Marquis of Bute was now the richest man in the world.

Jammy or what?

In the mid to late nineteenth century there was also a huge gothic revival. Castles and ruins were suddenly chic, and with his vast wealth and appreciation for all things historic, the Marquis poured millions into rebuilding Cardiff Castle and Castell Coch, and employed the greatest architects and craftspeople of the day to recreate his own mock medieval home. With Cardiff suddenly flush with cash and awash with gothic architects, designers and contractors, when Corbett bought and restored his manor house, he not only had the money to restore it, but also a string of experienced people on hand to do the work for him, people he would have already vetted when instructing them on behalf of the Marquis of Bute.

This is why I was fooled into thinking that this place was just a Victorian folly. It's because this is the period when so much of the work we see today was done.

2.10

THE PLYMOUTH ARMS, ST FAGANS

The English Civil War was a messy business. It raged on between the Cavaliers, who supported the King of England, and the Roundheads, who supported the Parliamentarians, between 1642 and 1646. And then, just when everyone thought it was all over, it flared up again, as tempers frayed over unpaid bills and who could and could not maintain defences and military forces.

It all gets rather confusing, and to make matters worse, in the second instalment of the conflict, lots of protagonists changed sides. It led to the biggest battle ever fought on Welsh soil, the Battle of St Fagans, which took place in the Spring of 1648. The fuse was lit when a number of defeated Welsh lords refused to hand over their castles. Then, the former leader of the Parliamentarians in South Wales, Major General Lord Laughan, decided to switch sides and join forces with the Royalist lords, leading an army against his former allies. They had decided to make their mark by marching on Cardiff, which had been a Parliamentarian stronghold.

Their opposition was led by Colonel Thomas Horton. Even though Laughan's rebel Cavalier army outnumbered Horton's Parliamentarian forces by near enough two to one, Horton was in command of crack troops of the New Model Army, equipped with modern equipment like muskets and cannon; Laughan's army, meanwhile, was mostly farmers, armed with clubs and sticks. Horton also knew that he had re-enforcements on their way, led by Oliver Cromwell himself, who must have managed to pull himself away from any number of pubs we have already looked at in this book, for long enough to lead an army into battle anyway.

Horton got to Cardiff before Laughan and pitched camp west of the town, in the fields and marshes around the riverbank in St Fagans, near where the Museum of Welsh Life stands today. This blocked Laughan's progress and meant he had to re-think his strategy. Determined to get the battle underway before Cromwell arrived, Laughan launched a surprise attack. To try and negate the effectiveness of Horton's artillery, the Royalists hid behind hedges and fought using guerrilla tactics. But this meant they were only able to attack the outposts of their opposing army. Once the Roundheads attacked in full, the Royalists panicked and ran. It was all over very quickly. The rebel Cavaliers were routed. 300 were killed and 3,000 taken prisoner. Laughan and his rebel allies fled to Pembroke castle, where they endured an eight-week siege before surrendering.

The village of St Fagans is very peaceful now. Lots of picture-postcard cottages, a castle, a historic church and a village green. The Plymouth Arms stands in a prominent position on the roadside in the heart of the village.

On a few occasions, when putting this book together, I have paused and mused to myself, 'Gosh! What a cracking pub that used to be. I haven't been there in years.' This is definitely true of the Plymouth Arms. There has been an inn on this site since the fourteenth century, but on first glance you cannot help but be impressed with its rather grand façade. It's certainly not your typical coaching inn.

The frontage was put up in 1859 by Lord Robert Windsor, Earl of Plymouth. He was famous as a host, liking nothing better than to entertain his aristocratic friends at St Fagans Castle. What is today the Plymouth Arms was then accommodation for the butlers and valets of his aristocratic party guests. So, wanting to make a good impression on his visiting friends, Lord Windsor decided this needed building up.

However, as his peers would only see the outside of the building, and only the servants would see the inside, that's where the finery ended. The inside was left as it was until relatively recently.

The Plymouth Arms is part of the Vintage Inns network. It is more focused on food than booze, but it has a good wine selection, decent food and always a couple of real ales on tap.

2.11
THE CAPTAIN'S WIFE, SULLY

The Captain's Wife only became a pub comparatively recently, but there is a lot to the building's history.

Over the years, Sully Island has seen its fair share of excitement. Once it had an Iron Age hillfort, which survived into the eighteenth century, serving as an infamous retreat for smugglers. Contraband would be unloaded at high tide, before at low tide being gathered up and hidden away. Some of the smugglers were believed to have been residents of a row of fishermen's cottages, later amalgamated into one large house, later again becoming the Captain's Wife.

In an attempt to stamp out the local smuggling problem, the Customs and Excise officer stationed in Sully was ordered to storm the island one night and commandeer whatever he could seize. He was a very nervous man, and did not like conflict, so he was delighted when he arrived on the island to find it was deserted. He was even more delighted when he found two large barrels of brandy. He took them back to his own cottage, thinking of presenting them to his boss the following morning. He hid them under his own bed for safekeeping and ran through the house to make sure all his windows and doors were securely bolted.

When he woke the following morning, both barrels had gone. His windows and doors all remained locked, from the inside, just as he had left them the night before. He fled without a trace, vowing to never again have anything to do with the godforsaken place.

It is believed that, years later, long after the smugglers had departed, the owner of the smugglers' once-separate houses was a ship's captain, and it was his wife who gave the pub its name. They were clearly a pair of local celebrities, because we have not one but three stories about them.

With apologies to readers of my first book, *Legends and Folklore of Bridgend and the Vale* (and with further apologies for the shameless plug), this is because of a practice I explored in great detail there. The truth is that, up until the twentieth century, most ordinary people in Wales could not read or write. Accordingly, the recording and retelling of history was the domain of the bards, who wrote them into songs, poems and stories.

The only issue with such a practice was their impulse to entertain, rather than to accurately inform. Exaggerations and sensationalism abound. A favourite technique was to take a classic story, dating from way back, and to re-tell it with a local contemporary as the main character. In my later chapter on the Old House, Llangynwyd, I will share with you the now famous legend of the Maid of Cefn Ydfa. There is quite a lot of evidence to suggest that the story is far older than the version known today; however, rather than let a good story go to waste, a talented bard clearly took the old story and re-cast local lovers in the lead role.

Conversely, as loath as bards were to let a good story die, they were sometimes reluctant to let a good character die too. A really famous local character might crop up in stories centuries after their death. For example, quite a lot of folklore about Robert Fitzhamon sees him slotted into the role of baddie long after the Norman conquest of Morgannwg.

We will encounter another example of this in my chapter about the Prince of Wales, Kenfig, where the death of a noble crusader precipitates the ruin of the town. The only problem is, this story takes place in the fifteenth century, while the Crusades were all over by 1291!

In other words, this knight would have been over 200 years old!

For all these reasons, I am always amused when people get hot under the collar about the correct version of a folk tale. 'No, no, that's not right, that's not the story I know!' they cry. Quite often there are several permutations, and equally often, none of them are true.

Anyway, enough commentary, here are those three stories I promised.

In the first, a sea captain and his wife lived in Sully House, and they loved each other very dearly. However, owing to the nature of his job, the captain was forced to spend months at a time at sea, away from her. One day he returned from a long voyage and was devastated to discover that she had died only a day or two before. Grief-stricken by his loss, he decided that he would never bury her body: that he would keep her coffin with him in their house together so they would never again be parted. The grisly truth was only discovered years later, when thieves broke into his house and stole what they believe to be a chest of treasures, only to discover her partially decayed remains inside. 'Serves them right,' as my mother would have observed.

Personally, I love that story. Plenty of twists in the tale, plenty of goriness and a really meaty plot. However, the others are equally good.

There is one that the local lord of the manor, Colonel Poyner (who was prominent in the English Civil War), took a wife who was much younger than him. She wanted for nothing materially, but secretly her heart belonged to the dashing sea captain who had been her childhood crush. It was futile for them to try and fight their feelings for each other, so one day they decided to elope together and start a new life overseas. But their plan was confounded when her husband caught them trying to leave together. The captain escaped into the night, but she could not escape her husband's grip, and in a fit of jealousy he murdered her on the spot, hiding her remains to avoid detection and the hand of justice. Her ghost still haunts the pub to this day; she appears as the spectre of a grey lady, pointing to where her remains have been hidden all these years, so that one day she might get a proper Christian burial.

And finally there's this one.

The captain and his wife were very much in love, and so that they would never be apart, he would smuggle her onboard his ship to accompany him on his voyages. Seafaring folk were very superstitious in those days, and it was considered bad luck to have a woman on board. When she was eventually discovered, one of his lieutenants was so outraged that he challenged the captain to a duel. In their ensuing contest, the lieutenant shot at and missed the captain, hitting instead his devoted wife, killing her instantly. He was left behind, wrought with guilt and mournful, and died shortly afterwards of a broken heart.

Now I know what you are dying to ask: 'Which one is true?' Alas, as boring as it is to say, I doubt any of them are. There is every likelihood that there really was a sea captain and his wife who lived in Sully, their love and devotion so evident as to be a frequent subject of conversation. I also believe that there was probably a particularly prolific bard in the area, who took the memory of these two lovers and cast them into this rather splendid triptych of tall tales. But all those twists and turns and tragedies? I have to think they're unlikely.

*

The Captain's Wife boasts one of the best beer gardens in Wales, with outstanding views across the Bristol Channel through the archipelago of islands that dot the seascape around Lavernock Point.

While supping your beverage of choice, looking out over this glorious view, you may well be treated to the sight of tourists walking along the rocky causeway between the beach and Sully Island at low tide, unaware that the sea in this area has one of the highest and fastest tidal flows in the world. When these walkers predictably get stranded, the coast guard has to come and rescue them. To anyone who fancies the adventure, it's worth pointing out that they will charge you for being such a numpty.

Today the Captain's Wife is part of the Vintage Inn Network. They always have a selection of real ales on tap and a typical pub chain menu: nothing too adventurous, simply all the usual pie and pint stuff.

2.12
THE BLUE ANCHOR, EAST ABERTHAW

Now here's a pub I have spent far more time in than I should have. It has many things going for it, not least proximity to my house. The sign outside proudly boasts 'Est 1380', which puts it firmly in the running for one of the oldest pubs in Wales. Paul R Davis estimated it to be early sixteenth century (which let's face it, is pretty old) but conceded that the building is another one made up of lots of earlier buildings subsequently absorbed into one. Most of the sixteenth-century features he refers to are in the main bar area on the upper level, which at some point would have been a kitchen. The stone arch over the door, now partially hidden by more recent masonry, is a particularly good example. The former hall on the lower level nearer the road, however, is probably the oldest bit of the pub, but by how much is hard to tell. The fourteenth century claim could well be genuine, but it is impossible to confirm.

It may be difficult to visualise it now, but there was a port on Aberthaw's river Thaw since Roman times. In particular, in the sixteenth and seventeenth centuries it was booming, to such an extent that the quayside Marsh House was fortified, to protect the valuable cargos that were unloaded there. There used to be two other pubs here, the Limpert Inn and the Ship Inn, both now gone, along with the ships, merchants and seamen who once passed through in their droves.

Not unrelated to its bustling maritime trade, this area, and this pub in particular, are closely linked to stories of smugglers and pirates. The Vale of Glamorgan as a whole was rife with it. A local vicar once complained of his flock, 'First they were pirates, next they were smugglers, then they became wreckers and by this time there is not an honest man left among them.' There is no doubt that this inn was a smugglers' haunt. There are even stories of a network of secret tunnels under it: one that runs from the cellar to the beach and another that runs to a safe house on the outskirts of the village. There is little in the way of evidence that either of these are real. It is quite likely that they were invented by local customs men, to account for how so much contraband escaped their supposedly watchful eyes.

The real reason was subsequently revealed by a smuggler in 1734, who had the misfortune of getting caught. He said (and I quote), 'We have always a spye on the officer; and when they find him on one side of the river at Aberthaw, they land what they have on the other.' There is no bridge at Aberthaw, so if you want to cross the river, you have to walk half a mile inland to the nearest bridging point, then back on the other side: enough time for smugglers to unload and make off with their contraband.

The pub is a free house and a permeant fixture in the food guides and the CAMRA good ale guides. They regularly have Wye Valley HPA, Wadworth 6X and Old Peculiar on tap, usually supported by a guest ale. They also do a good line in artisan ciders. This is a pub which has a string of celebrity visitors, most recently Simon Cowell and the Belgian Royal Family. Not both on the same night though.

2.13
THE OLD SWAN INN,
LLANTWIT MAJOR

As I mentioned in the preamble to this section, Llantwit Major was the site of Britain's first ever educational institution. If you are to believe the writings of a local antiquarian who went by the name of Iolo Morganwg (who is usually to be approached with caution), at its height it had over 2000 students enrolled. Its alumni included Saint David (the patron saint of Wales) and Saint Patrick (the patron saint of Ireland). There is even a widely held belief that it was from Llantwit Major that St Patrick was kidnapped and taken to Ireland in the first place.

With such a historical backdrop, it is hardly a surprise that, when you enter the square in the centre of the old town, three historically significant pubs, the White Hart, the Tudor Tavern and The Old Swan Inn, sit practically side by side. As you are about to discover, the Old Swann just edges the other two in terms of history and story value, but that is not to say that there is nothing to be said about the others. They are all medieval buildings, and the White Hart has a cellar believed to have once been part of a Romano-Celtic structure. This certainly goes some way to explaining the many regulars who have reported the apparition of a Roman soldier marching through the walls of the inn. There also used to be a trap door in the cellar, which opened onto a flight of steps. This is believed to be the entrance to a secret passageway which links to a series of tunnels dug from the old monastery at the

Cor – an escape route for when the university came under attack from Irish and Viking raiders.

The structure we see at the Swan today was originally a Tudor merchant's house, and like most pubs dating back that far, over the years it has absorbed other buildings around it, had bits added on and been partially modernised. However, most of what you see today is sixteenth century, and in remarkably good condition too, especially the rather ornate windows.

This was not the first building on this site. As I have mentioned, Llantwit was a significant settlement as far back as the fifth century. In the eleventh century, the last Welsh king of Morgannwg, Iestyn Ap Cwrgan, established a bank as well as a mint and a foundry here. He was ultimately defeated and deposed by the invading Norman army led by Robert Fitzhamon, Duke of Gloucester, and that saw this operation closed down. But it was not the last time the pub was associated with coin minting. In 1640 the then owner, Edward Maddock, was given licence to mint his own tokens in response to a general shortage of small coins at the time. The place was then a shop rather than an inn.

I mentioned in my chapter about the Blue Anchor in Aberthaw that, during the seventeenth and eighteenth century, smuggling and piracy was rife in the coastal towns and villages of the Vale of Glamorgan. The Swan was more than simply involved in this. It was the headquarters of the biggest operation of its kind in the area.

At its helm was Thomas Knight. He was a fearsome pirate and smuggler, originally from Lundy, and phenomenally astute in business. He had a fleet of large ships he had plundered from French merchants, and he needed to set up a harbour big enough to unload them but tucked away from prying eyes. In the end he built a quay on Barry Island which ticked all those boxes. At the time, Barry and Barry Island were two tiny hamlets with a combined population of around fifty people, quite different from the sprawling town we see there today. What really made his operation flourish, however, was the cooperation of the locals. There are sources that suggest that pretty much everyone in Barry was involved. So much contraband passed through Barry Island that Knight commissioned defences to be built there. It was becoming too valuable an asset to risk it being taken by customs officials. The enterprise was so successful he needed to recruit other smugglers from across the South Wales coast to distribute all the contraband.

He was landlord of the Old Swan Inn, running his entire operation from a small upstairs room. The pubs of the Heritage Coast were pivotal to the success of the operation, as they provided cellars where booty could be hidden and distributed. Even after customs officials had smashed his empire, he personally evaded capture and disappeared without a trace. No doubt he had a well-stocked war chest waiting for such an eventuality. Like I said, he was a very astute businessman.

The Old Swan has had its fair share of A list visitors. Its heyday in that respect was in the early twentieth century, when the nearby St Donats Castle was bought by the American newspaper tycoon William Randolph Hearst. He entertained many high-profile guests at his castle, and the itinerary for the day would quite often include a stroll into town along the coastal path, to grab a pint at the Swan. So it was that the likes Charlie Chaplin, Douglas Fairbanks, Errol Flynn, David Lloyd George, Winston Churchill and, of course, Hearst's mistress Marion Davies all frequented this out of the way spot.

Today there is always a good selection of ales and ciders, but not the standard ones you find everywhere. They tend to back ones you have never heard of, from more artisan breweries, although there is always Bass to fall back on if you're not feeling adventurous. The food here is very good too.

2.14

THE PLOUGH AND HARROW, MONKNASH

This pub might be tucked away in a remote backwater, but history exudes from every stone. The clue to this pub's antiquity can be found in the field behind the pub. Those overgrown mounds of stone and inexplicably high stretches of enclosure wall are all that remains of a monastic grange that was built here in 1130, by Richard De Glanville, as an annex to the Cistercian Abbey at Neath. The building the pub stands in was originally a barn on the monastery farm, much of which was rebuilt and extended in the eighteenth century. But it has had a number of uses since its early days, not all of them savoury.

Monknash is approximately a mile inland from the Bristol Channel, an especially treacherous stretch of the Bristol Channel at that. Just off the coast, to the east of Monknash beach, is the Nash, a submerged sandbank and a terrible shipping hazard. Many lives have been lost on the Nash, the worst single disaster being a boat called *the Frolic*, which struck the sandbank in 1831, with the loss of seventy-eight souls. Just to the west is Tusker Rock, a big black jagged rock that lies just below the waterline at high tide, ready to tear open the hull of any unsuspecting vessel that should drift too close. It has struck terror into sailors of these waters since the Vikings named it, over 1000 years ago.

In the seventeenth century a rash of ports sprung up along both sides of the Bristol Channel. Most traded between each other but some sent cargos further afield. This, along with the booming ports at Bristol and Gloucester, meant there was suddenly a lot of shipping in the channel, but precious little in the way of navigational aids or hazard warnings. Combine that with the unpredictable nature of the Bristol Channel generally, with its vast tidal ranges and propensity for waves, it was a disaster waiting to happen. And happen they did, and at such times the Plough was one of the buildings used as a mortuary and field hospital. The tables were frequently stacked with the bodies of perished mariners, awaiting a visit from the local magistrate and the priest to arrange for their disposal.

If drowned sailors were local, then at least their families would come forward to claim their bodies and give them a proper Christian burial. Sailors from further afield were not so lucky. They were disposed of in pits in nearby fields.

In the sixteenth century, there were a handful of locals who sought to turn the number of wrecks in the area to their own advantage. The most famous of these was a local brigand and pirate known as Matt of the Iron Hand. He got his name on account of losing a hand in a rather brutal altercation, and replacing it with an iron substitute. Matt of the Iron Hand is believed to have lived in Monknash. He lead a gang of ship wreckers who operated on the clifftops between Nash point and Dunraven beach, with the full blessing of the local landowner, Walter Vaughan of Dunraven Castle (more on whom later). Their modus operandi was to tie lanterns to the tails of sheep grazing on the clifftops. To the sailors out at sea, this mimicked the view of distant streetlights in Newton, which you would only see if you had sailed past the perilous Tusker Rock. Which, in fact, still lay ahead of them.

Once the ship had splintered and sunk, these gangs combed the beaches to collect whatever cargo, treasures and personal effects they could carry. Shipwrecking was a grizzly business. Even those survivors 'lucky' enough to be washed ashore would have their throats slit, to prevent them talking to the local authorities.

In the eighteenth century, the Plough and Harrow was still shrouded in this lawless world, used as a smugglers' lair to hide contraband. What a shocking outcome for a place that started out as a monastery.

But perhaps all hope is not lost. As recently as 2014, the monks were making a comeback.

The monks at the old monastery lived, worked and died within its walls. They were buried in a cemetery on the clifftops near Wick Beach. Over the centuries, successive rock falls and landslides meant that the cliffs around this burial place have slowly eroded away – to the point where, a few years ago, the thigh bones of an 800-year-old monk were spotted jutting out from the cliff face above the beach. This will not be the last time this happens, so it's well worth keeping an eye out for further skeletal appearances in the future.

The Plough and Harrow is a beautiful old pub. Full of character and ancient features, flagstone floors and exposed beams. There's always a good selection of real ales and ciders, and the food is pretty good too. Oh, and it is known to be haunted by a ghostly monk. And he isn't shy. Countless people have told me that they have seen him, independently of one another. Sometimes he is seen tending to the bodies of the victims of a shipwreck.

2.15

THE THREE GOLDEN CUPS, SOUTHERNDOWN

If you visit these pubs in the order I've presented them, then you would not break a sweat getting from the Plough and Harrow to the Three Golden Cups. It's barely a few miles between them. In fact, this is probably as good a time as any to share with you a top local tip.

There is a rural bus route that goes past all the best old pubs in this part of South Wales. Known locally as 'the ale bus', the 304 from Barry to Bridgend stops at (amongst others) the Blue Anchor in Aberthaw, the Old Swan and the neighbouring White Hart and Tudor Tavern in Llantwit Major; then it's on through the lanes to the Plough and Harrow, before St Brides Major and the Farmers Arms, and Southerndown and the Three Golden Cups. If at this point you can stagger your way back on, next up is the Pelican in Her Piety, opposite Ogmore Castle, before we finish our meander in Bridgend itself.

Being on a bus, of course, has other benefits. You can see over roadside hedges and out to the cliff line of the picturesque Heritage Coast, and you don't have to worry about having a drink or six. Not to mention, if you are of the right vintage yourself, it also has the benefit of being free.

We spoke in our last chapter about the shipwreckers of the area, and their patron Walter Vaughan of Dunraven Castle. You can see the remains of his castle, Dunraven, from the beer garden of the Three

Golden Cups. There are many legends about the place. It was originally an Iron Age hillfort. The name is believed to be derived from the Welsh *din dryvan*, which means 'triangular hillfort'.

It is believed by some to have been the home of Caradog (Latin name Caractacus), the enigmatic Welsh chieftain who managed to hold out against the might of the Roman army for over a decade. It was also linked to Arthurian legend by the colourful local historian and bard Iolo Morgannwg, who has already cropped up in a previous chapter. It is best known, however, for the legend of Walter Vaughan.

Walter Vaughan, to be fair to him, had a stretch of back luck. After a year in which his youngest child drowned in a shipwreck and his wife died of a fever, he turned to drink and gambling. It's an unhealthy combination. Very quickly he had squandered away the family fortune, and his two remaining children – his eldest son and his daughter – had disowned him and moved away. To restore his fortunes, he looked to the sea, which had taken so much from him.

As the coffers began to fill with his ill-gotten gains, Vaughan took stock of his life and decided that he needed to kick the drinking habit and try and restore his relationship with his children. He invited his eldest son and heir to come back to the castle and dine with him, and was delighted when he accepted. But the week before his son was expected, there was a terrible storm. Vaughan lit the light in his highest tower at the castle, to lure in any unsuspecting ships, and from his chambers in the dead of night, he heard the unmistakable sound of a ship wrecking on the rocks down below.

In the morning he went down to the beach to see what he could salvage. He spotted a dead man on the beach wearing very fine clothes, and thought to himself that they might be something to give to his son. But, as he turned over the corpse, he was devastated to recognise the man's face. It *was* his son. The young man had been so keen to rekindle his relationship with his father, he had come early as a surprise. Vaughan fell to his knees and let out a mournful cry, and from that day descended into madness.

Now, every year, on the anniversary of his son's death, their ghosts can be seen on either side of Dunraven Beach. Vaughan falls to his knees and raises his hands in the air, begging forgiveness from the ghost of his son. But the young man shuns his father's plea, turning away and disappearing. The ghost of Walter Vaughan cries out before disappearing himself.

Stirring stuff, I am sure you will agree. The moral of this story – don't have kids. Or have I missed something?

There is another legend about the castle, and this one relates directly to this pub and its rather unusual name.

As I alluded to earlier, there have been several castles on this site. In the twelfth century, Southerndown and Dunraven were part of the lordship of Ogmore Castle, which at the time was owned by the DeLondres family. We will hear more about them in a later chapter about Kidwelly.

The DeLondres family were served very loyally by a man of noble birth called Arnold DeBotler (his surname actually means Butler). Well, one day Arnold turned to his master and asked if he could be granted a plot of land, on which he might be allowed to build his own home. DeLondres agreed and gave him the estate at Dunraven; because De Botler had served him so well, he refused to take any payment from him for the land. Instead, they agreed that from that day forward, if a member or descendant of the DeLondres family were ever to visit Dunraven Castle, they would be served with three golden cups, full of the finest wine in the castle's cellar. And it is from this legend that the pub derives its name.

In more recent history, the Three Golden Cups has been no stranger to the A list. The picturesque beach of nearby Southerndown is now a staple backdrop in countless films and TV dramas. Devotees of *Doctor Who* will instantly recognise it as Bad Wolf Bay, the setting for a particularly iconic episode of the David Tennant era.

Of all these celebrity visits, perhaps most exciting is the day Bob Dylan walked into the pub. He had been shooting a scene from the 1987 film *Hearts of Fire*, in which Bob Dylan played, well, himself really, but called Billy rather than Bob. After the shot was in the can, as these Hollywood types say, he went for a drink in the Cups. He was very accommodating to the inevitable attention, even autographing the wall. Sadly a later, rather unimaginative landlord did not realise what the signature was and painted over it.

2.16
THE MARKET PLACE, COWBRIDGE

The inland area of the Vale of Glamorgan is altogether more genteel than the lawless coastal region. After all the cutthroat shenanigans in Sully, Aberthaw, Llantwit Major and Monknash, we can feel altogether more serene, refined and sophisticated in the ancient market town of Cowbridge.

The town has Roman origins, and archaeologists have turned up many interesting artifacts from that period over the years: a lot of pottery, a grave marker in the shape of a lion's head, the remains of long lost buildings (the most spectacular of which was the discovery of a bath house). On the old Antonine Itinerary, a town called 'Bomium' is listed somewhere between Cardiff and Neath. No one is absolutely certain where it was, but owing to all these discoveries, a lot of people (including me) back the theory that it was Cowbridge. That said, there are equally credible theories that it was on the banks of the river Ewenny near Heronstone, Bridgend.

After the Roman period, the town all but disappeared. We owe what we see today to its revival by the Normans around 1245. It became a flourishing commercial centre in the Middle Ages, and the layout of the high street and the town centre around it dates back to that period. The Bear, for example, is an early fifteenth-century building, although you would never know to look at it. Like much of the town, the Bear has been considerably updated over the years, its

Georgian façade being added in the late eighteenth century, like that of its namesake in Crickhowell.

As I have mentioned in earlier chapters, when the Normans invaded South Wales, they had a policy of banishing the Welsh to the mountains in the north, claiming the fertile land of the coastal regions as their own. As you can imagine, the Welsh were not especially thrilled with this arrangement, and they launched reprisals and uprisings, burning to the ground any Norman settlement they could storm. To protect themselves, the Normans built defensive stone walls around their towns, as can be seen in Cowbridge. The original south gate and a small section of wall still stand in the street behind the Duke of Wellington, next to the old school. At one time these walls would have completely surrounded the town, a formidable obstacle, particularly the west wall, which was insanely thick – the reason being that the west gate incorporated another pub, the Market Place (formerly the Masons Arms).

Those sections of the old west wall that did not form part of the pub were demolished in 1754. Having been built in the thirteenth century, the walls might indicate that the Market Place is another contender for the oldest pubs in Wales.

The building still remains remarkably unchanged by the progress of history. In the seventeenth century the medieval hall was modernised, with the addition of an upper floor and the conversion of the open hearth to a stone fireplace. In the eighteenth century a small brewhouse was built at the back. But there are many wonderful original features to look for. The stone arched doorway by the main entrance is one, as are the intricate, narrow, pointed windows on the exterior wall.

The building is quite unique. It is also haunted. It used to be an inn, and there is a report of the landlord opening up one morning to find a guest sleeping downstairs in the lounge. When questioned he said that the ghost of a 'pale lady' had walked through the wall into his upstairs room.

The Market Place is more of a restaurant than a pub these days, and I have eaten well there on several occasions.

2.17
THE BUSH INN,
ST HILARY

The Bush Inn is an exceptionally pretty pub, and it is in an especially pretty village too. It wouldn't look out of place on the lid of a box of fudge.

At the heart of the village is the Bush Inn, which sits in the shadow of a magnificent village church. The oldest bits of the church date back to the twelfth century, but pride of place is a rather grand tower, funded by a local family of sixteenth century nouveau riche called the Bassets. There is an effigy of Sir Thomas Basset in the church itself. He and his family lived close by, in an initially fairly modest manor house, which they rebuilt with their newfound wealth into an extravagant Renaissance castle. Its remains can still be seen today in Old Beaupre, not that far from the village on the road to St Athan; it is worth a visit, but be warned that the path leads across fields, so be prepared for mud.

The Bassets were pretty ruthless people. Once Thomas Basset got into an argument with a local farmer about the prices he was charging, and the future knight of the realm employed the interesting negotiation technique of stabbing the man and killing him. A very ornate tomb is dedicated to the family in a nearby church at Llancardle.

But enough about churches and Bassets. The Bush has enough to keep us busy.

Like many, the pub was built in the reign of Henry VIII (or possibly his son, Edward VI), but it is a rare example for how much remains unmodernised, untouched and authentic to its origins. The thatched roof, the exposed masonry, and the great open fire are particularly lovely features, along with the massive oak lintel. The floor is limestone flags, and dark beams support a low ceiling. It is exactly what you would hope for from an old inn.

Its aesthetics were not lost on the makers of the modern day, edgy Sherlock Holmes stories, with Benedict Cumberbatch in the leading role. The Bush served as a location for the episode based on *The Hound of the Baskervilles.*

The pub and its village stand on the edge of a large expanse of open common land called Stalling Down. It is claimed – and contested – that Owain Glyndŵr routed the English at an epic battle here. It is also where a particularly hapless highwayman by the name of Ianto Frank came to a bad end.

The crossroads on Stalling Down was a notorious black spot for bandits and highwaymen. The people of the county even went to the lengths of erecting some gallows there, in the hope that the sight of a hanged felon might dissuade others from following the same path. But to no avail. The robberies continued unabated.

The extent to which Ianto was involved is unclear. We get the impression that he was just an opportunistic petty criminal, but that after downing a few pints in the Bush, he used to swagger about, boasting that he was the ringleader of these cutthroats, and informing his fellow patrons that they should pay him more respect than they evidently did. No one really took him very seriously, but his boasting came back to haunt him when he was caught stealing a sheep.

When he was brought before the magistrate, a question was asked about his character. All of his stories started to come out: his dastardly exploits on the downs, the countless victims he had robbed at the point of a pistol or a sword. Ianto bleated anxious denials, offering explanations from the dock, only to be silenced by the magistrate, who believed he had before him the mastermind behind this blight on the county. He passed sentence that Ianto 'be hung by the neck 'till he be dead at Pant-Y-Lladron' ('thieves' hollow' in Welsh, this was the name given locally to the gallows on Stalling Down).

But when the bailiffs of the court came to take him down, Ianto surprised them all with a sudden burst of athleticism. He leaped out of the dock and into the courtroom (which was in the lesser hall at Cowbridge Town Hall) and ran like a gazelle through the open door and out into the street. By the time the bailiffs had got to the door themselves, he was gone. Vanished from sight.

A search party was assembled and went door to door in Cowbridge and the surrounding villages of Llanblethian, St Hilary and Aberthin. But Ianto was nowhere to be found. They turned their attention to hedgerows and farm buildings, and the glades on Stalling Down. Eventually he was discovered, hiding in a cave on the edge of a small, wooded area near St Hilary on the down, dragged out and made to face the hangman. When asked for some last words, he defiantly told the authorities that hanging him would not make a blind bit of difference to their highwayman problem. Unsurprisingly, he turned out to be right.

There's a lot of folklore about caves and hideaways and secret passageways in and around pubs. Normally, once you scratch the surface, there is no evidence behind them. But Ianto's cave is a real place. The green hilltop west of St Hilary is pitted with shafts and caves opened up long before the Industrial Revolution, early mines, which, up until the eighteenth century, are claimed to have yielded lead and galena, supposedly even some silver, though I cannot swear on the latter.

The Bush Inn is a great little pub. If you want to go there for Sunday lunch, you'll need to book weeks in advance. Its menu features home cooking with local ingredients, and it has its own specialist pie menu, with all the classics plus a few more specialist delights, like rabbit and game. There's a few hand-pulled real ales to choose from, usually Doombar, Abbot and Wye Valley Butty Bach; they tend to swap them round fairly regularly, though, so don't hold me to that.

2.18

THE LALESTON INN, LALESTON

Laleston has always been quite a quiet little place. I should know. I grew up there. Nothing seemed to happen here at all until the late sixteenth century, when, towards the end of the reign of Elizabeth I, two rival families in the village fell into a frantic game of one-up-man-ship.

For whatever the reason, both households started to kit out their homes in spectacular fashion. The winners were undoubtedly the owners of what is now the Great House Hotel, on the main road through the village. This was, by the measure of its day, the last word in architectural fashion, a mini Hampton Court, with rows of mullioned windows, exposed masonry, clusters of chimneys and an ornamental garden (now lost to a tarmac car park).

However, it had quite a rival. Behind the church on the other side of the village, in Wind Street, is the building that now houses the Laleston Inn. Originally this would have been quite a modest medieval farmhouse. But its owner had grand designs of their own. The two-storey bay window at the front is a very rare feature and would have been very striking, the road in front of the building being then set further back than now. There is a lot of ornamental carved stonework, which would have been very expensive, and what is today the main bar, a long room with a fire at each end, would have been partitioned into two rooms. You can still see the slots on the central beam where it would have stood.

The restaurant stands in what would once have been a kitchen and bakery, and the old bread oven can still be clearly seen in the inglenook fireplace, which is a lovely feature.

2.19

THE JOLLY SAILOR, NEWTON, PORTHCAWL

The ancient village of Newton is now absorbed into the town of Porthcawl, although it has an unmistakable character and identity of its own. The hub of the village is the green with the Jolly Sailor at one end, the twelfth-century church of St John in the middle, and at the far end, by the entrance to Beach Road, a thoroughly unassuming stone wall with barbed fencing along the top. If no one pointed it out, you could be forgiven for not noticing it. But it is in fact an ancient well, a holy relic and a former sight of pilgrimage. The pub began its life supplying refreshments for pilgrims who came to visit it.

The well has a magical property that, right up until modern times, could not be explained away by science. Intrigued? Well, let me tell you more.

The well was established when a knight called Sir Thomas De Sandford returned from the crusades. He was a knight of the order of St John, who have a fascinating history all of their own. They, like the better-known Templar Knights, were a warrior band of holy men. Having been sent to fight in the crusades, they were left behind in the region to guard Jerusalem from future attack. They set up headquarters in Cyprus and Rhodes, and after being chased out by the Ottoman Turks they were gifted the island of Malta by the Pope, where their mark is still indelibly felt to this day. St John's order was known as 'hospitaller' knights, meaning that they founded hospitals and tended to the wounded on the field of battle. It is a tradition maintained to this day by the St John's ambulance service.

Anyway, Thomas De Sandford returned to Britain after fighting alongside members of Robert Fitzhamon's family, possibly alongside the great man himself. As a result. De Sandford was well looked after by the Fitzhamon family. After his conquest of Morgannwg, as a dowry Fitzhamon gifted Sandford land around Porthcawl, hence why both the well and the church at Newton are dedicated to St John. However, it is unclear whether De Sandford himself ever actually spent any time there. He also had estates in Shropshire, which is where he made his home.

During the Middle Ages, the waters of the well were said to have incredible healing powers. Numerous miracles were reported: life-changing injuries healed, the lame made able to walk. No doubt they were all related to the hospitaller traditions of the order of St John.

But the well had another peculiarity too, which has made it a talking point throughout the ages. When the tide at the nearby beach is fully in, the well is always empty, but when the tide is out, the well is always full. Over the centuries this phenomenon has had everyone perplexed. Even RD Blackmore, the novelist who grew up in the area, wrote:

'It comes and goes, in manner, against the coming and going of the sea, which is only half a mile from it: and twice a day it is many feet deep, and again, not as many inches. And the water is so crystal clear, that down in the dark it is like a dream... The children are all a little afraid of it... partly because of its maker's name... and partly on account of its curious ways, and the sand coming out of its nostrils when first it begins to flow.'

Such a phenomenon has attracted tales, legends and superstition in abundance.

The well was seen as a conduit to the saints, a magnet for flagellants scourging themselves with whips or tree branches, to atone for their sins. It was believed that if you were to take water from the well and bottle it, that it would remain pure, clean and fresh for a whole year.

But if you were to spill some, this was an omen of bad luck. Also, if two people wanted to wash at the well at the same time, they had to make the sign of the cross before proceeding.

There is, of course, a perfectly rational, scientific explanation for the anti-tidal nature of the well. I am not a scientist, but I can summarise: it is all down to a freak geological occurrence, where the movement of the tide creates pressures on plates running along the spring source of the well. This causes it to fill and empty in reverse countenance with the moving tides.

It's hard to say exactly when the Jolly Sailor (previously known as the Ancient Mariner) was built, but it is more than likely early seventeenth century. At this point in history, the area started to flourish, as Newton became a bustling port, the only one between Aberthaw and Briton Ferry. With the ensuing commerce passing through the area, there were fortunes to be made, not least by the landlords of the pubs that sprang up as a result.

Like other pubs of similar age in the area, the Jolly Sailor was always associated with pirates and smugglers, and there is once again a legend that a tunnel runs from the pub, under the church, to the beach on the other side. As ever though, there's not much evidence of it at either end.

Most pubs have a ghost story attached to them, but the Jolly Sailor has one with a difference. It was once visited by a commonly reported phenomenon in this part of Glamorgan throughout the seventeenth and eighteenth centuries. It was known as *canwyll corff*, which translates as 'death candle'; this was as a ghostly looking candle that foretold the route of an impending funeral. If it stopped outside your own front door, it meant you were a goner. But in the story that follows, the phenomenon was more of a phantom funeral. Let me explain.

A notorious drunk from Newton had been whiling away the day at the Ancient Mariner, when the landlord decided he had had enough and threw him out. As he staggered through the winding streets to his home, he saw a ghostly funeral procession shuffling past him in silence.

Whether through the drink or the darkness, it was very difficult for him to make out any more than vague shapes as they passed him by. One mourner, however, caught his eye; he was wearing hunting pink (the red jacket worn by fox hunters). The procession continued to roll past him, but instead of heading for the church as you might expect, it headed towards the Ancient Mariner. Then it just disappeared.

The man told the pub landlord and anyone else who would listen, but no one took his account very seriously. Not until a few years later, when the landlord of the inn died suddenly when on a trip to Neath. His body was brought back by road to the inn, where it rested in state, prior to burial in Newton Churchyard. In the funeral procession the next day, the most prominent mourner was a man dressed in hunting pink.

2.20
THE OLD HOUSE, LLANGYNWYD

The aspect of this old pub is quite magnificent. It is located opposite the church gates in the ancient village of Llangynwyd, which is a heritage preservation area, due to the unique construction of its old dwellings. All the exterior walls, rather than being made up of large stone blocks and boulders, are instead made up of thin stone slats.

Behind the pub, you will find the beer garden, and the most beautiful view across the mountains. To the front is the village and the thirteenth-century church, which were both established by a saint called Cynwydd in the sixth century. He didn't get here first though; there has been a settlement on this spot in one form or another for thousands of years.

I have a personal connection with this pub. In the 1970s it was run by a couple called Ivor and Winnie, who were very good friends of our family.

On one occasion my father bought a horse from Ivor and Winnie. The horse's name was Tommy, and his old home had been in a field behind the pub car park. Ivor brought him down to us from Llangynwyd to Laleston, and we kept him in a fenced off field and orchard. One day, we woke to find that the gate into his enclosure was open and Tommy was gone. We started to search the lanes around our house but could not find him anywhere. Then the phone rang. It was Ivor. 'Have you lost something?' he asked.

It is quite common to hear stories about cats who trek vast distances back to former homes, but more unusual are similar accounts of horses. Llangynwyd was over eight miles away from where we lived, and the route at the time involved navigating a webbed network of lanes that ran through Cefn Cribwr. Clever horse.

As you can imagine, for the next week talk in the pub was of little else. Tommy's homing instinct was the toast of the village, and as one of the regulars at the Old House was a journalist from *the Glamorgan Gazette*, he asked my father and Ivor if he could bring a photographer over to cover the story in a small piece in the paper. In the ensuing photo shoot the photographer called to Ivor, 'Can you go and pull a pint and hold it up to the horse's mouth?' That, as it turned out, was a moment of genius.

The piece was run in the local paper. It raised a few smiles in the pub, but what no one appreciated was that it would soon be picked up by the national press. Then the international press. For weeks afterwards, we were receiving letters from all over the world, sending us 50p coins so we could buy Tommy a pint. That's right: back then you could buy a pint for 50p. Even if it was stuff like Worthington E and Watney's Red Barrel.

It was also during Ivor and Winnie's tenure that the Old House had its most famous visitors. Yes, even more famous than Tommy. One evening, it was graced by none other than Richard Burton and his then wife Elizabeth Taylor, much to the incredulity of everyone there.

Llangynwyd's Wikipeida page says the pub was established in 1147. I will give the establishment the same benefit of the doubt that I have extended to everyone else, and say that maybe this refers to a building that formerly stood on this site. What we see there today is clearly old, with its thatched roof, low doorways, inglenook fireplace, spiral staircase, exposed masonry and dark ceiling timers. But the oldest part, the main bar, is most likely sixteenth century. The property was clearly vastly extended in the eighteenth and nineteenth centuries all of which are somewhat dwarfed by the very adventurous, modern extension the new owners have put on the back of it. It is sympathetic to the older parts of the building, but it is colossal.

When I was little, the pub was the hub of the revival of an ancient Welsh Christmas tradition called 'the Mari Lwyd'. The sign outside used to depict the practise in full swing.

'What on earth is the Mari Lwyd?' you may well be asking. Well, bizarrely, it is another equine reference. The name translates as 'grey mare', and at the centre of it is a rather grisly prop: a horse's skull festooned with ribbons and bells, the lower jawbone wired on so it flaps as it is carried, as if chattering or laughing. It is a ceremony that dates back into pre-history, and in its most stripped-down form it consists of a man wearing the horse's skull like a hat, with his actual head and upper torso covered by a sheet. He is then led from door to door in the village on the night of Christmas Eve, asking for entrance and entertainment through a series of rhymes. The origins of this tradition are long forgotten; it is one of those pre-Christian festivals which the new religion rebranded and adopted to help win over local pagans.

When it had long become a Christian tradition, in the Middle Ages, the Mari Lwyd was usually carried by three mummers. Gradually the religious significance dwindled, and it became a form of revelry and comedy show rolled into one, the protagonists chosen for their quick wit and ability to make up rhymes on demand, larking around like an oversized Punch and Judy show to entertain the gathered throng. Sadly this quaint and good-humoured tradition was brought to an end when a rough element infiltrated it, using it as a rouse for ransacking and robbing people's houses.

It is impossible to write a chapter about Llangynwyd without at least mentioning the legend of the Maid of Cefn Ydfa. It is a tale that started out as a hauntingly beautiful Welsh folk song called 'Bugeilio'r Gwenith Gwyn', which translates as 'Watching the White Wheat'.

This song and these words are said to have been written by a Welsh bard and poet called Wil Hopcyn. Wil was a peasant who earned a living as a thatcher in the village of Llangynwydd, near Maesteg. The words capture his feelings of love for a local girl he is forced to worship from afar as their social circumstances keep them separated.

The girl in question is Ann Thomas. She was born in 1704 to a wealthy landowner, William Thomas, who lived at the ancient manor house at Cefn Ydfa, in the parish of Llangynwyd. Two years after her birth, her father tragically died, so Ann (the maid of Cefn Ydfa) was placed in the wardship of Anthony Maddocks, a wealthy lawyer from Cwm Risca Farm near Bridgend who had looked after her father's affairs. He had long planned that she would marry his son, who was also called Anthony. However, much to everyone's consternation she instead fell in love with the penniless poet and thatcher Wil Hopcyn. When their romance was discovered, Ann was forbidden from seeing Wil. She was kept as a prisoner, locked in her room at the manor. The Thomas and Maddocks families were both determined that her rightful suitor was Anthony Maddocks.

But they had not banked on how deeply Wil and Ann were in love, and how determined they were to be together. They continued their relationship by writing love letters and poems to each other in secret. Ann would have hers delivered by a servant girl when she was running errands to the village. Wil would post his replies in the hollow of an oak tree on the Cefn Ydfa estate.

When this was discovered, Ann's mother confiscated all writing materials from her. Undeterred, and desperate to communicate with her lover, Ann is said to have plucked leaves from the tree outside her bedroom window and written love letters to him in her own blood.

But in the end, Ann was forced to marry Maddocks. Knowing the hopelessness of his situation, Wil Hopcyn moved away from the area, and Ann is said to have pined so heavily for her lover that soon after her marriage she became very ill. On her death bed she sent for Wil. He came running to her side, and on his arrival, they embraced, and she died in his arms of a broken heart.

Ann's body lies buried in the churchyard in Llangynwyd, and a cross has been raised outside the church gates dedicated to Wil Hopcyn. Ever since, their story has been a staple of Welsh folklore; it was made into a silent film, and the composer William Parry incorporated the folksong into an opera.

I recently heard an exchange between two local historians, where one asked the other if they believed the legend to be true. The questionee replied that, as a historian, the lack of contemporary evidence suggests that it was not true, but as a Llangynwyd local, 'Of course it's true.'

2.21

PRINCE OF WALES, KENFIG

I mentioned earlier that someone has collated a league of the most haunted pubs in Wales. Straight in at number one is the Skirrid Inn, with Monmouth's the Queen's Head in at third. I say this without actually being able to find the league itself. It is just 'oft quoted'. Anyway, the Prince of Wales is a likely contender for that coveted second place spot. Maybe the Queen's Head eyes it up with envy and resentment on a daily basis? Why not.

It certainly has its fair share of ghost stories. There is a phantom often seen on the dunes (the Hag of the Moors), disembodied hands, even a ghost who makes the place smell of rotten fish. Although to be fair that could just have been an electrical fault.

In the 1980s the landlord reported hearing phantom music, and a team of paranormal investigators came to the pub and set up recording equipment. The tapes picked up something, but exactly what is inconclusive.

There is no doubt that the pub itself has a very interesting history. When you arrive, it is easy to see why. It is located on the edge of a vast system of windswept sand dunes, which encase a seventy-acre lake filled with still black waters. The pub you see today may be eighteenth century, but it is actually built on the remains of a guildhall from the fourteenth century. You may well be thinking that this setting seems rather desolate for a guildhall. You would be right. Its location reflects another, hidden history.

You will recall from previous chapters that I wrote about Trellech: the lost city uncovered by an amateur archaeologist, forgotten by history and now a tiny village. Similarly, the thin row of cottages at Aberthaw, which bely its history as one of the major ports of the Bristol Channel.

This is also the history of Kenfig. Before the Norman invasion, this was where the kings of Morganwg held their court. And once their grip had been smashed, newcomers were keen to move in and develop their own port and commercial hub. For many years the town thrived. So what happened?

I can offer two explanations. One is a legend captured by the ineffable Iolo Morganwg, who never let the truth get in the way of a good story. The other comes from more dependable sources. So, let us begin with the more entertaining version.

One day, a peasant living in Kenfig fell in love with the daughter of the great earl who ruled over the people of the county. He declared his love for her on the spot, but she refused him. Being the daughter of an earl, she knew that a union with a peasant boy would be impossible. Before they parted however, she gave him her silk glove as a 'favour', so that he knew that secretly she reciprocated his love.

This was a desperate plight for a young peasant boy with no money or prospects. He tried to think of ways he could prove himself worthy of winning her but could think of nothing. At his wit's end, he hatched a dark plan.

He went to visit a noble knight, who had fought in ancient wars but was now old and frail and dedicating the remainder of his days to God. The peasant boy asked the old knight to lend him the trappings of a rich man so he could convince his love that he had succeeded in amassing a fortune. But the old knight would not hear of it and scolded him. He warned the boy that winning a bride by deception was no basis for love, and that he would come to regret his actions when the truth was inevitably discovered.

The young boy, hot headed and fuelled by passion and lust, could not cope with the old man's wisdom. In a fit of temper, he slashed out with his trusty sword. Though old, the blade was still razor sharp, so with a single blow the boy cut the old knight's head clean off. To cover his tracks, he tossed the remains into a nearby lake and helped himself to the knight's money, fine clothes and riches. Then he paraded himself before the earl and his daughter, claiming the old knight's fortune and lineage as his own.

The girl and her father were very impressed, and she agreed to marry him. They were married in the Church of St James in Kenfig and had a great wedding feast in the old guildhall. But just as the festivities were getting underway, the ghostly voice of the old knight rang through the rafters, calling out, 'Vengeance will be mine!' The terrified guests ran in fear, but the boy, in the knowledge that he had incurred this wrath, stood fast. He asked the ghostly voice, 'When will this happen?' and the reply came, 'Vengeance will come with the ninth generation.'

When he told the others of this they laughed and said, 'In nine generations' time we will all be long gone!' But when a child was born soon after, the locals were oblivious to the fact that he was the first of the ninth generation to be born in the town of Kenfig. The voice echoed once more, threatening, 'Vengeance will be mine!' Terrified, all the people of the town ran to their homes and bolted their windows and doors.

But to no avail, for suddenly a huge tidal wave rushed in from the sea, up the river Kenfig, and completely engulfed the town, obliterating all its fine buildings and depositing a wall of sand to keep the lake from ever draining. All the inhabitants were drowned, and the only sign that the town had ever been there were the chimneys of the houses, still smoking above the water line. On the shore were found the gloves of the old knight, which washed up by the feet of a young descendant. As they were discovered, the voice of the old knight was heard from the sky praising God.

Legend has it that, on a clear day, when the water of the lake is still, you can still see the houses at the bottom of it. And if you listen carefully, you can occasionally hear the bells of the old church still ringing, warning of an approaching storm.

How close is this to the reality? As we have already mentioned, the Norman conquest was a bloody affair, and displaced locals did not take kindly to having their land confiscated by the invaders. Skirmishes and backlashes were commonplace everywhere, and in Kenfig in particular. The town was a Norman enclave within what was, for a while, the wild western flank of Norman controlled Wales.

It is amazing it survived its early years at all. But as time went by, the raids and sieges became more and more infrequent, and the town grew, drawing in Welsh as well as Norman inhabitants looking to make their fortunes in its prospering trades and markets. Soon Kenfig was a significant trading post, its burgesses given a charter allowing them to levy taxes and pass by-laws. We have on record that they used this authority to set high standards around the quality of food and drink produced and sold in the town, and in regards to the cleanliness of the streets. Kenfig had a town hall, a guildhall, a hospital, a church and master measures to ensure fair weights and measures in sales. They had strict rules against gambling and fighting. They had the right to hold fairs, and every year they held an event to celebrate their patron saint and benefactor, St James. It was held every November and was called the Mabsant.

So, what went wrong? Well, the tale of the peasant boy and the heiress got one thing right: it was mother nature who decided the fate of Kenfig.

A series of terrible storms in the fourteenth century caused regular flooding, eventually forming the seventy-acre lake that we see now at Kenfig Pool. But alas, the stories of the town being at the bottom of the lake are a romantic invention. It makes for a cracking, almost biblical end to the legend, but in reality the old town was located quite a bit further north than where the lake is today. It lay pretty much alongside where the London-to-Swansea railway line is now. So, if it's not under the lake, why did the town disappear?

The storms that formed Kenfig Pool brought in a lot more than just torrential rain. They also blew in sand, a lot of it, and once it got a hold and started to form dunes, it was the beginning of the end for Kenfig. With the prevailing westerly wind blowing in every day, bit by bit, the sand progressed, slow but impossible to stop. Soon gardens could not be cultivated, and the routes in and out of the town were constantly blocked with swirling sand. District by district, the town was abandoned, as sand claimed the once thriving streets, until only a small number of dwellings on the higher ground remained – as they are to this day.

By the time Leyland, the sixteenth-century chronicler, visited, Kenfig was no more than 'a little village on the est side of Kenfik and a castel booth in ruine and almost shokid and devoured with the sandes that the Severn Se there castith up.'

The Blue Anchor, Aberthaw

The Plough and Harrow, Monknash

The Cross Keys, Swansea

*View from the beer garden of
the Worms Head, Rhossili*

The Rummer Tavern, Cardiff

The City Arms, Cardiff

Ye Olde Murenger House, Newport

The White Hart, Llangybi

The Bush, St Hilary

Llanthony Priory, Llanthony

The Bear, Crickhowell

The Radnorshire Arms, Presteigne

Y Talbot, Tregaron

Ty Mawr, Gwyddelwern

The Horse and Jockey, Wrexham

*The view from the beer garden of
the Groes, Ty'n-y-Groes*

The Laleston Inn, Laleston

The Welcome to Town, Llanrhidian

*The view from the beer garden of
the Harp, Old Radnor*

The Angel Vaults, Camarthen

The Priory, Milford Haven

Penlan Fawr, Pwllheli

The Bull Inn, Llangefni

The White Lion, Llanelian-Yn-Rhos

The Aleppo Merchant, Carno

The Black Boy Inn, Caernarfon

The Harp, Abergele

The Plough, St Asaph

The Llindir, Henllan

*The view from the beer garden of
the Anchor Inn, Tintern*

The Glyn Arms, Howarden

The 100 House, Bleddfa

The Three Cocks Inn, Three Cocks

The Jolly Sailor, Porthcawl

The Prince of Wales, Kenfig

The Old House, Llangynwyd

The Plymouth Arms, St Fagans

The Queens Head, Monmouth

The Travellers Rest, Thornhill

The Skirrid Inn, Llanvihangel Crucorney

THE ANCIENT KINGDOM
OF DEHEUBARTH

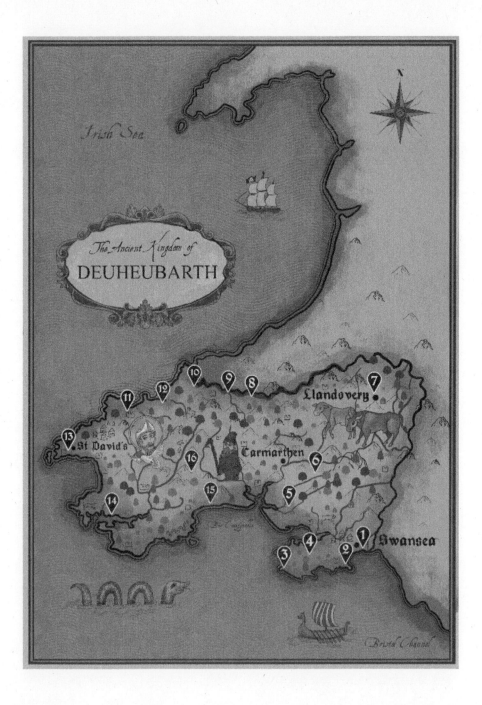

I could easily describe the area covered in this chapter as West Wales, or even less romantically by its 'SA' postcode. But the borders of Wales' ancient kingdoms suggest something more tangible. They give us a clearer idea of the historic patchwork of identities which exists in what we now call Wales. In turn, that explains a lot of entrenched loyalties, hostilities and general attitudes that survive today. Little things, like why people who live in one town might feel more affinity to the city to the east than the city to the west.

Some may put the rivalry between Cardiff and Swansea as simply down to neighbourly proximity. In reality it is a historical hangover from when Wales was separated into individual kingdoms. Deheubarth (Swansea) and Morgannwg (Cardiff) were pretty much constantly at war. If either side had had the foresight to unite against their common enemy, the Normans, we might have had a very different outcome when they invaded. In reality, knights from Morgannwg fought alongside the Normans to help them subdue Deheubarth, and vice versa. Both sides contributed to their mutual downfall. Isn't there a lesson for us all there?

The kingdom was established in 920AD and was a quite distinct entity from the rest of Wales. It had its own court and capital in Carmarthen, the birthplace of Merlin the magician from Arthurian legend. In early Welsh history, right up to the Middle Ages, Carmarthen was by far the biggest and most important town in the southern half of Wales.

In later history, it was Pembrokeshire which became the biggest force in the area, yielding yet another King of England, in the form of Henry VII, and the start of the Tudor dynasty. Then finally, as Pembrokeshire and Carmarthenshire's lights began to flicker, the wealth and influence passed to its eastern corner, as Llanelli and Swansea boomed in the industrial age – Swansea in particular, becoming 'Copper-opolis', the copper-producing capital of the world.

Not only was Deheubarth a kingdom in its own right, but throughout history it also experienced far more inbound immigration than the rest of Wales. In addition to the Roman and Norman settlers, which we saw all over coastal Wales, in earlier history West Wales saw influxes of Irish, Saxon and Viking settlers; then, in later history, Dutch and French Huguenots fled here to escape persecution. Each new arrival added an extra bit of spice to the melting pot, and today Pembrokeshire's cosmopolitan roots can be seen in its rich variety of place names, as well as its nickname, 'little England beyond Wales'.

Anywhere with such a unique heritage is always going to have its fair share of colourful folklore. And when you add in characters like the wizard Merlin, and the saints who made places like St Davids hubs of early Christianity, you have a recipe for some great stories. And some great pubs in which to tell them.

3.1

THE OLD CROSS KEYS, SWANSEA

I have a special place in my heart for Swansea. Swansea feels like the biggest village in Wales. It may have a population of nearly 250,000, but everyone seems to know each other. If you go out in town with a local it is just ridiculous. You can't pass anyone without stopping for a chat. I am told you experience something similar out on the town in Helsinki and Reykjavik. Maybe it is a culture left over from the city's founding fathers? Unlike anywhere else we have been to on our travels thusfar, Swansea was originally established as a Viking settlement.

The Vikings never really made much of an impact in East Wales, but in West Wales, place names like Skomer, Skokholm, Stakk, Emsger and Worm's Head show that they more than made their mark. But while most of the aforementioned are islands off the coast, in Swansea we have a large, mainland settlement. The name of the city is derived from the Norse *Sweyns Ey*, meaning 'Sweyn's Island', as it was established by Sweyn Forkbeard, who went on to be a Viking king.

The oldest part of Swansea is the area immediately around and in front of the castle. Wind Street follows the route which has for centuries run from the castle to the old port. Virtually all the buildings that once stood there have been demolished and replaced, some in a vast modernisation programme undertaken in the Victorian era, but most during the Second World War, when the whole city was flattened by German bombing raids.

Pretty much the only building that seems to have survived intact is where the Cross Keys now stands. This is a building of substantial and verifiable antiquity. It also has a fascinating history all of its own.

It was built by Bishop Henry de Gower (Bishop of St Davids) in 1330, not as an inn but an almshouse and early hospital. The charter of 1332 says that it was established for 'the support of other poor chaplains and laymen deprived of bodily health.' It was not only there to look after people taken ill or injured, but to support the destitute, poor and starving.

The institution must have had some significant patronage, as it survived right up until the Reformation. It was then confiscated by the Crown and sold to Sir George Herbert, who you may remember from our chapter about the Baron's Court in Penarth. He was a man of very different moral fibre to Henry de Gower. As there was no money to be made from feeding the starving or tending to the sick, he closed down the hospital and almshouse and broke the estate up, turning the old buildings into shops and an inn. Later all the other buildings were demolished, but the inn thrived.

By the beginning of the twentieth century the pub was very dilapidated and run down. By that time in its history, its origins had largely been forgotten, so it was a very brave undertaking to get it all restored and renovated. But when the rendering got stripped away, to the delight of the owner who oversaw the work, a lot of the original features, like the stone arched windows and medieval timber, were re-discovered. The two bays on the St Mary Street side were added onto the original building in the seventeenth century, and it is believed that when they were built, they contained two narrow shops separated by a passageway which ran to the back of the building.

Inside there are some lovely features. The massive ceiling beams tell a story of all the walls and partitions that have been added and taken away in the last 700 years, and there are fragments of medieval roof trusses on either side of a small seating area in the lounge.

The layout suggests that, before conversion into a drinking house, the building that remains had two uses. The old hall would have been located on the first floor, which suggests that this was a cleric's living accommodation, situated above another part of the hospital, possibly a ward.

Several celebrity drinkers have supped pints here, most notably Dylan Thomas, who worked in the vicinity as a journalist at *the Swansea Evening Post*; it must be admitted, however, that Thomas used to drink in *every* pub within a mile's radius of his old offices. Another patron was a pillar of the Welsh political landscape in the 1950s. A former train driver who rose to become a county councillor in the old county of West Glamorgan, and an MP; Llewellyn Heycock. He was granted a life peerage in 1967, after which he became Lord Heycock the Baron Taibach. Loyal to his working-class roots, despite his high office and peerage, Heycock lived all his life in Port Talbot, the town of his birth, in a comparatively modest house.

On one occasion, in response to what they saw as the rising tide of sin and godlessness in Port Talbot, a team of Christian missionaries had been going door to door to try and drum up support for the local chapel. One afternoon, they knocked at the door of Lord Heycock. The door was opened by his housekeeper, who politely enquired how she could help. The minister, who was predisposed to grandiosity, held his hands aloft to heaven and dramatically enquired, 'Is the Lord in this house?' To which the housekeeper calmly replied, 'No, I'm awful sorry. He 'ave gone to Porthcawl.' For the first time in anyone's memory, the baffled minister was lost for words.

3.2
THE WHITE ROSE, MUMBLES

Mumbles is a pretty little fishing village on the end of Swansea Bay. In 2018 it was listed by *the Sunday Times* as the best place to live in Wales. I am guessing this list was compiled by someone who has not had to sit in nose to tail traffic on the road from Swansea on a sunny Saturday afternoon.

Supposedly Mumbles got its name when Norman invaders first arrived, saw the two humped hill tops above the headland, and thought that they looked like a pair of breasts. They called the area *les Mamelles*, meaning 'the breasts', which got corrupted to Mumbles. So many possible jokes... but let's not milk it (I thank you).

The White Rose is a pretty enough place. Not especially old. Nineteenth century with some renovation work to make it look older: bits of mock Tudor timber, that sort of thing. Its inclusion in these pages is mainly down to it being an integral part of an institution: the now world-famous Mumbles Mile.

What's the Mumbles Mile? Let me explain.

Back in the 1970s, students from Swansea University were looking for a theme around which to stage what used to be called 'Rag Week'. Rag Week was a thinly veiled excuse to get ludicrously drunk in order to 'raise money for charity'. Participants would dress up in fancy dress and go from pub to pub carrying buckets, collecting loose change from revellers for some local good cause. To try and distinguish that year's event, the students declared that this year they were to do 'the Mumbles Mile': pub to pub along the seafront in Mumbles, from one end to the other. It became an annual event, growing and growing in popularity until everyone wanted a go. A pub crawl along the Mumbles Mile became a rite of passage, an ever present on the bucket lists of people from all over the UK for the past forty years.

At its height, there were twenty-six pubs on the Mumbles Mile. It is a depressing reflection of the fate of so many pubs in this country that today there are just five.

The White Rose has traditionally been the starting point of the Mumbles Mile, but it was popular long before the tradition existed. It stood opposite the terminus of the old Swansea to Mumbles tramline, and it was always filled with people waiting to catch a tram. Today the lines have gone, but its former route has now been turned into a lovely walkway and cycle path that hugs the coastline around Swansea Bay, with spectacular views and access onto the beach.

3.3
THE WORMS HEAD, RHOSILLI

The Gower Peninsula was Britain's first designated area of outstanding natural beauty, and it is easy to see why. This dramatic landscape is very easy on the eye. It is also an area full of fascinating distractions for the amateur historian. The oldest human remains ever discovered in Britain were found in the Paviland Caves here. 'The Red Lady', as she was called, dated back to 31,000 BC, making her the earliest example of a ceremonial burial in Europe. There is also Arthur's stone, which is a Neolithic burial chamber with a vast capstone perched on top of the windswept Cefn Bryn common. The views from this vantage point are quite spectacular.

Like the Vale of Glamorgan, in the seventeenth and eighteenth centuries, the area had more than its fair share of pirates and smugglers. Do you remember Thomas Knight, who ran his smuggling empire out of his pub, the Old Swan? Well, the collapse of Thomas Knight's operations on Barry Island were a hollow victory for the law enforcers, because it was pretty soon taken over by one of Knight's contemporaries, a smuggler called William Arthur (who became known as 'the Smuggler King'). He already ran a very successful operation out of Gower. At the height of his power, he was reputed to have a gang of over 100 men and, a smuggling operation that spanned right across the southwest Wales coast. Arthur ultimately got his comeuppance on 13th April 1804, when customs officers raided his farm near Oxwich on the Gower, seizing 420 casks of contraband spirits (about 3,000 gallons).

Given the Gower's rich history and incredible beauty, it is disappointing how few old pubs survive. Sadly, until the boom in camping holidays in the twentieth century, the area's rural isolation meant there was never enough trade to support them. However, the Worm's Head is such a gem it makes up for it by the spade load.

Not for the first time in this book, I must confess that this is technically a hotel. Technically. I would argue that it is more a pub with rooms. The beer garden behind the Worm's Head, for my money, has the best view of any that I know. It is absolutely spectacular, and it alone makes the establishment worth mentioning.

The Worm's Head was originally a row of fishermen's cottages built in the eighteenth century. They all got absorbed into the one building we see today, which stands perched on a clifftop facing west across Rhossili Bay, making it the perfect spot to sit and watch the sun set, with a pint in hand on a warm summer evening. Below it is the vast Llangeneth beach, littered with the carcasses of ancient shipwrecks. Their semi-fossilised timbers poke up through the sand like the rib cages of giant skeletons. The bar is named after one of them, the Norwegian barque•Helvetia. It was carrying timber from Canada when it ran aground at Rhossili in 1887.

3.4

THE WELCOME TO TOWN, LLANRHIDIAN

The northern coastline of the Gower may not have the glamour and allure of the south coast, but it has every bit as much history. This old pub dates back over 300 years, but by the early twenty-first century it had become so neglected and run down it was in danger of being lost. It was for sale for over two years, until it was bought by Paul and Natasha Crowther in 2015. They lovingly restored it and have made it into a very comfortable boozer, popular with the local branch of CAMRA for its selection of real ales and good reputation for food.

The Welcome to Town has a very interesting history.

Like many rural villages, there was no money in Llanrhidian for municipal or public buildings other than the church (which was not to be used for secular matters) and the public house. Accordingly, the pub was not just where villagers went for a pint. In its time, the Welcome has been used as both a courtroom and a gaol for local outlaws awaiting trial. It was also for a while a food hall, as well as a masonic temple and a meeting place for local landowners to discuss business.

With such a chequered history, the Welcome has, as you would expect, a few ghosts. First thing in the morning, it is quite common to hear the footsteps of a tormented soul trudging slowly across the floorboards of an upstairs room above the main bar, from one end to the other. That is the room that used to be used for court hearings, and the footsteps are believed to be heading from where the dock would have been, in the direction of the prisoner's exit. So maybe those reluctant footsteps are recreating the steps of a newly condemned man towards the gallows in Swansea. There is also a corner of the pub that is notoriously difficult to heat, where guests have sometimes spoken of feeling a 'presence'.

3.5

THE OLD MOATHOUSE
KIDWELLY

It is impossible to miss the clues of Kidwelly's twelfth-century origins. The remains of the vast castle are a dead giveaway.

The town's founder and benefactor was a very ambitious cleric called Bishop Roger of Salisbury. He may well have been a man of the cloth, but he was descended from a family of accomplished Norman warriors, and he had a reputation for being a canny operator.

He had a clear plan for Kidwelly. He wanted to establish a Benedictine priory, an extension of the one on the other side of the Bristol channel, at Sherborne in Dorset. And he had no interest in appeasing the locals whose land he built it on. The fortress therefore, was a very necessary addition to the priory, which suffered frequently from attacks.

One of the most celebrated was led by a warrior princess called Gwenllian. She was said to be very beautiful, and she was married to the rightful heir to the king of Dehauberth. His name was Gruffyd ap Rhys, and he was the son of the old king, who had been slaughtered in battle by the Normans. The husband-and-wife team raised an army in the mountains around Brecon and marched on the Anglo-Norman settlements around Swansea and the Gower, with a mission of pushing the invaders back into the sea. They fought in several small-scale battles, but Gwenllian had her mettle tested when she met a vast Norman army in battle on the Lougher estuary, somewhere between

Llanelli and Gorseinon. There, she smashed the Normans, killing over 500.

Her husband saw this as a sign, an opportunity to take back the kingdom that was rightfully his, ridding West Wales of the villainous Normans once and for all. He rode north to Gwynedd to enlist re-enforcements to fight alongside him and his talismanic wife. But while he was gone, Maurice De Londres, who was Lord of Kidwelly and Ogmore, counterattacked.

De Londres was, even by Norman standards, hard as nails. The two forces met in battle on a field around five miles north of Kidwelly, which to this day is known as 'Gwenllian's Field'. The battle was a brutal and bloody affair which in the end went the way of De Londres. Not only was Gwenllian's army defeated, but she herself was decapitated in battle. Her head was positioned on a stake exhibited on the gate at the entrance to the town, to remind the troublesome Welsh of the likely outcome of any future reprisals. Legend has it that the ghost of her headless corpse still haunts the battlefield, while she helplessly searches for her skull to reunite with her body in the grave.

As a deterrent, the head-on-stake thing didn't achieve much. Attacks didn't seem to abate in either regularity or severity as history progressed. There was a constant need to upgrade the defences and fortifications. The inadequacies of the original timber fort very quickly became apparent, and bit by bit it was rebuilt in stone, until it was one of the strongest forts in Wales. In the thirteenth century the town was given a grant to build a defensive wall. This may have defended the residents against attack, but it was rather limiting in regards to future buildings, which is why all the newer buildings went up on the other side of the river, near the priory.

Most of the old town wall has crumbled away now, but bits of it remain in pockets behind houses and along garden walls, and also in the general outline of the old part of the town. A part of it is incorporated into the outside wall of the Old Moathouse itself.

In the fifteenth century, the town was sacked by Owain Glyndŵr and his rebel army, in their fight for Welsh independence. They attacked the old walled town and the castle and flattened them. Once the town had been destroyed in this attack, it did not recover for centuries. Nearly a hundred years later, in 1536, John Leland, who we spoke about in our chapter on the Baron's Court in Penarth, visited Kidwelly and wrote, 'the old toun is near desolate.'

Even by the seventeenth century, a survey of the town only noted eighteen properties within the old town wall, with most of the land given over to gardens. It also referred to an inn, meaning the Old Moathouse is one of the few remaining domestic buildings from the medieval period.

However, as always, we have to concede that a lot of the building has been modernised or rebuilt, and it is hard to say how much of it is original. But it has some great features, such as thick stone walls, a massive chimney stack and an inglenook. When the work was done to reveal the inglenook, which had previously been bricked up, a zinc fire mark dated 1740 was found, more than likely also dating most of the building we see today.

The layout of the rooms is quite common in an eighteenth-century Carmarthenshire cottage, featuring original rough-cut beams. You'll never guess what these beams are claimed to be made out of? Yep. The usual. It's a wonder that the Royal Navy had any ships left, given the voracious appetite for their masts. Mind you, Kidwelly is at least near the sea, so in this instance the claim is at least plausible, although still unlikely when contemporary records suggest that, at the time of its rebuilding, many old cottages would have lain in ruins all around. There would have been no end of free roof timbers to be recycled from neighbouring buildings.

One of the more unusual stories about the Moat House is that there is an outhouse, little more than a shed really, located at the end of the pub's backyard, dating back to when it was a cottage. Formerly this building was let to a barber who was inexplicably popular with the men of Kidwelly. Even those who were as bald as a coot. That in itself aroused suspicion amongst their wives, but when the youngsters of the village were so long getting their hair cut, eyebrows really started to rise. One day the mystery was solved when it was discovered that the barber was running an unlicensed bookie. If he was cutting the hair of some young lad, the boy would have to sit in the chair and wait while the barber disappeared into a back room, to place a bet or cash out winnings. On days when the Cheltenham Gold Cup or the Grand National were taking place, a short back and sides could take hours.

In 2018 the building was described as a 'neglected listed building', but I am delighted to see that it has been taken over by someone who really cares about the place. In the last two years the new owners have set about some very bold plans for sympathetic restoration, and the results have been pretty dramatic. The ethos of the owner when choosing his ales is, 'If you can buy it in the supermarket, we won't sell it on tap.' He specialises in artisan independent breweries, with a special emphasis on what is local. He also has plans for a Welsh take on tapas, offering small platters and homemade nibbles for people wanting a bar snack with a difference. He also has a wine list with fifty wines on it

Just round the corner from the Moat House is the Masons Arms, which is worth a mention too. It claims to be fourteenth century and was featured in *Most Haunted*, for its poltergeist who likes to move furniture around.

3.6
THE WHITE HART THATCHED
INN & BREWERY,

The little village green at Llanddarog and the 'Best Kept Village' signs scattered thereabouts give you an idea of how much its residents love where they live. And you can see why. Perched on top of a hill, crowned by the old church and one of the prettiest pubs I know, it is a very romantic little idyll, a quintessential Carmarthenshire village, reminiscent of the 1944 British black and white film *the Halfway House*.

The White Hart is heralded by many as the prettiest in West Wales, with everything you could want from an ancient pub: thatched roof, stumpy chimneys, bare stone walls and leaded windows on the outside; on the inside, the inglenook fireplaces and beams exuding the comforting reassurance of great age. So how old is this place? Well, as with all great pubs, opinion is divided. Which is great. If you ask me, there are four primary measures of a truly great pub: (1) real fire (2) real ales (3) no mobile signal (4) conflicting stories about its ancient history and a lack of clear evidence either way.

There is a popular story that the pub was built to provide accommodation for the craftspeople and workers who built the village church. That would make it fourteenth century. There is no doubt that in such rural locations as Llanddarog people brought in from outside the village to work would have needed accommodation. And once the church was completed, many of its new parishioners would have had to travel a fair distance to worship there; in other words, some refreshment would have been called for. That co-dependency between pub and church continued for long centuries. And not just for Sunday worship. It was traditional for pallbearers to rest the coffin containing the deceased on the stone bench outside the White Hart while they popped inside for a quick stiffener before the funeral service at the church. It is all slightly reminiscent of the White Hart in Llangybi, where mourners were occasionally diverted through the pub to maintain a right of easement.

But not everyone is convinced the White Hart is fourteenth century. There are those who point to the floor plan, saying that the room layout is more characteristic of traditional eighteenth-century Carmarthenshire cottages.

3.7
THE KING'S HEAD, LLANDOVERY

If there was one corner of Wales that would have been disappointed to see the downfall of Richard III, at the hands of the Welsh born challenger Henry VII, it would have been Llandovery. Richard once wrote a charter for the town which included the decree 'there shall be no tavern in this land... except in the borough of Llandovery' thus granting Llandovery a monopoly on pubs in Carmarthenshire. Which, if you lived in Llandovery, was probably a good thing. But it's no wonder the rest of the county ran to Henry Tudor's side and marched to Bosworth with such vigour. They wanted their pubs back!

In essence, that's what the War of the Roses was all about. No simplification whatsoever.

The King's Head is the oldest surviving building in the town. The only other contender would be the castle, but that is sadly in ruins. What remains today betrays that this is another town with a turbulent history. As usual, it has something to do with Norman domination of good fertile land, and the reprisals and raids of the displaced Welsh they had taken it from. Like Kidwelly, Llandovery was also decimated in an attack from Owain Glyndŵr in the fifteenth-century, and also like Kidwelly, it took the town centuries to recover from it.

It did, however, manage to emerge as a thriving commercial centre during the Middle Ages and later pre-industrial history. The King's Head was very much at the centre of it all. In much the same way as

Lloyds of London and the Stock Exchange can trace their roots back to the coffee houses of the City of London, so too can the global financial institution Lloyds Bank trace its roots back to this pub.

We spoke in an earlier chapter about the tradition of droving. Well, in the seventeenth and eighteenth centuries, Llandovery was essentially a drover town. Many teams of drovers either lived or operated from the town, and as such this was the starting point of many herding journeys across the ridgeways of Wales to the markets of England. It was a very tough, spartan way of life but there was good money to be made. The challenge was hanging onto that money, as there was always the threat of attacks from bandits and highwaymen. To say nothing of farmers and landowners, who were often less than willing to pay a fair price for such a demanding job.

In the latter part of the eighteenth century, an enterprising young lad called David Jones, who was himself from a droving family, worked at the King's Head. He knew all the regulars and clearly built up a lot of trust with them, as they took to giving him their money to look after while they were out of town. Trust was a very rare and, as such, very valuable commodity in those dark times, and theirs allowed him to build a small cottage in a yard behind the pub, which he called 'the Black Ox Bank'. His reputation as a safe custodian of the drovers' hard-earned money grew, news of his reliability spread, and the Black Ox Bank flourished under his stewardship, making him a very wealthy man. He became high sheriff of Carmarthenshire, and his sons and grandsons carried on the family business, expanding it until there were branches throughout the county. In 1909 it was incorporated, along with other similar Welsh merchant banks, into Lloyds bank. The black ox became a black horse and it now has interests all over the world.

The King's Head is one of the few remaining medieval pubs left in Wales although it would be hard to put an exact date on it. And as with all places of that age that have remained in perpetual use, it has been modernised, altered and rebuilt many times over. The original floorplan is still there to be seen though. A hall and cross-passage and lateral fireplace. Also, a lot of original features have been revealed by more recent renovations in the 80s and 90s, such as the original inglenook fireplace and the oak panelling. The fireplace and thick stone walls are part of the original medieval building, but sadly the passage has now been lost. A lot of modernisation was carried out during the reign of the monarch whose head it was named after, King Charles I.

In addition to the pioneering banker David Jones, there are plenty of other characters who were regulars at the King's Head. None more so than a notorious sixteenth-century highwayman and swindler who was known as Twm Sion Catti (far more interesting than his real name, which was Thomas Jones).

They do not come much more colourful than Twm. He was born in 1530 in Tregaron, the illegitimate son on a local aristocrat. As a young man, when he was already living the life of an outlaw, he was based in Llandovery but operated across West Wales. When he was on the run from the authorities (which was often) he used to hide out in a cave at Ystradffin, between Llandovery and the village of Rhandirmwyn. You can still visit it today (although proper historians take delight in telling you he probably never actually stayed there at all).

His story became popularised in the 1760s, when a book was published featuring stories of him and his exploits. In Welsh folklore he is always tag lined as 'the Welsh Robin Hood' which seems a little generous. He got the 'steal from the rich' bit down to a tee; it was the 'giving to the poor' he never seemed to get to grips with. So why was he so revered if he was just a common thief? How, like Dick Turpin, did he somehow end up being remembered with fondness.

The first reason is that he was not like other bandits and highwaymen. They were generally the most horrific brutes. Dick Turpin for example once famously burned a housekeeper by holding her down on a hot stove to torture her into telling him where the valuables were hidden in her house. Pretty horrific I'm sure you would agree, but this was not unusual. They would beat the living daylights out of their victims, regardless of whether they needed to or not. And if they beat them to death, then so be it.

This was not how Twm operated. He was not interested in hurting his victims, only lightening their purses. One of his signature moves (which may have played more than a small part in the Robin Hood comparisons) was firing an arrow that would pin his victim, by their clothes, to their horse's saddle. It was enough to scare them, and show he meant business, but not something that would injure or kill.

Another reason for his enduring popularity is that he was an ordinary man getting one over on the greedy landowners. I have mentioned a few times that in the eighteenth and nineteenth centuries, wealthy landowners and the church in Wales were taxing ordinary people into the gutter. Amongst the public's growing unrest, this dashing and cunning outlaw, outsmarting and humiliating the fat greedy aristocrats, proved a very popular anti-hero, even if he didn't share out his spoils.

The main reason, though, is that his antics were sufficiently brazen and cunning to make for very entertaining stories. One which springs to mind, personifies what I mean by that.

Twm had not long arrived in a new neighbourhood and had taken a lease on a cottage. As a shrewd outlaw, he made it his business to find out the identities of the wealthy people of the town and where they lived. In these early days after his arrival, the town knew little about Twm. He clearly, however, already had a bit of a reputation. When a wealthy farmer found that his prize-winning bull had been stolen, suspicion immediately fell on this new brigand about town, who he had heard his fellows talking about over a tankard of ale. The farmer got on his horse and rode into town, to discover where he could find this rogue and question him about his bull.

He arrived where he believed Twm to live and straightened himself in his saddle, to look up at the house. Sitting in front of it there was a beggar dressed in rags. The farmer boomed out to him, 'You there. Is this the home of Twm Sion Catti?' The beggar looked up at him. 'It is,' he replied, 'but I have not long seen him go out.' The farmer, wanting to seize this opportunity to search Twm's garden and orchard for his bull, started to dismount. 'Would you like me to hold your whip and steady your horse for you while you dismount?' the beggar asked. 'I would be most obliged,' the farmer replied. He handed the beggar his whip and climbed down off his horse as the beggar held the reigns.

Once the farmer had pulled his feet from the stirrups, he turned to the beggar and snarled, 'Mind my horse for me while I am gone, if you want to be spared a beating?' The beggar bowed graciously and replied, 'I would be much obliged to you, sir.' But no sooner had the farmer taken a couple of steps toward the house, than the beggar had flung off his rags revealing himself to be a young, athletic and handsomely dressed man: Twm Sion Catti. He leaped onto the farmers horse and rode off into a cloud of dust, leaving the farmer shouting and swearing and waving his fists in anger.

Twm rode to the farmer's house, where he ran up to the farmer's wife and announced that the farmer was in terrible danger and urgently needed money. He showed her the farmer's horse and whip as proof that he was running an errand under his command. The farmer's wife dutifully ran through the house, gathering all the money, jewellery and valuables she could lay her hands on. She poured them into a sack and gave them to Twm. He loaded it onto the horse, climbed into the saddle and rode off, never to be seen in the area again.

In later life Twm became a reformed character. He married very well and lived out a very comfortable life as a landowner himself. He even, somewhat ironically, became a justice of the peace, sitting in judgement over the miscreants of the county.

Having one such larger than life character associated with the King's Head is kudos enough, but believe it or not, Twm Sion Catti has a rival in a direct contemporary. He was a local vicar called Rhys Pritchard. He was a priest with a penchant for a pint (or ten), famous around Llandovery for his overindulgences. It was not uncommon for him to be delivered up to his housekeeper at the vicarage in a wheelbarrow, after a session in the town's pubs. For everything the burly, beer swigging drovers might put away in the pub, they could only shake their heads and say, 'Bad as we may be, we are not half so bad as the parson.'

That is, until Pritchard had his own road to Damascus moment at the whim of a goat. Let me explain. There was a goat tethered to a rope in the yard of the pub. The animal had been bought by the inn keeper to provide milk for his guests. One night, after Pritchard had been drinking heavily, he thought it would be a laugh to give the goat beer. He offered it to him from his own tankard, and the goat duly drank and drank until the two of them collapsed into a drunken stupor. The following day Pritchard thought he would try the same trick again, but the goat took one sniff of the ale and turned his head away in disgust. Pritchard proclaimed, 'My God! Is this poor dumb creature wiser than I?' and he never touched another drop for the rest of his life.

He went on to write a series of religious homilies which were called *Cannnwyll Y Cymry* (which means 'Candle of Wales'). Published in the seventeenth century, it was like a Welsh counterpart to the popular English book *Pilgrim's Progress* and was published around the same time.

3.8
BUNCH OF GRAPES, NEWCASTLE EMLYN

Newcastle Emlyn stands on the Carmarthenshire bank of the river Teifi. The village of Adpar, on the opposite bank, is in Ceredigion. But this was once an altogether more hostile frontier, marking the furthermost outreach of Norman Wales. There was a lot of conflict and a lot of bloodshed here. It is no wonder that the castle lies in ruins.

Since it was built, in 1215, it has spent more time in ruins than intact. Everyone and his brother has had a go. Displaced Welsh kings and princes took it, lost it, took it, then lost it again; Owain Glyndŵr flattened it; Parliamentarians took it from Royalists, the Royalists took it back, and the Parliamentarians took it again.

And it was not just people the castle came under attack from. There is a legend of a 'winged wyvern' (a type of dragon) which flew down from the mountains, curled up on the walls of the castle and fell asleep.

The town was divided on how to deal with it. There were those who felt it best to just leave the beast be, but others were more agitated, believing that the wyvern meant them harm.

The fearful met in secret and decided that the risk was too great: the beast must be slaughtered. They pooled together for a bounty and sent for a mercenary.

The mercenary asked the women of the town to weave a shawl of many bright colours and textures, which he took to the riverbank, in plain sight of the wyvern's sleeping place. He spread it out on the grass and hid under it with his sword drawn. When the wyvern woke and saw the shawl, he was curious and swooped down to investigate. With a cry, the mercenary leaped out from under it and drove his sword up through the beast's soft underbelly. It keeled over into the river and died. But the wyvern's blood poisoned the river water, and a plague ravaged the town for 100 years.

The moral of this story: let sleeping wyverns lie. But just how long do wyvern's sleep for anyway?

During the English Civil War, the castle at Newcastle Emlyn changed sides like a ping-pong ball. When the Parliamentarians were faced with having to take it for the second time, they wanted to ensure that, this time, they finished the job. They blew the defences to smithereens. The people of the town, not wanting to pass up on this sudden windfall of free stone, helped themselves. It was from these ruins that most of the older properties we see in the centre of the old town today were constructed, including the Bunch of Grapes.

The Bunch of Grapes was built in the seventeenth century, which was a very significant period for the town. A bridge was built across the river, which saw traffic and trade blossom, and a man called Isaac Carter took rooms at the Salutation Inn (no longer there) and had a printing press installed. The town was now at the cutting edge of modern communication. The press published religious books and became quite celebrated, and there is now a blue plaque to commemorate it.

3.9
THE THREE HORSESHOES, CENARTH

Only a few miles downriver from Newcastle Emlyn is Cenarth, the triangulation point between the counties of Carmarthenshire, Ceredigion and Pembrokeshire. It is best known for its waterfalls, along a stretch of the river Teifi that runs through the town. At the right time of year, you can spot spawning salmon leaping over the rocks to get upstream.

There is a medieval mill on the riverbank and a historic bridge over the river by the falls, which was built around 1787. If you have ever seen the old bridge over the river Taff at Pontypridd, you might notice some similarities. They were both designed and built by the same man, William Edwards. There has been a bridge over the Teifi at this point since the twelfth century, and that, along with the rich fishing, is the main reason for the village's existence.

There is a very strong tradition in Cenarth of fishing on the river, using a rudimentary craft known as a 'coracle'. There is a museum dedicated to the history of coracles in the village. At one time they were used all over Wales, but they have a particular association with the Teifi and Carmarthenshire, where they were in continual use for so much longer than anywhere else.

In essence, a coracle is an animal hide pulled tightly over a circular wooden frame. It is a design that no doubt dates back thousands of years, into prehistory, and one that appears to be quintessentially Welsh.

However, coracles have popped up in a most unexpected place.

According to an ancient bit of Welsh folklore, when the father of Madoc ap Gwynedd died, his two eldest brothers fought over who should succeed to the throne, dragging the whole kingdom into civil war. Madoc was so disillusioned that, in 1170, he put to sea in search of distraction and adventure. In 1584, Humphrey Llwd wrote an account of this legend. He described the exploration thus: 'sailing West, and leaving the coast of Ireland so far north, that he came to a land unknowen, where he saw manie strange things.'

The story claims that Madoc found a beautiful and peaceful land that no one had known existed. He left a detachment of men there to establish a settlement, then returned to Wales to tell everyone of his amazing discovery. People were excited at the prospect of this exciting new land, and a flotilla of ships was launched to sail families of settlers back with Madoc, to start new lives there. What happened next, no one knows. They sailed off over the horizon, and none ever returned or were seen again. The legend ends on a note of mystery.

That mystery persisted for the best part of another 500 years, until 1660. A ship captained by a Welshman named Morgan Jones had been stranded off Oyster Point (modern day South Carolina, in the good ole US of A) for eight months. His situation was getting pretty desperate. The crew were virtually starving; they had long since run out of food. They were miles off course, nowhere near any British colonies, and their range of options was pretty slim: accept certain death by remaining where they were, or probable death by swimming to shore and trekking through the wilderness until they came to 'civilisation'. Given that stark choice, they plumbed for probable death and set off, on foot, across the uncharted terrain, in search of salvation.

Jones wrote in his journal that he and his men encountered a tribe of indigenous people who took them prisoner. In his own words, 'That night they carried us to their town and shut us up close to our no small dread.' Jones and his men were terrified that they were about to be executed, so when Jones was dragged from his cell and dropped on his knees in front of a warrior gripping a thick wooden club, he pleaded for his life in his mother tongue: '*Ydw i wedi dianc rhag cymaint o beryglon dim ond i gael fy nharo ar fy mhen fel ci?*' In other words, 'Have I escaped so many dangers, just to be hit on the head like a dog?' The warrior looked back at him quizzically, before a tribal elder pushed forward and gave an instruction to spare these men's lives... in Welsh!

They remained as guests of the tribe and observed them in their day to day to life, documenting the use of Welsh words in conversation and of coracles for fishing. Once they were fit enough to travel, their new native hosts freely allowed them to leave and rediscover the British colonies they had been in search of.

They finally made it, and on returning to his home in New York, Jones told his pastor of his discovery, sharing his journals about the encounter. Being a man of South Wales, Jones had never heard of the old legend of Madoc and his new world. The presbyterian minister, however, a man by the name of John Williams, a scholarly man of North Wales descent, was very familiar with the story, and immediately started to join the dots. He took Jones's account and wrote it up in a book entitled *An enquiry into the truth of the tradition concerning the Discovery of America, By Prince Madog ab Owen Gwynedd, about the year, 1170*. It was published in 1791, and it told the world of Jones' experiences and story. It was met with great excitement. In fact, finding this tribe became an obsession for many early settlers in the States, among them the country's third president, Thomas Jefferson.

Before we too get all excited, it is worth pointing out that, as much as Williams and Jones were verifiably real people, and both swore that the accounts were true, the story raised huge political issues. If the two men proved that, in 1170, 300 years before Columbus, Prince Madoc had discovered America, the legitimacy of Spain's claim to her American colonies was undermined. It meant that America had been discovered by a Welshman, and by modern association, a servant of the English crown. Therefore, these colonies should be English not Spanish.

These two superpowers of their day had been battling over their individual claims of sovereignty in the Americas for over 100 years. Every possible bit of leverage they could find to bolster their own position was grasped with both hands – this story, quite possibly, among them. Of course, the continent already had its own indigenous people, who had a far better claim to sovereignty than any European power. Unfortunately, the one thing the English and the Spanish agreed upon was the total rejection of any such claim.

Having said all that, there genuinely were Native American tribes who used craft very similar to coracles. But to be fair, it is not exactly a revolutionary design. I am pretty sure different groups of people could have come up with it independently of each other, in the same way as they did with the wheel.

Anyway, I've ended up in quite a lofty place, talking about contested claims for the discovery of America, the legitimacy of colonial sovereignty, and so on, without yet even mentioning the pub this chapter is meant to be about. If you were waiting to get to this bit before buying a pint here, I must apologise. You must be parched by now.

So, what can I tell you about the Three Horseshoes? Well, it is an eighteenth-century building which boasts a lovely cottagey feel, with bare stone walls, beams, a recessed fireplace and a lovely wood burner. There are plenty of craft and real ales to choose from and a fish-oriented menu.

Bizarrely, it is not the pub itself that has earned its place in this book. It is the small thatched cottage in the yard behind it. It was refurbished and made into a second bar in the 90s, but it is likely to be the original alehouse of the village, referred to in a document dated 1760. The building is really difficult to age. The beam over the fireplace says 1805, but that has clearly been added; it is quite likely that much of the rest of this building dates back to the Middle Ages, and it optimises the simple and humble design that you would expect from such a building, of such an age, in this remote corner of rural Carmarthenshire.

3.10
THE PENDRE INN, CILGERRAN

I accept that I am taking a gamble by covering the Pendre Inn, as at the time of writing it is for sale. I really hope it finds a sympathetic custodian soon. It deserves its chance, as it is one of the oldest pubs in West Wales, possibly dating back to the fourteenth century. If you have visited the Laleston Inn, which we spoke about in an earlier chapter, you may well recognise several similar features: not least the two-storey stone bay window at the front of the building. Flagons of ale used to be handed through these windows in the days before they were glazed, for the men who tended to the horses of visiting travellers.

The bay is more than likely a late sixteenth- or early seventeenth-century addition, to tart up what would have been a fairly modest building. Today, the oldest part of it, though quite plain, drips with conspicuous antiquity, with its thick slate-stone walls, an inglenook fireplace and blackened beams. It was formerly the hall of the original medieval house, which more latterly became the pub's lounge. In its original form, it would have been open to roof level and heated by an open hearth on the floor. You can see from the outline of the outside wall that the building was at some point extended upwards and an upper floor added. The stairs leading up to it were also built into an extended wing on the side of the original building.

One unusual feature, or omission, is the lack of a flue where the original fire would have been. Where did the smoke go? Well, in this part of Wales, something rather unique to buildings of this age was the construction of a wattle and daub hood, which would have hung over the fire and vented the smoke out of the building. Sadly, as the rest of the building is made of stone, it would have been an easy feature to remove, to make way for the new upper level. None of it is still visible today.

3.11
THE ROYAL OAK,
FISHGUARD

In the 1990s, on his TV show *Here Comes Barry Welsh*, the actor and comedian John Sparkes used to have the nation in stitches with his character 'Hugh Pugh'. Hugh was a fictional news reporter on a program called *Look Out Wales*, and he was always reporting 'live from Fishguard'. His sketch involved black and white film footage of old age pensioners doing an awkward piece to camera, no doubt lifted from some local news item from the early 60s; their responses would be interspersed with the questions of a black and white Hugh, so that their answers were either rude or absurd. One of Hugh's most regular 'interviewees' was a putative former mayor of Fishguard, who had been voted out in the last election after seventy years in office. The name of this great public servant? Kenny Twat.

They just don't make them like that anymore.

I say he had the nation in stitches. Not, apparently, in Fishguard. They were really quite cross about it. Maybe I shouldn't have brought it up.

Fishguard is the second stop on our national pub crawl to have originally been a large-scale Viking settlement. The name is a corruption of the Norse word Fiskigarðr,•meaning 'fish catching enclosure'. There is little left of the Vikings' legacy today, although at low tide we can still see how the place got its name. It is sometimes still possible to see the 'V' shaped stone structures its founders used to support their wooden fish traps, which would have caught larger fish as the tide went out. It was a technique quite common in ancient Scandinavia, and also used by the Saxons, but not so common in Wales.

Most of the buildings in Fishguard, including the Royal Oak, are seventeenth and eighteenth century, which is when the town saw a period of expansion and prosperity. At this time, it was a key port for trade between the southern half of Britain and Ireland. It was also during this period that Fishguard played a crucial part in an episode of British history that is nothing like as well-known as it should be.

When do you suppose was the last invasion of mainland Britain by a foreign force?

Battle of Hastings, 1066? Oh please!

William of Orange landing in Brixham in 1688, with an army of 14,000 Dutch soldiers?

Nope.

On 22nd February 1797, an incredibly inept detachment of the French Naval Fleet was heading for Ireland to launch a surprise attack, when they found they had miscalculated and inadvertently landed in Pembrokeshire.

Surprise!

Not wanting to waste the opportunity, they decided to launch an attack on the harbour, possibly with a view to holding it until they could send for re-enforcements. However, they were hardly the cream of the French fighting elite, mostly convicts drafted in to make up numbers. As such, they were easily distracted from their mission, not least by some barrels of Portuguese wine that local farmers had salvaged from a shipwreck and stacked on the quayside. When the French soldiers stumbled upon them, they could not help themselves, cracking them open and drinking their contents.

The effect of 1,400 drunken men might have somewhat diminished the element of surprise. But before the local militia arrived, the invading French first had to face down an adversary they had not anticipated: the women of Fishguard. They came out with pitchforks and clubs, and the sight of them scared the troops half to death. By the time the local militia came, the French were in no mood to fight. The invading troops were rounded up and imprisoned within two days. By 24th February 1797, it was all over.

The French and the British commanders came together to sign a treaty, and the place they chose to sign it was the Royal Oak – and yes, it was a pub at the time. There is an inscription above the door as you go in that commemorates the historic moment.

In case you are wondering what ever happened to John Sparkes, you will be delighted to know that, in animated children's TV programmes like *Fireman Sam* and *Peppa Pig*, his voice lives on.

3.12

GOLDEN LION, NEWPORT

The Preseli Hills start on the edge of Newport. They are unprecedentedly beautiful, steeped in myth, legend and folklore. The great work of Welsh mythology, *the Mabinogion*, describes it as a land of mystery and enchantment. If you are not familiar with the *Mabinogion*, it was the first secular book ever in Britain, written by a monk from Gwynedd in the eleventh century, a compilation of stories about Welsh folklore and legends. What kind of fool would write a book like that?

Immediately north of Newport, there is a hill called Carningli, which dominates the landscape all around. It used to be an Iron Age hillfort but more latterly has been revered as a holy shrine. It dates back to the very earliest days of Christianity in Wales, and no doubt before that too. The name is a corruption of its original Welsh name *Carn Yngely*, which translates as 'summit of angels'. According to legend, there was a sixth-century monk called St Brynach, a contemporary of St David while he was bishop at the nearby cathedral, who used to retreat to the hilltop to 'commune with angels'. It is claimed that if you fall asleep on the hilltop, you will dream of angels yourself. As such, the area has long been considered very holy, and even now there is a Christian retreat nearby.

The spiritual tradition in the area is not something that was introduced with Christianity, however; it goes back way further than that. You may have noticed the Preseli Hills in the national news in the early part of 2021, when a convincing theory was put forward that they were the original location of Stonehenge. It suggests that the monument was only subsequently moved to its current site on Salisbury Plain. If this theory is on the money, it perhaps speaks to why these hills are one of those areas that, for whatever reason, have always felt spiritual to people, like the island of Lindisfarne or the area of south west France around Lourdes.

Even if you are not convinced by these spiritual credentials, it's worth a walk to the top, as the views of the coastline and surrounding countryside are stunning.

Newport itself is a quaint little village with a varied history. In the early days of the Norman occupation, it was the capital of a lordship called Cemais, which had its administrative centre at the castle. The remains stand on a spur on Carningli, possibly on the same site as the former hillfort. In the Middle Ages, its principal form of industry was pottery, but across its history it has been best known for its port. In the old harbour area in Parog, you can still see the remains of the ancient quayside and some early lime kilns for the production of iron. Both are believed to date back well over 2000 years.

It is a very pleasant place to stop for a pint and a bite to eat, and there are few places better for that than the Golden Lion. The building was most likely built in the eighteenth century and is a hodgepodge of old cottages and outbuildings merged into one. It does not have much in the way of original features, but there is a series of steps leading to a plinth on the front that, when this building was a dairy, would have been used to load milk churns onto a dray; once the building became a pub, it would have been just as handy for unloading barrels of beer. The pub has bare stone walls and roof beams, but these are the result of comparatively recent renovations and improvements.

3.13
THE BISHOPS,
ST DAVIDS

As I am sure you are aware, the city of St Davids is named after the patron saint of Wales. In the sixth century, he established his mission in a monastery that used to surround the beautiful cathedral here. Thanks to this cathedral, the 'village' it stands in is officially Britain's smallest city.

I mentioned earlier that some Arthurian legend might feature in this chapter, and Saint David is the reason why. Or at least his mother is: she was, so legend has it, King Arthur's niece, not to mention a saint in her own right, known as St Non. It just goes to show: it's not what you know, it's who you know.

In the hours leading up to Saint David's birth, the peninsula which now bears his name was being battered by a terrible storm. But as he was born, the clouds parted and an unearthly light shone down, and all became calm and still. A spring of crystal-clear water burst forth from the ground, and to this day you can still see that spring, high on the clifftop above St Non's Bay, to the south of St Davids. It is called St Non's Well, and a simple stone arch covers it. There are legends that, from time to time, rather than running with water, it runs with milk or wine. It is still a place of pilgrimage to this day, and for centuries provided the holy water used in the fonts at the cathedral.

It must have been good stuff, as Saint David is meant to have lived to the ripe old age of 147. He died on March 1st 588, and was buried in his cathedral, where his tomb can still be seen in the west wall of the chapel of the Holy Trinity. He has long been a prominent figure in the pecking order of Catholic saints. I mentioned in my chapter about the Anchor Inn that, in the Middle Ages, pilgrimages operated on a sort of point system. The more revered the relic you visited, the more points you would score, and the greater the chances of your entering heaven. Visiting the remains of Saint David was worth half one visit to the Vatican. (Side note: someone really needs to make a sixth-century saints Top Trumps set.)

The Bishops is actually one of St David's newest pubs. It is pretty unmissable, as it is located on the central square, opposite the old cross. It is made up of two separate buildings that have been incorporated into one. One is eighteenth century, the other seventeenth century. The interior is all stone walls and beams, and an industrial-looking wood burner, but there is not much of genuine antiquity. One nice touch is that the tables are named after nautical features in the area. There is much schoolboy guffawing at the one called 'bitches', but it is not as derogatory as you might think, named after a tidal race just off Ramsey Island. The beer garden is something truly special, and it has great views of the historic cathedral.

It is known for simple hearty fare.

3.14
THE PRIORY INN,
MILFORD HAVEN

I remember from my Geography O-Level that Milford Haven is a 'rea', which is defined as a flooded river valley. Historically it was the port from which multiple invasions were launched by Norman or English rulers against the poor Irish: Richard De Clare in 1167, Henry II in 1171, John I in both 1185 and 1210, and Cromwell in 1649.

It hasn't all been one way traffic though. In 1405 Jean II de Rieu landed a detachment of French troops here to support Owain Glyndŵr's rebellion against the English. And it was not the last time Milford Haven had strong French connections either.

The fortunes of the town have always been inextricably linked to the port, which really started to grow in prominence at the turn of the nineteenth century. At the time, a lot was being invested in Britain's defences; Milford was a naval port and a Royal dockyard, and a fair number of other activities grew up around the town to capitalise on this. Unusually for the time, the dockyard had a strong Gallic flavour, being managed by a Frenchman called Jean Loiuse Barrellier. Under his influence, a lot of French shipbuilders and craftsmen were brought in to work there, and it led to quite a sizable French community in this part of Pembrokeshire.

The Priory does not escape a French connection either. A very pious and hard-working order of monks from l'Abbie de Tiron, in the Brittany region of France, came to Britain to establish missions here.

Their order was very strict, even by comparison with other monastic orders. They craved hardship and suffering and lived out their lives in total devotion to God, with no contact with the outside world. They effectively worked, lived and died within the walls of their monasteries.

They established an abbey at St Dogmaels near Cardigan. A Norman noble, Adam de Rupe, lord of Roche Castle (near Haverfordwest) also gave them land above a *pil*, which is a Welsh word meaning a tidal waterway with access onto a wider navigation, usually used as a harbour. This particular *pil* was on the shore near Milford Haven. Around 1200, de Rupe gave the monks patronage to build a priory cell there and to operate a port.

During Henry VIII's Dissolution of the Monasteries in the sixteenth century, the priory cell was seized by the crown (much like the Cross Keys in Swansea). The buildings were sold off to secular landowners, who stripped them of anything of value (such as lead and other expensive building materials) and they were either put to new use or left to rot. The latter was the fate of the old priory church, which was not a flexible enough building to be converted to a secular use. However, the south cloister was converted into a farmhouse, and this is where the pub now stands.

Architecturally it is a bit of a patchwork of styles, a mishmash of the various buildings it is made up of. We have lots of small windows at irregular intervals, with mismatched gables and stumpy chimneys. A central wall also seems to incorporate what at one time would have been the gable end of a mediaeval building, likely to have been the abbot's private quarters. On the first floor there is a Tudor doorway which would have led into it. The heart of the inn, though, is the remains of the cloister range. Wrapped around that is the Tudor farmhouse with its beamed ceiling and large inglenook fireplace. What at one time would have been a separate cottage is now the lounge.

The central lounge is the most historically significant bit of the building. It is housed in the vaulted undercroft of the medieval range. This would at one time have been a storeroom or barn, but more recently, large windows have been cut into those deep stone walls, to let some light in. The main living area originally would have been above it on the first floor. Overall, this layout is similar to the central part of the Cross Keys in Swansea.

The pub is in quite a rural, remote spot and is located close to the waterfront. In 2018, after continuous heavy downpours, the pub was badly affected by flooding. A great deal of effort went into trying to salvage what could be saved, and in repairing the damage – only for the exact same thing to happen in 2019. A newspaper report in *the Milford Mercury* said that the pub was now closed indefinitely: undoubtedly the oldest pub building in Wales looking like it was about to be lost to us forever. However, when compiling this book in June 2021, I paid the old place a visit, just on the off chance that someone might have bought it. I was delighted to see some signs of life. So watch this space: its doors may be about to open once more.

3.15
NEW INN,
AMROTH

These days, south Pembrokeshire is a hot bed of tourism. But while Tenby itself, as well as Pembroke and Carew, have some really interesting ancient architecture, there is surprisingly little in coastal south Pembrokeshire. Pretty much all of what you see is no older than eighteenth century. Which might seem odd when places like Milford Haven and Pembroke were always very important places. The fact is, once you stepped outside them, the rest of the coastal area, especially places south-east of Narberth, were very remote and isolated. Long sandy beaches have not always held the same draw as they do now.

The village of Amroth, however, is dripping with history.

If you are a fan of ancient history, there are the remains of a petrified Neolithic forest just off the coast. When the tide retreats to its lowest point, the gnarled roots and timbers are revealed from their briny hiding place. These fossilised trees date back to around 5,000 BC, a point in history when the sea was a long way further out than now.

The village itself is also very old, established more than 2000 years BC as an Iron Age fort, taking advantage of the spot's commanding views out to sea. A nearby site was also developed into a villa by the Romans in the second century, and in the ninth century the village attracted Viking settlers, who named it Earewear, which is Norse for 'sandbank'.

They didn't muck about with naming places, the Vikings. 'Oi, Sven! What do you think we should call this village by the sandbank then? Alright, I was only asking!'

The New Inn stands right on the seashore. It is a stone building and is believed to be sixteenth century. For my money, it is made up of two cottages that originally stood back-to-back. I would say the rear one is the older of the two, with the one at the front perhaps being eighteenth century. In the front part, there are two large stone fireplaces either side of a long bar, which has been made from recycled bits of sea chests. This room at one time would have been partitioned into lots of smaller rooms. The lounge to the rear has flagstone floors and a vast inglenook fireplace peppered with nooks, crannies and ovens, and I feel it looks a lot older.

In the sixteenth and seventeenth centuries, this remote coastal village would have had a very similar look and feel to other coastal areas in South Wales, like the Vale of Glamorgan and the Gower peninsular. It was just as reliant on shipwreckers, pirates and smugglers for commerce, and there are a lot of similarities between the history of the New Inn and the Plough and Harrow in Monknash or the Blue Anchor in Aberthaw. It was another smugglers' inn, a place for vagabonds to negotiate the sale of barrels of contraband hidden in the cellar, and a makeshift mortuary for the bodies of shipwrecked mariners.

In later history, it is quite likely the village was visited by JRR Tolkien, author of *the Lord of the Rings*. He is, after all, known to have spent time in Wales, and he often acknowledged the country, its folklore and language as inspirations for middle earth. In particular, the kingdom of Gondor features a fortified settlement looking out to sea from a promontory, called Dol Amroth.

3.16
THE BLACK LION,
ST CLEARS

The inclusion of the Black Lion in a book about historic pubs might raise a few eyebrows. But it is not so much the pub that is of interest: it is the white marker that stands outside it. This rather innocuous white cast-iron plinth, sunk into the outside walls of the pub, is a monument to something that in the nineteenth century ignited this hitherto tranquil corner of Wales into revolutionary fervour.

The main road which runs through St Clears, what is now the A40 to Haverford West, was the front line of the unrest. At the time, it was a turnpike. Remember them? They were the points where, from the seventeenth century, landowners would charge travellers for use of the roads – charges which quickly became excessive, arbitrary and exploitative.

If St Clears' only problem had been the turnpikes, it is unlikely that the hard-pressed farmers of West Wales would have exploded to the degree that they did; however, these unpredictable charges were compounded by an agricultural crisis. Ordinary people were already buckling under the weight of grinding rural poverty, and the turnpike tolls were the final straw. In the 1830s the people rose up against them, in what were known as 'the Rebecca Riots'. A lot of the worst trouble was in the towns of Whitland and St Clears.

It all started with the tollgate at Efailwen. An attack was led by the stirring figure of 'Rebecca' – a man with a blackened face, wearing a wig and women's clothes, astride a white horse and waving a sword. There was a great deal of irony intended in the protestor's getup: women traveling alone were exempt from paying a toll. The name Rebecca, meanwhile an allusion to the most beautiful woman in the Old Testament (her name becoming the Hebrew word for 'alluring') had its own barbed significance. If such figurative subtleties registered with the landowners, we will never know. But they couldn't have missed the protestors' destroying the gate and attacking the toll collector.

Shortly after this first attack, a new tollgate was placed near the Mermaid Tavern in St Clears itself, on November 18th 1842 (the Mermaid, incidentally, is another historically significant inn lost to the sands of time). This new imposition upon the locals became the site of a four-month battle between the rioters and the authorities. The mob's modus operandi remained consistent throughout: they would descend without warning, led by the figure of Rebecca, before just as quickly disappearing into the night. There are claims that their numbers reached as many as 100 men, armed with scythes and billhooks.

Police and troops were called in to help protect the gates, but Rebecca and her daughters were consistently one step ahead of the law. The protests came to an end in 1844, partly because a Commission of Inquiry was set up to reform the Turnpike Trusts, but mainly because the introduction of railways meant that the turnpikes lost their monopoly on the movement of people and goods around the country.

I cannot find any records which specifically earmark the Black Lion as the scene of any action. But today it is broadly representative of the kinds of places where the rebels would have met up to plan their raids, and stock up on Dutch courage before taking to the road. It is, after all, a nineteenth-century building, even though it has been extensively modernised.

These days, the Black Lion is both a public bar and the official club house of St Clears Rugby Club. So if you are looking for a hostelry to sit in a quiet corner by a roaring log fire, this possibly is not the place for you.

*

Now also seems as good a time as any to tackle something that perplexed me for decades: the spelling of St Clears. Why is it spelled this way, when it is pronounced 'St Clairs'? Was there an early Welsh saint whose name was Anglicised to St Clear, in the same way as St Dunwyd ended up as St Donat?

Well, it is an Anglicisation, but the root is not Welsh but French.

The Norman lords who governed the area in the thirteenth century prized its forests around for their bounteous supply of wild boar. The area was declared an official hunting park, where keepers were employed to manage the boar population so there would always be plenty of hunting. The French word for wild boar being *sanglier*, it is this, rather than a saint called Clair who couldn't spell, that provides the root of the town's name. You're welcome.

3.17
THE ANGEL VAULTS,
CARMARTHEN

armarthen is another one of those places with such a massive
weight of history that there is no way I could do it justice in any
preamble. It was established well before anyone thought to record
history. The twelfth-century castle stands on the remains of a Roman
Fort from 75 AD, which in turn stands on the site of an Iron Age
hillfort, possibly dating back another 2000 years before that.
Carmarthen was the capital of the Dematea tribe, then became the
Roman capital of West Wales, known as Moridunum (meaning sea
fort); from the ninth century it was where the ancient Kings of
Deheubarth held their court. Until the Industrial Revolution shifted
the balance of power east, this was the most significant settlement in
the southern half of Wales by some margin. And if all that wasn't
enough, Merlin the Wizard, King Arthur's sorcerer at Camelot, was
born here too.

So, is there a pub in Carmarthen that does all this history justice?
Well, the first thing to note is that there are less candidates than you
might expect. And those that do remain have been modernised or
rebuilt or made into hotels or some such other purposes. There is,
however, one that stands out to me.

Formerly the Angel, now the Angel Vaults, this lovely old pub
stands right next to Carmarthen's historic castle. It has a room called
the Castle Room, which has some great views over the old ramparts,

while the frontage faces onto Nott Square, which is named after Major General Sir William Nott. Nott may well be best remembered for his military contribution to the British imperial expansion in India and Afghanistan, but coincidentally, he was the son of an inn keeper. His family used to keep the Ivy Bush, which is now a hotel just down the road.

Nott Square used to be the medieval market square of Carmarthen, so undoubtedly there would have been an inn in the vicinity, although whether or not it would have been this exact site, we cannot be sure. But however you carve it up, this is the oldest pub in the oldest part of what claims to be the oldest town in Wales.

The Angel as we know it now dates back to the turn of the eighteenth century, but like so many buildings of this type, it is a hodgepodge of the remains of multiple buildings from different periods, all cobbled together into what we see today. Every now and then it yields clues to its past; for example, in 1983 some remedial repair work was being done, and behind some old plaster the builders discovered a stone mullioned window dating from the Tudor period hidden in one of the walls.

This window is quite likely to have originally been part of the exterior wall of the lost church of St Mary. How do you lose a church? Surely, for once, the question 'Where were you when you lost it?' would actually be helpful when it came to a church. The answer in this case is that there is documentary evidence of this church standing immediately to the east of the guildhall in 1252, but by 1701 it was described as 'dissolved'. Most likely it was another casualty of Henry VIII's Dissolution of the Monasteries. No doubt the people of the town took advantage of the free masonry and timber for use in other buildings, and I would hazard a guess that the building the Angel Vaults stands in today was one of them. There is also every likelihood that, given where the building stands, some of the masonry, in the foundations at least, is contemporary with the Celtic/Roman period.

THE ANCIENT KINGDOMS
OF BRYCHEINIOG, POWYS
AND CEREDIGION

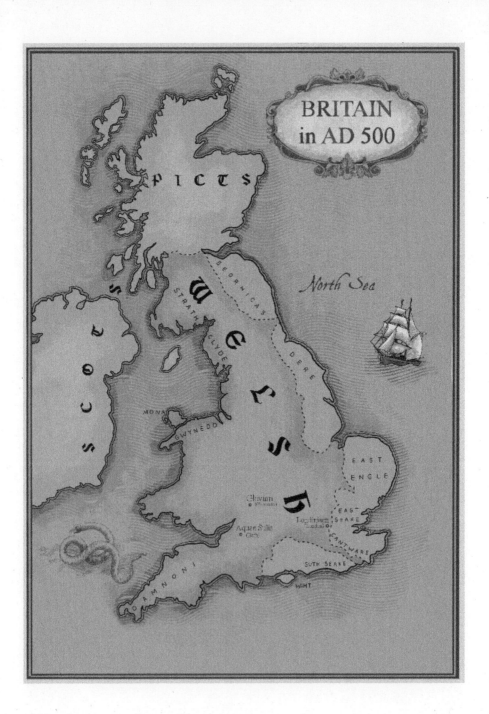

BRITAIN
in AD 500

PICTS

North Sea

SCOTS

BEORNICAS

STRATH CLYDE

DERE

WELSH

MONA

GWYNEDD

EAST
ENGLE

Glevum
(Gloster)

EAST
SEAXE

Aquae Sulis
(Bath)

Londinium
(London)

CANTWARE

DAMNONI

SUTH SEAXE

WIHT

In the year 500, the land of the Welsh was a lot bigger than it is today. And no wonder: it included most of the Midlands and southern and southwest England, as well as the lowlands of Scotland. Its eastern border was modern day London, and further north it stretched all the way across the island from west to east, between Cardigan Bay and the Wash. It also extended along the northwest of the country, through the kingdom of Strathclyde, as far north as the beginning of the Scottish Highlands, the land of the Picts.

I accept that this observation may raise some eyebrows. All the way through this book, I have been ducking the question, 'What is the oldest pub in Wales?' claiming that it entirely depends on the criteria you judge it by. Well, the complexity of that question is a drop in the ocean compared to 'How do you define the Welsh?'

But if you had asked in the sixth century, any Welshman would have told you that the territories listed above were the home of the Cymry, one of the four original peoples of Britain. This goes some way to explaining why the name of the English region 'Cumbria' sounds so close to *Cambria*, (the Latin name for Wales), and also why a lot of place names in the rural northwest of England have a distinctly Welsh sound to them. To the Saxons, Welsh just meant 'foreigner'.

I was once told a story by an old man in a pub (so it's bound to be true): when he was a boy, he was staying with his parents in a guest house in the Lake District, ran by a family of sheep farmers. They claimed that their family had been farming there for centuries. The young lad was from Llanelli and had no real experience of country ways. To him, at his age, the farm seemed to be a magical place. He went out with the farmer every day, and on one particular day, they went to the moor so the farmer could count in his flock.

The old farmer began counting, '*Un, dau, tri, pedwar, pump...*' Seeing the young boy looking back at him in astonishment, he stopped and said with a smile, 'Oh, yes, of course. You wouldn't be able to understand what I am saying. This is a very ancient way shepherds in these parts count their sheep. It must sound strange to you.' With a grin, the young boy chirped up with, '*Chwech, saith, wyth, naw, deg...*'

The shepherd's eyes nearly popped out of his head. He had never known that this ancient tradition was just plain and simple Welsh.

I mention this blurring of modern-day boundaries to explain why it was that the ancient kingdom of Powys did not just cover mid-Wales. The court of the king of Powys is likely to have been modern day Shrewsbury, and his kingdom would have included large parts of what in the twenty-first century is Shropshire and Herefordshire.

The re-drawing of the map started in earnest with the battle of Chester in 616, when the forces of Northumbria defeated Powys, pushing them back to the floodplains of the River Severn. Progressively, over the ensuing 100 years or so, Powys drew back to what we might today recognise as the border between Wales and England – a border that became enforced in the eighth century, when the Anglo Saxons invaded, claimed the kingdom of Mercia, and their king, Offa, built a dyke to ensure clear demarcation.

Compared to the kingdom of Powys, Brychieniog (which after the Norman conquest became Anglicised to Brecknockshire) and Ceredigion were the poor relations. Brychieniog was little more than a buffer between the English to the east, Morganwg to the south, Deheubarth to the west and Powys to the north. It was ruled by the Tudwal dynasty, only coming into being because ancient Welsh inheritance law meant that all surviving sons inherited a portion of their father's estate (even illegitimate sons). All of their neighbours were far more wealthy and powerful, and any one of them was liable to kick off at the drop of a hat. Likewise, Ceredigion was never much more than an enclave of Deheubarth.

Today the area is divided into the beautiful counties of Ceredigion in the west (which mirrors very accurately the boundaries of the old kingdom) and Powys. Between them, they cover the largest area with the lowest population of any of the counties of Wales. They're great places to seek a bit of solitude, to experience a sliver of how life would have been in a simpler time.

It is one of my great pleasures in life to plan a long walk through these beautiful counties, along an ancient path, to a beauty spot or up a mountain, and to end the walk at any one of the pubs I am about to introduce you to.

4.1
THE GRIFFIN INN, LLYSWEN

L lyswen is a village on the Wye and stands on what used to be the Builth to Hay turnpike. The village is said to date back to 1127, and it got its name (which translates as 'white court') when Prince Rhodri Mawr established his baronial court there.

As far as history goes, that's pretty much it really, although one rather eccentric footnote is the story of John Thelwall's time as a hermit here in the late eighteenth century. Thelwall was a very controversial intellectual of his day, who could never settle on what he wanted to do with his life. Though descended from a Welsh family from Denbighshire, he grew up in Covent Garden. He qualified in the law before discovering an interest in anatomy and attending lectures at Guys and St Tomas' Hospital in London. After deciding that this didn't really float his boat either, he diverted his focus to writing, predominantly journalism but also Romantic poetry. As with everything he tried, he was really good at it, and he soon developed a following of influential literary friends. But soon even his successful writing career fell by the wayside.

He found his feet as a radical political speaker. However, his subjects and views made him a lot of enemies. For example, he was a very outspoken anti-creationist, as well as part of a movement that believed blood to be a mystical, magical substance. His fascination with blood influenced a friend, one Bram Stoker, who used these notions as a springboard for his masterpiece, *Dracula*.

At the time of the French Revolution, Thelwall started giving talks about the merits of a republican Britain. This, in particular, made him a target for some very powerful people.

When the heat got too much for him, he went off grid and moved to a farm in Llyswen, living in a hermitage in its grounds. In August 1789 he was visited there by some of his friends, including the poet Samuel Coleridge and both William and Dorothy Wordsworth. It is believed that the character 'the solitary', from Wordsworth's poem *The Excursion*, was based on Thelwall in this period.

It is likely that Coleridge and the Wordsworths would have retired to the Griffin to discuss the plight of their friend over a pint. It is also believed that they stayed there.

When they visited, the Griffin would have looked pretty much as it does now. As with so many old pubs, it is a series of buildings, outhouses, extensions, and lean-tos, which over time have been absorbed into the one unit. There is a general belief that the inn existed since 1467, and if that is true, it occupied what is today the central bar area. The two adjoining rooms and the exterior of the building probably date from the turn of the eighteenth century. The upper lounge has a beautifully restored inglenook with a brick bread oven to one side. No doubt this was at one time the kitchen.

The Griffin has traditionally had a very good reputation for food and is listed in *the Good Pub Guide*. They also offer rooms.

4.2

THE HARP INN, OLD RADNOR

The use of adjectives like 'new' and 'old' in place names is, as you might expect, quite subjective. Especially in rural village communities like this one, where the pace of change is slow. My father grew up in a small farming community, and he distinctly remembers a family that all the residents of the village would refer to as 'the new people'. It was a practice that continued well into his adulthood, even though he knew full well that they had moved to the village before he had been born.

In this case, New Radnor became 'new' in the thirteenth century, when the Normans established their own settlement a few miles away from the original Welsh one. All that is left of Old Radnor today is a small cluster of cottages, this wonderful pub overlooking the Summergill valley, and the fifteenth-century church of St Steven. If you get the chance, it is well worth taking a look at it.

The church building that is St Steven's today is a replacement for one burned to the ground by Owain Glyndŵr, but even that one is believed to have stood on an even older site, possibly dating back to pagan Celtic times. The current building still has its pre-Reformation rood screens intact, and they are very good examples, well worth a look by themselves. Its real pièce de resistance, however, is its font, a vast, hollowed-out boulder on stumpy legs. It is believed to be both the biggest and the oldest font in Wales, and legend has it that it was made from a megalithic standing stone by early Christians in the eighth century.

These standing stones (which stand at the foot of the hill near New Radnor) have a legend of their own. When the church bells of St Steven's ring, they are believed to move by themselves, to a nearby pool, and start to drink from it.

The church also boasts a beautiful renaissance organ covered in intricate carvings, supposedly contemporary with the church building itself. To my knowledge, it is the only working organ in Wales claimed to date back to the fifteenth century. Granted, such claims are not an area of personal expertise, but however you carve it up, there cannot be many organs contemporary with this one still in use anywhere in the world.

Visitors to the Harp Inn will enjoy a wonderful location, a bare stone exterior, and a largely unrenovated interior featuring ancient, polished slate floors, oak beams, antique settles and a huge open log fire set in an inglenook with an offset bread oven. The current owners are the coveted winners of *The Good Pub Guide*'s Country Pub of the Year award 2020. It is a pretty hotly contested accolade, even in a year when all the pubs were closed (an irony not lost on the owners). It is also recommended in all the other main pub and food guides, including Michelin and CAMRA. Their menu focuses on local, seasonal produce and simple dishes done really well.

It has not always enjoyed this reputation, however. In 1645, after the battle of Naseby, Charles I did a tour of Powys, the Marches and Monmouthshire to garner support for his struggle against the Parliamentarians. On this tour, he is believed to have visited the Harp Inn, and while he was there, he complained about the food. No chance of that happening now, although it's probably a bit late in the day to invite him back.

The Harp is also dog friendly, offers rooms and has a beer garden with some of the most spectacular views you can imagine.

4.3

THE RADNORSHIRE ARMS, PRESTEIGNE

B eing a border town, Presteigne has a rich cocktail of influences to its history, culture and architecture. The name, for a start, rather than Welsh, is believed to be derived from an ancient English word meaning 'the priest's house'. This was a Saxon settlement, quite different, therefore, from any other we have looked at so far in this book. Their influence can still be seen in some of the earlier masonry in the church.

Like everywhere else with good, workable land, Presteigne fell to the Normans in the twelfth century. Its heyday, however, would have been in the seventeenth century, when its streets would have been crammed with black and white half-timber structures like this old coaching inn. Sadly only a few remain now, but that just makes the Radnorshire Arms all the more special. About this time, Presteigne saw a boom in its economy, becoming county town of the old county of Radnorshire, and as such serving as an important trading gateway to this part of Wales.

There is a rather spectacular bit of folklore associated with Presteigne, concerning a haunting by a terrifying and malevolent ghost called 'Black Vaughan'. The story starts seven miles down the road in the town of Kington.

Hergest Court is a large, black and white, half-timber manor house on the edge of Kington. It was once the home of the infamous Black Vaughan, who even in life was a pretty sinister character. He was a knight and when fighting in the War of the Roses was decapitated by one of his adversaries in battle. As his head fell to the ground, his trusty bloodhound let out a deafening, blood-curdling howl.

The beast ran up to where his master had fallen, gathered up the severed head in its jaws and ran at full pelt in the direction of Hergest Court. But neither dog nor head ever made it home. The knight's body was brought back to the court and was buried in the churchyard. But his ghost remained at large. He would sometimes appear as a headless apparition, sometimes as a black bull, but always with his ghostly bloodhound at his side. He terrorised people in the towns and villages for miles around. It got so bad that the terrified residents would not dare even leave their homes for fear of encountering him.

Something had to be done, and thirteen parsons were summoned. They gathered at the church and began the incantations to exorcise Black Vaughan once and for all. No sooner had they started than the apparition of the headless knight and his drooling hound appeared before them. Twelve of the thirteen fainted from the shock of it, but from somewhere the thirteenth found the strength to proceed with the exorcism on his own. As he went through his ritual of bell, book and candle, he saw the ghost of Black Vaughan shrink and shrink before his eyes, until he was no bigger than a fly. Then the parson bent down, scooped up the ghost in a snuff box and buried it under a rock at the bottom of a pond.

The ghost was finally laid to rest. But the ghost of his hound... lives on.

Pretty spectacular stuff, I'm sure you will agree. This hound, incidentally, is credited as the inspiration for Sir Arthur Conan Doyle's Sherlock Holmes story *The Hound of the Baskervilles*.

A timber above the porch of the Radnorshire Arms is dated 1616. This could be accurate, but for once I will suggest that, if anything, the pub might actually be older than that. My reasoning is that this building was originally a house, and there is documentation to say that it was once the home of one of Queen Elizabeth I's favourites, a courtier by the name of Sir Christopher Hatton. But Hatton died in 1591. So if this was his home, unless he was camping in the garden, it must be older than this beam records. Maybe the porch was put up in 1616, as an addition to an already existing house. If so, we have a true rarity: a pub that is actually older than it claims to be.

An archived title deed shows that this was once the property of a man called John Bradshaw. This was a discovery that a former landlord latched on to, as there was a Cheshire-born man called John Bradshaw who was instrumental in the execution of Charles I. However, it is very unlikely to be the same John Bradshaw. Some rough arithmetic would suggest that the regicidal John Bradshaw would have been fourteen at the time he was recorded as residing here.

But even without such supplementation, the pub has such a rich history, evident from the moment you pull up outside. The white walls and black timbers that mark its exterior still speak to the boldness and confidence of the Welsh gentry of the Stuart era. The bulk of the building has survived relatively unmolested by future renovations (besides a bit of Victoriana round the back). Inside you have some lovely old oak panelling, with lattice leadwork windows facing onto the old formal gardens, and in the lounge bar a line of mullioned stone windows lets the light pour into an otherwise quite dark space, typical of its time.

Some renovations were done at the turn of the 1900s, and during the work a priest hole was uncovered behind a false panel. Even more impressive was the discovery of a diary kept by a Catholic priest over the course of two years of hiding out in it.

At some point there was a legend of buried treasure at the inn, and several broken wall panels are indicators of a night when some gullible locals broke in to rob the place, hoping that this legend might be true.

These days the inn is more of a hotel than a pub, but given all of this amazing backstory, I hope my reader will forgive the inclusion. As with all the borderline cases I have allowed, you can still go in and ask for a pint if you want to.

4.4

THE THREE COCKS, THREE COCKS

This rambling old coaching inn is pretty much all there is to the village that now shares its name. It was originally a set of farm buildings, separated by a yard with quite a mature tree growing in it. All these buildings ended up getting amalgamated into one enormous building, absorbing the old yard, tree and all. In the kitchen and rooms which spin off it, you can still see how the builders incorporated the old tree into the structure of the building. And a very fine building it is too, with plenty of exposed stone, carved timber and huge private gardens to the rear, which are stunning in their own right. Bits of this structure are believed to date back as far as the fifteenth century, with its conversion to an inn coming in the eighteenth century, a response to the increase in traffic brought about when the road running in front of it became the turnpike between Hereford and Brecon. Despite many obvious stories to the contrary, the name 'three cocks' did not come about as the result of an anatomical abnormality. Instead, rather boringly, it is a reference to the coat of arms of the Williams family, who were the lords of the manor here. They lived in a grand old country pile nearby, called Old Gwernyfed Manor. It was at one point quite dilapidated, but it has since been saved by a chap called Ian Burgess, who bought it in 2013 and bit by bit is restoring this magnificent grade 1 listed Tudor manor house and outbuildings to their original splendour. The Williams family were very influential in the area. Sir David Williams and his son Sir Henry Williams were both MPs. Sir Henry was also a Royalist during the English Civil War, and he entertained Charles I at Old Gwernyfyd Manor when the king did his famous tour of the Marches, which has cropped up a few times already in other chapters.

4.5
THE HUNDRED HOUSE INN, BLEDDFA

When it comes to historical buildings, the tiny little village of Bleddfa really punches above its weight. As you approach on the road from Knighton, you cannot miss the mighty Monaughty House, one of the earliest stone-built buildings in Radnorshire and a fantastic example of a Tudor mansion. It was originally built as an abbey but was converted into the very elegant residence we see today after the Dissolution of the Monasteries.

It is not the only historic building in the village to have had two lives. Our chosen pub is another.

In 1524 it was the court of the Hundred Townships of Cefnlls, a sort of council of elders. The committee met at the village inn to discuss public business, church affairs, settle disputes and hear criminal trials. In time this led to the inn being referred to as the Hundred House, as it is called to this day. Circuit judges used to come and hear serious criminal trials here, with guilty parties often being condemned to hang at the gates of Monaughty House.

How much of the original building still survives is hard to say; most of what you can see today is late seventeenth century. It has some beautiful old features, including heavy dark beams and large inglenook fireplaces, one of them apparently haunted by an apparition only animals can see. Sometimes in the bar dogs sleeping peacefully will simultaneously leap to their feet and start howling and barking at the fireplace for no discernible reason. There is also an apparition of a lady in medieval costume seen from time to time.

Recently, however, the ghosts have had to reckon with an even scarier presence in Hundred House. In 2013, while tables were being set ready for the evening, a cattle truck, driving past along the main road, lost control and came crashing through the walls of the gentlemen's toilet. Fortunately, the pub was not busy at the time, but as you can imagine it gave everyone quite a turn.

4.6
THE ALEPPO MERCHANT, CARNO

The A470 is the longest road in Wales, 186 miles from end to end. It starts in Cardiff in the south, cuts straight through the Valleys and then meanders through the rolling hills of Powys to end up in Llandudno in the north. In recent years, the odd stretch here and there has been made into a dual carriageway, to bypass bottlenecks like Pontypridd, Merthyr Tydfil and Brecon. Most of it, however, is single carriageway. It takes you through some very dramatic and beautiful landscapes, but it is not a route you choose if you are on a tight deadline.

The Aleppo Merchant is at the side of this road, and it is a welcome stopping point for motorists navigating the winding stretches that lead up to the village of Carno. If you have spent the preceding forty minutes stuck behind a caravan at 20 mph, it is perfectly located for a break, to soothe the urge to scream or punch something inanimate.

Carno is a very quiet place, but just because it is remote, doesn't mean nothing ever happens here. As unlikely as it may sound, in the 1970s Carno was the LSD capital of the world, reputed to have supplied over 50% of the entire world's supply of the hallucinogenic drug of choice for the hippy generation.

A Cambridge chemistry graduate from Tregaron called Richard Kemp is credited with first synthesizing LSD in 1969. He used the manor house at Plas Llyswen in Carno to set up a lab where he could manufacture the drug far from the prying eyes of law enforcement. Not too long after setting up operations, however, he was involved in a road traffic accident just outside Carno and was recognised by one of the police officers at the scene. His connections with the drug world already known to the police, he was put under surveillance as part of a massive sting operation known as 'Operation Julie'. In March 1977 drug enforcement officers raided the manor house (and several other locations key to their investigation), seized all they found and brought the culprits to trial. The song 'Julie's Been Working for the Drug Squad' by the Clash was inspired by the whole event.

I wish at this point to make it absolutely clear that there are no links between this story and the pub in this chapter. It's just the single most exciting thing that has ever happened in Carno, and I simply had to mention it.

The Aleppo Merchant dates back to an altogether more sober chapter in the village's history. The building was once part of a medieval hospice, ran by the Knights Hospitaller of the Order of St John, an order of warrior monks we have already encountered in previous chapters, established during the crusades to tend to the wounded. In Carno, their role was to provide succour to the incurable, and also rest and accommodation to pilgrims. In that respect, they operated much like an inn.

The inn has always had a maritime association, which might seem odd for somewhere so far inland. A sea captain retired here in 1850 and renamed the pub after his merchant vessel, which had traded between Liverpool and Aleppo in Syria. There are tales that he was a rather lawless man, who indulged in a lot of skulduggery.

The building as we see it today dates back to 1632, and at one time it would have been a traditional black and white, half-timbered structure. It would, in fact, have looked very similar to Plasnewydd House, which stands on the hillside just east of the village, only its gable ends would have been built of stone, to safely house fireplaces and chimneys. Most of the old woodwork has now been replaced with masonry, but there are still some original old oak beams on the inside that survive.

4.7
THE BUCK INN,
NEWTOWN

Newtown lies on the banks of the River Severn, near the site of a historic ford crossing over the river. Similar to New Radnor, Newtown isn't really all that 'new' anymore. In fact, it hasn't been since 1279, when King Edward I granted the powerful Marcher Lord Roger Mortimer the right to hold a weekly market here. All that remains from that period are the castle mound and the shell of St Mary's church.

Newtown has quite a different history from other towns we have visited so far in Wales. It was established in the thirteenth century, but only really came to prominence in the early part of the Industrial Revolution. It became a centre of textiles manufacture with the 1819 construction of the Montgomeryshire canal, and reached its peak with the establishment of the Newtown Mills in 1856. The trade became closely associated with the area, and clothing and textiles have been made in the vicinity ever since; until relatively recently, this included the Laura Ashley factories.

The town was also the birthplace of an oft-overlooked figure in the world of influential political thinkers, a paragon of social reform by the name of Robert Owen. He was born the son of a town saddler in 1771 but rose to the cream of society as an industrialist. He used his wealth and influence in pursuit of establishing the cooperative movement, and he was a pioneer of free education and improved working conditions for mill workers. There is now a museum dedicated to him in the town.

Not much went on in the town until the eighteenth century, and accordingly it still boasts a few medieval buildings, although pretty much all of them have been modernised with Georgian or Victorian frontages. You would never know it, looking at it now, but this is just the heritage of the Black Boy Inn on Broad Street. Today the frontage is pure Georgian, but had you visited back in the 1990s, you would still have been able to see the interior timbers that revealed its true age. Now, after unsympathetic renovation by the JD Wetherspoons group, its current owners have put paid to all that; it has been thoroughly Starbucked.

Still, there is no danger of missing the Buck Inn's age. Surrounded by modern brick buildings, its white walls and black timbers scream antiquity, and most of its original features remain intact. One in particular that stands out is the heavy oak door in the entrance hall, its iron hinges engraved with fleur-de-lys. The inglenook inside is particularly interesting too, as the hearth has an early cobbled surface, where the stones have been set side-on to better resist the effects of the heat.

There is also evidence of building alterations carried out in the Georgian period. They are not as all-encompassing as with the Black Boy Inn, but it appears that a wing was added onto the back, with a dog-leg staircase that rises to the full height of the building. There are some old timbers in the wall by the fireplace, which suggest that this was where the original stairs would have been.

A blocked-up door in the cellar is said to be the entrance to an old secret passageway that ran under the road outside, to where the old Newtown Hall stood before it was demolished in the 1960s. The passage is believed to date back to the English Civil War. The owner of the old hall was a staunch Royalist and was hell-bent on rebuilding the old castle as a Cavalier stronghold. It is even believed that King Charles I himself came to inspect his progress, staying at the inn while he was there. Charles I must have loved a good pub; it seems he couldn't get enough of them.

4.8

THE TRIANGLE INN, RHAYADER

Unusually, I am going to begin by writing about a completely different pub to the one that gives this chapter its name. That's just typical of the crazy, messed up and unpredictable world we pub chroniclers live in.

The pub in question is the Old Swan Inn in Rhayader. The reason it does not have a chapter of its own is that, sadly, it stopped being an inn back in 1860. Prior to that it had been trading as an inn since the Middle Ages.

As I have mentioned previously, generally speaking in Wales we did not go in for the purpose built inns synonymous with the medieval period in England: places like the New Inn, in Gloucester, or Ye Olde Trype to Jerusalem, in Nottingham. Most of Wales' old pubs started out as cottages, farms or shops. But in the Swan, we have one of the few medieval pubs of Wales.

It was built for the same reason as the two English examples I have just highlighted: to cater for pilgrims. In the Middle Ages, Rhayader was a popular stop for pilgrims travelling to the abbey at Strata Florida. It was also on one of the major drovers' routes. All in all, ideal conditions for a pub to flourish.

It is difficult to say with any certainty exactly how old the Swan is, but the architecture seems to be early Tudor, albeit modified across the centuries. In a document reliably dated to 1676, the pub was mentioned as one of Rhayader's two inns; we also know that the triple chimney stack in the centre of the building was built in 1683, a date also carved into some of the old timbers on the inside of the building.

In 1815 an artist by the name of Paul Sandby Munn made a wood carving of the building, which shows the pub in all its half-timber glory, chimneys in full smoke. If you look really carefully, you can spot one of its most interesting features, an engraved wooden bracket just below the roof line on the east-facing gable, on the outside of the building. It depicts the head of a lady wearing a pointed medieval hat and veil. Since the Swan's days as an inn have come to an end, it has housed any number of shops as well as a tourist information office.

Despite not being a big town, Rhayader has lost many interesting inns down the centuries; not all had the same vintage as the Swan, but all the same, they are evidence of a boom-and-bust economy, where one day lots of travellers passed through the town, and the next they dried up. Another casualty was the town's principal coaching inn, the Red Lion. This was at its height during the town's boom period, when a turnpike was first put through it in the eighteenth century.

If you were planning a trip to Rhayader today, you would most likely first check any number of review sites, to see what people have to say about the local pubs. Tripadvisor is all well and good, but what about the thoughts of some actual patrons of the Red Lion from the eighteenth and nineteenth centuries?

We have mentioned Sir William Colt-Hoar in previous chapters. In the late 1790s he travelled around various parts of the country, keeping a journal of the places he visited and the standards of hospitality on offer, and in 1796 he wrote a one-word review of the Red Lion: it simply read 'bad'. Not many shades of grey there. However, the keepers of the Lion clearly got their act together, as a few years later, another traveller, George Lipscombe (an antiquarian better known for writing about Buckinghamshire), wrote gushingly, 'I was amazed to have a meal of roast fowl, ham, veal cutlets, cold beef, tarts and beer – all for a shilling.' No doubt tempted by this glowing review to give the Lion another go, Colt-Hoar returned in 1802, and even he remarked on the general improvements and 'very decent accommodation'.

The Red Lion was a stop for stagecoaches, and you have to wonder whether Colt-Hoar's first, disappointing experience has something to do with that. Let me explain.

The stagecoach was an incredibly uncomfortable mode of transport. The coaches themselves had the same unsophisticated wishbone suspension you would these days associate with a Silver Cross pram; plus, of course, the wheels had no air-filled tyres to cushion the passenger. And the roads, even after the introduction of turnpikes, were still in pretty poor order. When a gentleman of the Welsh borders was asked how it was possible to travel between Wales and England, given the state of the roads, he replied, 'We drive around in ditches.' With the average stagecoach managing no more than seven miles per hour, people took every opportunity for a break, a stretch of the legs and some food and refreshment.

But so doing, they put themselves at the mercy of swindlers. Inn keepers where stagecoaches frequently stopped would offer soup, gruel or casserole – something that could be prepared in one big pot and then slopped out onto a bowl while hungry customers waited for a change of horses. However, the dish would be served at a temperature so hot that it was impossible to eat without burning your mouth. When the coach driver called out that it was time to resume the journey, the hapless passenger would have no choice than to leave their meal half eaten. The inn keeper would then gather up the bowls and pour whatever had not been eaten back into his cooking pot, serving it up again in exactly the same way to the next batch of poor saps who came by. Sometimes the same dish could last for days at a time. It is no wonder that people back then did not travel unless they absolutely had to.

As much as the turnpike brought commerce to the town, it also brought unrest. You may recall from our chapter about the Black Lion Inn that the Rebecca Riots saw locals marching on the toll houses, and Rhayader saw similar scenes. In fact, six separate local toll gates got smashed up in the unrest.

As in Pembrokeshire and Carmarthenshire, to plan their attacks the rioters would have met up at pubs like the Swan, the Red Lion and the Triangle. Of the three, the Triangle is the only pub that remains. Even though technically it is just outside Rhayader, in the village of Llansantffraed Cwmdeuddwr, it thus wins the prize of the title of this chapter: for surviving where the others have not.

The building is sixteenth century, with some seventeenth-century alterations. It is in quite a lovely location on the edge of the village, on a narrow lane that winds down to the banks of the burbling river Wye. It is built in the style of the traditional old cottages of the area, with plenty of old timbers on view and a beautiful stone inglenook at one end of a very low ceiling. They do some traditional Welsh real ales, such as Hancock's HB and Reverend James, as well as home-cooked food.

It promotes itself as a dog friendly pub, but if you do take your dog along, heed this warning: when walking along the banks of the river Wye, in the countryside around Rhayader, keep them on a lead. There is reputed to be a vampiric beast in the area, which is known to kill and drain the blood of any small animal unlucky enough to encounter it.

The Pugh family, owners of a 2000-acre farm in the area, were the first to raise the warning, reporting curious goings on in the fields near the river Wye. They had started to find the carcasses of sheep with startling regularity. It is relatively common to find the bodies of livestock, victims of foxes or dogs, but generally there are signs of attack, whether biting, tearing or ripping. There were no such tell-tale signs on these animals. In fact, the only detectable injury was a single small, deep penetration below the neck. The flattened patches of grass in front of the carcasses suggested that whatever had inflicted this injury was quite large. A long line of flattened grass leading to and from the scene, meanwhile, hinted that it might be a serpentine creature, which had arrived via the river and left by the same means. In all, thirty-five sheep were lost over the period of a few months. Bloodhounds were used to try and track down the assailant, but its trail always disappeared once it had returned to the river. The carcasses were sent away to be inspected by experts, but no one could determine what had caused these unusual injuries, nor why a creature would kill so many animals without devouring any, only draining them of their blood.

Now, you might be forgiven for thinking the story I have just told dates back to the Middle Ages. But these events actually took place in 1988. Comparatively modern techniques and processes were employed to deduce the culprit, but they all drew a blank. To this day no one knows the true nature of the Beast of Bodalog, where it came from or what happened to it. All we know is that it came from the river, it was a fair size, it attacked at night, it could strike faster than a sheep could get away, and it was vampiric. Sleep well.

4.9

THE GEORGE & DRAGON, KNIGHTON

K nighton has no end of reminders that it is a border town, not least the two defensive dykes. The one everyone has heard of is Offa's Dyke, built on the orders of the Saxon King of Mercia, who reigned from 757 to 796. It was built either to defend against Welsh attack or to control traffic between Wales and Mercia, no one is entirely sure which.

Then there is its lesser-known counterpart, Wat's Dyke. It is believed to be the amalgamation of two different structures, the first being a Romano-Celtic fire line, the second a subsequent rebuild from the ninth century, possibly by the Mercian king Coenwulf.

The two run pretty much parallel with each other, between the Dee estuary in the north and Maesbury in Shropshire in the south. Sometimes they are no more than a few yards apart, in other placcs up to three miles apart. No one knows for sure what Wat's Dyke was for either, but it is generally accepted that both were intended as defensive structures.

But as we know, the Welsh are happy, peace-loving people. What would provoke their neighbours in Mercia to build not one but two defensive dykes to keep them out?

To answer that, we need to try and forget what we know about the border between England and Wales today, and think instead about the map of ancient Powys which appears in the preamble to this section. As I said there, at the turn of the sixth century, the kingdom of Powys stretched a lot further than the area we might recognise as Wales today. The people who were at the time known as the Welsh could just as easily have been known as the ancient Britons, having once lived and farmed in places like Shrewsbury, Ludlow and Leominster. But they had been displaced by the invading Saxons, who pushed them further west, to places like Knighton. This inevitably led to the displaced 'Welsh' mounting countless reprisal attacks, to try and win back their land in what these days is Shropshire and Herefordshire.

So, if anyone ever tries to tell you that these dykes were built to 'stop the Welsh invading England' you must stop them in their tracks. England had already been invaded. It was the invaders who built these dykes. They were trying to hold onto the territories they had seized, and to keep out the people they had taken them from. Just saying.

Knighton is another town, like Newtown, which at one time had a thriving wool and textiles industry. Here in Knighton, however, it was established much earlier, reaching its peak in the 1500s, way before the Industrial Revolution. It was also a drovers' town, on the route from Aberystwyth to the markets of London. Our pub, the George and Dragon, would doubtless have been a popular haunt with the drovers. It was originally a coaching inn, with stabling for horses in the buildings to the rear, which now provide accommodation for modern day tourists. It is believed to have been built in 1637; at least, that is the date inscribed into the building, not over the front door or anywhere obvious, but on the side of the building, which you can only see if you walk down the hill and turn into a lane below the lower gable end.

As you would expect with a pub of this age, it has its supernatural stories. When new owners took over in 2005, they reported a lot of activity, including an incident when, one night, the trays in the till all filled with water, despite there not being any detectable leakages anywhere. It is also said to be haunted by the ghost of a woman who lost her baby in childbirth.

4.10

Y TALBOT,
TREGARON

Tregaron is in central Ceredigion and has been around since Edward I granted Geoffrey Clement a charter to hold a weekly market here in 1290. The town peaked in the mid-nineteenth century, when it found itself at the forefront of droving, the hardy but well-paid drovers assuring pubs like Y Talbot of swift trade.

Situated in the centre of this small, quiet town, Y Talbot is believed to date back to the seventeenth century. While the frontage is plainly Georgian, once you step inside, you can feel the weight of history weighing down on you. It has all the trappings of antiquity that you would expect, with log fires and dark timber beams in abundance.

But it is neither beams nor drovers that have assured Y Talbot a place in our pages. It is the quite spectacular story of the elephant buried in its garden.

As we have gone from pub to pub, we have come across plenty of wild and far-fetched stories, but perhaps the wildest part of this one is that there is actually quite a lot of evidence to back it up.

The elephant, who is locally nicknamed Jwmbi, was part of a touring circus troupe, quite possibly Batty's Travelling Menagerie, who entertained extensively in the area. According to an 1840 article in *the Cambrian News*, the chapels of Tregaron were empty on the day the circus visited the town, with everyone lining up to see Batty's exotic animals. Sadly, the young elephant became ill and died after drinking contaminated water at Bronmywn Farm. There was a lot of lead mining in the area at the time, and presumably this had something to do with it. Land belonging to Y Talbot Inn was made available for the burial of the creature, and there he has remained ever since.

Over time this story has passed into the realm of myth, with no one really quite certain if it is true or not. Accordingly, in 2011, an archaeological dig was commissioned to try and track down Jwmbi's final resting place. Early attempts were confounded by the discovery of an 1840 title deed which revealed that, at the time of Jwmbi's burial, Y Talbot had over 200 acres of land. Undeterred, project leader Dr Jemma Bezant led a team of volunteers, including children from the local primary school, to take a part in a series of small-scale excavations. However, after a five-day dig, the archaeologist from the University of Wales Trinity St David had to concede that they had found no signs of the elephant, and so the mystery continues.

Perhaps noting Wild Wales' author George Borrow's 1854 remarks that Y Talbot offered 'a warm welcome to English persons', over the years the pub has played host to some very distinguished guests. In 1986, none less than former US President Jimmy Carter stayed there, clearly sufficiently enjoying himself to return again in 1988. Prince Charles visited in 2011, as (randomly) did the president of Ukraine in 2015. Perhaps they all wanted to secure their legacies by being the one to find the famous elephant.

If you visit Y Talbot today you will find excellent food and drink, which has earned it a coveted place in the Michelin Guide. Cardigan Bay crab and lobster, fresh fish and locally reared beef and lamb are just some of its specialities. It also boasts a range of draught Welsh Ales and ciders such as Purple Moose, Evan Evans, Monty's and Gwynt y ddraig.

With such a good reputation for food, no wonder it is haunted by the ghost of an eighteenth-century cook, who is frequently seen revisiting his old kitchens, no doubt to ensure that standards are being maintained.

4.11
THE GREEN INN,
LLANGEDWYN

In a few previous chapters of this book, I have mentioned how many of our historic towns were at one time burned to the ground by Owain Glyndŵr. Well, it was the people of the village of Llangedwyn who actually did much of the burning. This was very much Glyndŵr's stomping ground, and his heir, Sir Watkin Williams-Wyn, lived his final years on the family estate at Llangedwyn Hall.

This is a very rural spot so, apart from that, there is not a lot to report – besides, of course, this gem of an ancient pub. Built in 1740, the

Green Inn is the shape of a fairly typical period cottage for the region. Its location, in the beautiful Tanat Valley, is its main selling point. The building itself has been modernised through the ages, but it still has beams and fireplaces and serves locally sourced food and real ales.

On several occasions this place nearly disappeared. There was local uproar back in 2014, when it emerged that the then owners, Punch Taverns, had put in a planning application to convert it into two houses. The local community rallied around to save it, and they try hard to make it work, frequently putting on music and beer festivals. There might not be much to say about its history, but it is beautifully located, and I hope its inclusion in this book is enough to keep it bobbing along for a few more years.

THE ANCIENT KINGDOM
OF GWYNEDD

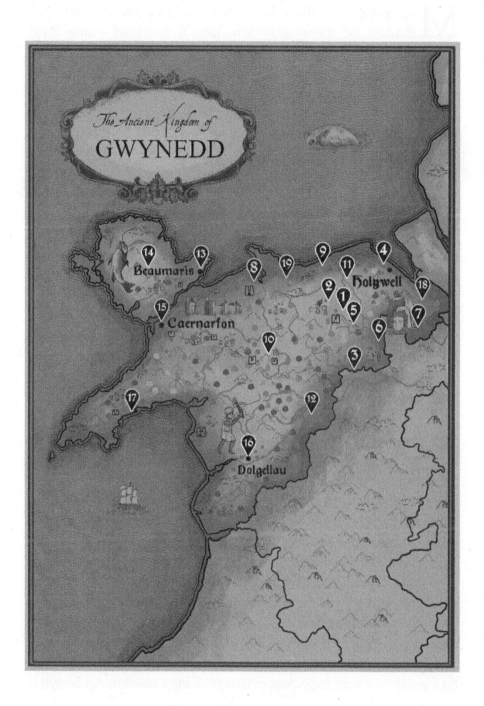

The Ancient Kingdom of

GWYNEDD

M uch like Powys, the modern county of Gwynedd is a rather pale shadow of the mighty kingdom it takes its name from. Gwynedd used to stretch across all of North Wales and Anglesey, and it owes its boundaries to the old Roman province it replaced. Its kings were very wealthy and powerful, and as we touched upon earlier, one of its princes, Madoc, just might have discovered America. The kingdom incorporated some of the most beautiful landscapes you will see anywhere in the world, most famously the national park at Snowdonia.

By the measure of its time, Gwynedd had a very sophisticated and cultured society. Its aristocracy used to play heavily on their Roman ancestry, and Latin was the language of court. The kingdom maintained links with Rome long after the empire had retreated from British shores. Professor Bryan Ward-Perkins of Trinity College, Oxford, wrote, 'It took until 1282, when Edward I conquered Gwynedd, for the last part of Roman Britain to fall [and] a strong case can be made for Gwynedd as the very last part of the entire Roman Empire, east and west, to fall to the barbarians.' It's worth adding to this note that it took the English king twenty years to subdue Gwynedd, and even then peace could only be maintained by building massive stone castles at every step.

I know what you are thinking. 'Did this mean Gwynedd's pubs were really posh?' No, but you have to admit that a pub whose toilet walls bear the graffiti '*Quia tempus bonum voca X1 11 1V petere quia Trixy*,' is a bit classy.

It also meant that Gwynedd had one thing the rest of Wales did not: towns. Businesses need customers. The only places a medieval inn could generate enough business to be viable was either a town or by a holy shrine, and Gwynedd had both. In fact, in its heyday, Wrexham was one of the most significant settlements in the British Isles. As we travel to North Wales, for the first time we start to see an abundance of purpose-built medieval inns.

Gwynedd rose to the height of its power in the eleventh century. As a result of a very expedient marriage, King Llewelyn Ap Seisyll of

Gwynedd inherited the kingdom of both Powys and Gwynedd, making him ruler of the whole of the northern half of Wales. Not satisfied with that, his son Gruffudd the Great launched a successful military campaign against both the kingdoms of Deheubarth and Morganwg. The outcome of that was when Gruffudd sat on the throne, he was king of all of what we would recognise as Wales today. This kingdom of the Welsh peninsular lasted for seven years, from 1055 to 1063.

And he's not the only famous regal son of Gwynedd: this is the stomping ground of Owain Glyndŵr, a man who has cropped up in pretty much every chapter in this book.

5.1
THE GUILDHALL TAVERN
INN, DENBIGH

Denbigh was once upon a time a fortified medieval town in the shadow of a mighty castle. You would never know it now: the part of the town that was once the centre is all but abandoned, and the castle in ruins. It has been abandoned for some time. The poet and antiquarian John Leland visited in the sixteenth century and wrote about the perplexing mystery of this derelict part of the town: 'I have not yet lernid the certente how this wallid toune decayed... wither it were by fier or for lak of water.'

There is a distinct possibility that it suffered the same fate as Kidwelly in South Wales: that, after being burned to the ground in 1400 by Owain Glyndŵr, it never really recovered. It was easier and cheaper to build new houses elsewhere than try to salvage the ruins within the walls.

Another theory is that people just got fed up of the town's steep hills and instead built a town on the lower slopes of the hill, where the inclines are a bit more forgiving.

An eerie old, abandoned town is bound to conjure up any number of scary ghost stories and manifestations. One of Denbigh's scarier ones is 'Black Bob'. Bob is a dark, shapeless figure seen dashing around the Goblin Tower, and is said to be the son of the castle's builder. He was falsely accused of having an affair with the landowner's daughter and was thrown to his death from the partly completed tower. There have been sightings of Black Bob as recently as 2000.

There is also the ghost of a grey lady, while another local legend says that a dragon once resided in the castle. A man with eight fingers on each hand finally killed the creature. If you walk just a mile or so to the moors, there have also been sightings of a glowing skeleton near the Sportsman's Arms.

Even though nothing much remains of the medieval town, we still have some very old inns here, trying to soldier on.

In the sixteenth and seventeenth centuries, new buildings were constructed around the old market square and in the streets running off it. The Golden Lion, in Back Row, is one of the oldest surviving. It would once have been a half-timber building, but timbers on the outside have largely been hidden by a thick layer of cement and pebbledash. The first floor overhangs the doorway, and according to Cadw, the frontage was decorated with close studding, a pattern of vertical strips of wood designed to look impressive. In other words, this was the owners showing off their wealth to passers-by.

Inside, the lounge and bar are separated by a very original partition; indeed, the layout generally was quite unaltered down the centuries.

The building was once two adjacent properties, both shops. We know from old records that one of them was at one time a jewellers. With a little imagination you can still fathom the old layout: two small shops to the front, with the living quarters behind and a hall at the back which would have had no ceiling or floor.

The Golden Lion was once the venue for meetings of the district's Female Friendly Society. The society was wound up in 1877. Before the welfare state was introduced, friendly societies were sort of like a mutual insurance programme, collecting fees from members, who would then receive payments if they were unable to earn money.

Just a few yards away from the Golden Lion is the much older Eagles, a house with a gable-fronted lobby, dated 1643, which gives an idea of how the frontage of all the buildings in that area, including the Golden Lion, would once have looked.

The coaching inn of the town was what is now the Guildhall Tavern (formerly the Bull) which dates from 1666. It is a three-storey building that, like so many coaching inns, is made up of several buildings that have all been absorbed into one. What were once the stabling and coach houses are to the rear. Like the Golden Lion, those upper floors jutting out over the lower floors are a display of wealth.

During the English Civil War, Denbigh Castle was under siege from the Roundheads, and the generals Mytton and Myddleton are believed to have held their headquarters in this pub. Even though it has antiquity and history by the bucketload, unfortunately it has been thoroughly refurbished, and not much of the original building or its interior survives. Even the timber frontage, though similar to what would have been there originally, is part of a more modern facelift.

5.2
THE LLINDIR INN, HENLLAN

The Llinidir Inn is a Grade II listed building that stands opposite the historic church of St Sadwrn. The church has an unusual architectural quirk in that its tower is separated from the main building. It stands instead on a rocky mound, in a far corner of the churchyard. No one knows exactly why. I came across one suggestion that it has some acoustic virtue, allowing the sound of the bells to carry further. I would have thought a connecting roof would act as a sounding board, but what do I know.

The pub itself is an archetypal thatched country inn. It is another claimed to be one of the oldest in Wales, with a suggested 'established' date of 1229. The layout, however, is more typically seventeenth century. But who knows, maybe the cellar or some of the interior walls attest to a greater age, or maybe an earlier building occupied the same site. Whatever the truth of its origins, the interior retains a lot of its old charm, with beams and tiled floors and lots of copper and brassware.

The Llindir is supposed to be haunted by, of all things, a randy ghost.

She is known to locals as Sylvia, and it is said that she was once married to a sea captain. While he was away on sea voyages, she had needs she would satisfy with the help of the obliging young men of the village.

Until one fateful occasion, when her husband decided to surprise

251

her by taking some shore leave. Arriving home unexpectedly, he caught her in the arms of another man. In a blind rage, he stabbed the man and strangled Sylvia, leaving their bodies limp and lifeless as he fled into the night. To this day, Sylvia's spirit roams the upstairs rooms of the inn.

Dewi Roberts says in his book *the Old Villages of Denbighshire and Flintshire* that pub goers report seeing the spectre of an attractive woman in white, although there are other accounts of her being dressed in blue. It is said that she is seen exclusively by women, flitting from room to room. However, the odd male customer has reported the sensation of feeling her hands running through their hair. I sat there for hours. Nothing. Gutted.

I have read one rather cynical account that suggests that no one had ever heard of this ghost until the 1940s, when the then landlord spun the story as a ruse to amuse American GIs stationed in the area. What? A pub landlord making up stories to lure in customers? I am lost for words at the suggestion.

Not that I am levelling such an accusation at the current owners, who are lovely people. She is a chef looking to create a casual artisan feel, with lots of locally sourced seasonal produce. He is a master brewer, having set up his Heavy Industry brewery in an old disused slaughterhouse nearby, using the pub as 'the brewery tap'. These days, he is looking to set up a new micro-brewery on the premises, and wishes to showcase ales and craft beers from his own and other local independent breweries.

5.3

TY MAWR,
GWYDDELWERN

The tourist route between Ruthin and Corwen, the road which passes the Ty Mawr pub (formerly the Rose and Crown), has for centuries been associated with holidays. When the Ty Mawr was built, however, it was more associated with 'holy days', a road well-trodden by pilgrims en route to the holy shrine at St Winfried's Well, in what is today called Holywell. This is also the same road taken by Owain Glyndŵr and his followers as they began their rampage through Wales.

In 1797, the Revd Warner passed through the Dee valley and was startled to see a 'fierce gigantic figure' painted over the door of the Owain Glyndŵr Inn at Corwen, just a few miles up the road from the Ty Mawr. He shouldn't have been so surprised. This was Glyndŵr's stomping ground. His castle was nearby, and it was from there that he marched to take his first swipe at the English, sacking Ruthin in September 1400.

One day in the Middle Ages, the people of Corwen were building their village church, but work ground to a halt owing to the Devil stealing building materials off the building site. After all, when building materials go missing, that is the only logical explanation. A wise old man of the village came forward and said that this showed they were building the church in the wrong place. The only way they could be sure of keeping Old Nick at bay was to find a new site for the church.

'How will we know when we have found a more appropriate spot?' the villager asked. He replied, 'You will know it as a white stag will be standing there marking the spot.'

The people of the village scattered into the countryside in search of this white stag, and sure enough, he was spotted. He allowed the people to come close enough to mark the spot before he bolted into nearby woodland. Work on the building of the church recommenced and carried on without interruption. The Devil had been confounded. Or at least had managed to pinch everything he needed.

I find it fascinating how often stags pop up in early Welsh Christian legends. Living as I do in the Vale of Glamorgan, I am more than familiar with the legend of St Cadoc, who was assisted in the building of the Clas monastery in Llancarfan by two stags; also how St Cadoc's cousin St Petroc (patron saint of Cornwall) is usually painted with a stag at his side, and that his best mate, St Illtud, saved a stag from a hunt. And it doesn't end there. Both St Derfel and St Brynach had carts pulled by stags, and when a nobleman offered to give as much of his land to the poor as St Teilo could cover between dawn and dusk on the same day, the saint rode a stag. *Stags and Saints*: maybe a title for another book.

But back to the building. I wrote earlier 'when the Ty Mawr was built', as if this is some fixed point in time. It is not. It is a pub made up of lots of buildings, and another to have a claim to be the oldest in Wales. However, claims that it dates back to 1081 might raise an eyebrow or two. To be fair, the owners have always maintained this means 'a building on this site' rather than the building you see today. Even that is undoubtedly very old: more than likely late fifteenth or early sixteenth century. In the 1990s you could be forgiven for not realising that, as it was then covered in thick pebble dash and cement. This has all now been taken away as part of an extensive renovation project, revealing the original timbers and beams.

The pub's connection to the pilgrimages is more than just its situation on the road they would have walked. In the Middle Ages, this was a priest's lodgings, providing accommodation to the clergy making their pilgrimages, so they didn't have to hang out with the riff-raff. Over the centuries it has been extended, absorbing other buildings to grow to the sizable structure we see today, which is estimated to have been completed round about 1572.

One interesting discovery stands out above any others: when the Ty Mawr was renovated back in 1999, a 'jetton' or gaming token dating from 1521 was discovered tucked into a crack in the beam above the main fireplace. It was similar to the type of chip you get in a modern day casino. Interestingly, it was absolutely identical to six that were found on board *the Mary Rose*, Henry VIII's flagship, when it was raised off the coast of Portsmouth.

5.4

THE OLD TAVERN INN, LLANERCH-Y-MOR, HOLYWELL

Holywell may not seem it now, but for much of its history it was as well-known as Lourdes. It is home to one of Wales' most celebrated holy shrines, the Well of St Winefride. Over the centuries the miraculous healing qualities of its water attracted a seemingly never-ending list of royalty, stretching as far back as King Richard I (the Lionheart) to as recently as Queen Victoria.

One of the most celebrated miracles of the well was when James II and his second wife, Mary of Modena, visited in 1686, having failed on numerous attempts to produce an heir to the throne. Shortly after their visit, they produced little baby James.

The well is believed to be the oldest continually visited pilgrimage site in the UK. The building that greets pilgrims today is Grade 1 listed, and the inner walls are covered in inscriptions from those who have visited the shrine, many attesting to miraculous cures to all manner of illnesses, injuries or deformities.

You may recall from my earlier ramblings that, up until the nineteenth century, when Britain's road network had sufficiently improved to make it possible to travel simply for pleasure, the only location for an old inn to be viable was in a town or a place of pilgrimage. For such a significant site of pilgrimage as this one, there was a very busy inn and a brewery just next door. The well gardens, an outdoor space beyond the shrine where visitors can wander in silent contemplation, stands on the site of the former St Winfried's Brewery. It was cleared to create the outdoor space in 1930.

The legend of how the well came to be tells us of Winifred, a virgin martyr. She was pursued by a local prince called Caradoc but refused his advances. In a fit of fury, Caradoc drew his sword and cut off her head. Her uncle, St Beuno, happened to be passing and ran to his dead niece's side. He prayed, then lifted her head off the ground and put it back on her shoulders. Miraculously she came back to life, and the place on the ground where her head had fallen produced a gushing spring.

Today, the Talacre Arms stands nearby, rather derelict and awaiting its fate. It is not especially old, a typical nineteenth-century inn, but it is worth a mention for its many ghost stories. It was claimed to be haunted by a particularly active poltergeist. Not only did this spirit do all the usual things poltergeists do – flinging chairs and glasses, etc. – it also used to pour its own pints, cause electrical disturbances and make the bulbs in table lamps and light fittings glow like a supernova. One night, terrified that the bulbs might explode, a quick-thinking barmaid went through the pub unplugging all the lamps. But they burned just as brightly as before, even without electricity.

Most of Holywell's folklore centres around Basingwerk Abbey. This was a Cistercian abbey established in the twelfth century that suffered what by now should be a familiar fate at the hands of Henry VIII. In the 500 years it operated, it was a very wealthy and powerful body, owning vast estates of land as far away as Derbyshire. But it wasn't all rosy for the monks of the abbey, who found themselves terrorised not just by a witch, but a witch capable of transforming herself into a werewolf.

So transmogrified, she preyed on lone monks who strayed outside the abbey walls on the night of a full moon, leaving their bodies mutilated and lacerated with her claws and teeth. Then at dawn she transformed into the form of an innocent girl, confounding those hunting the beast. Her reign of terror seemed set to benight the abbey forever, until one night the abbot begged heaven for intervention, and the curse on the werewolf was altered so that the witch was no longer able to change back to a human. She was trapped in the form of a wolf. Unable to hide she ran… straight into the path of King Henry II's hunting party. After a vicious fight the creature was slain and the monks were free.

If you think that's a bit strange, get a load of this one. In a later time, one of the abbey's monks fell through some kind of rift in time. He was spotted centuries after the abbey had been ruined, looking startled, panicked and confused. He asked some passers-by why the abbey was in ruins and where all his fellow monks had gone. Feeling sorry for him, they offered him some food and water. As soon as his fingers touched the food he turned to dust and dissolved into the air.

On the banks of the river Dee is the Old Tavern Inn. It is an ancient coaching inn dating back to at least 1664 (that date is inscribed on one of the fireplaces), although it is quite likely to incorporate a far older building, possibly dating back to the fifteenth century or even earlier. It has some very interesting architectural features, in particular the roof trusses in the thatched section of the roof. They are vast, rising up from the ground then arching through the natural curvature of the timber almost as high as the apex, supporting the roof. This is a very ancient technique known as 'cruck trusses', and there are not many examples of it remaining in Wales. Another lovely architectural quirk is the leper's window, which now marks an internal wall, indicating that this inn, like so many, has been extended over the centuries.

Lepers were forbidden from entering an inn, to protect customers from the transmission of the disease. This leper's window was an opening in an external wall through which they could receive food and drink without coming into contact with anyone. Just to the right of this narrow aperture you can see a slight indentation in the wall. There would once have been a bowl here, containing vinegar and holy water. The lepers would pay for their fare by dropping coins in the bowl. The vinegar was believed to clean the disease off the coins, and the holy water would protect the inn keeper from infection when he retrieved them. A nice balance of science and religion just to make sure.

In these pages we have come across many pubs claiming to have a tunnel or a secret passage. In the case of the Old Tavern, there is an opening in one wall of the cellar which certainly has the appearance of a walled-up tunnel. It is believed that it was originally built by smugglers under the coast road, so they could smuggle their booty ashore and into the cellar of the pub without being detected. The tunnel would most likely have been blocked up when the road outside was widened.

Tales of ghosts in the pub abound. One ghost's appearances are said to be accompanied by the smell of casks; he is the spirit of a former legless landlord (a double amputee rather than a drunkard). Another ghost appears as a small woman with grey hair who likes to sit on the steps. Bar workers have also reported hearing a child behind them, calling for its mother, and turning to see nobody there.

5.5

THE KING'S HEAD, LLANRHAEADR

T his is an absolute gem of a pub in the little village of Llanrhaeadr, just off the A525 between Denbigh and Ruthin. The 'rhaeard' part of the village's name means 'waterfall', which is strange as there is no waterfall here. However, before a bypass was added, the old road used to go straight through the village, crossing the stream over a ford next to the pub; on the opposite bank of the stream was a very steep incline, which may at one time have had water flowing down it. Apparently the hill was so steep that spare horses were kept at the smithy, to help out coaches who otherwise would not have made it. In the twentieth century, with the advent of town planning and groundwork machinery, the incline was dealt with in more permanent fashion, when it was flattened out for good. The groundwork meant that the inn had to move its front door to the back, and it also gave it its rather sunken look.

Opposite the inn is a very interesting thirteenth-century church. It is Grade 1 listed and well worth a visit for its celebrated 'Tree of Jesse' window. This is early sixteenth-century stained glass representing the genealogy of Christ, by depicting a family tree growing out of the body of his ancestor Jesse. It shows the line including King David, King Solomon, Isaiah and Moses all the way to Jesus, with all the characters dressed in medieval costume, as was the custom at the time.

The church also has a rather unique holy well, called St Dyfnog's well, which is another candidate to be the missing 'waterfall'. It is just behind the churchyard, a gushing spring which flows into the baptistry. Its gushing is one of its most famous features, as was recorded in the sixteenth century by Leland, who described it as 'a mighty spring that maketh a brook running scant a mile.' In the late Middle Ages, it was a significant place of pilgrimage, as it was claimed that the water had miraculous healing powers. No doubt it was in order to cater for these pilgrims that the King's Head came into being as an inn.

Inside, you can see that the King's Head has been very sympathetically restored. It is a warren of small, thick-walled rooms and passages with low beamed ceilings of polished wood. The original seventeenth-century lobby has been greatly extended at the back, and the old hall has been converted into the 'Witch and Warlock' bar.

5.6

THE MORNING STAR, RUTHIN

There is an extricable link in British culture between alehouses and the gallows. It may sound odd, but with the benefit of some context, it becomes clear why. For the best part of 500 years in Britain, executions were held in public. The practise of hanging as a means of execution was introduced by the Germanic tribes of Saxony, and as such was not a common practice in ancient Wales. When the Normans took the English throne, William the Conqueror thought hanging was barbaric and removed it as the primary form of punishment for crimes other than murder or treachery.

It was Henry I who reintroduced it. Under his edict, there were no less than 222 crimes defined as capital offenses, including things as trivial as 'impersonation of a Chelsea pensioner' and 'damaging Westminster Bridge'. As such, the spectacle of a hanging soon became very regular.

Every big city or province had public gallows, some of the most famous being on the Knavesmire in York (near the racecourse) and at Tyburne in London (roughly where the Marble Arch stands now); and of course, right here in the town square at Ruthin, at the top of the hill from the gaol which stands opposite the Morning Star.

Turning up to watch the hangings was like going to a football match. It was seen as a day out, good old fashioned family entertainment. Vast crowds would gather, especially for a particularly notorious criminal. This sketch from the eighteenth century gives you an idea of what it was like.

If you were a landlord of the time, a crowded scene like this would of course guarantee a very swift day of trade indeed. But this is not the only reason for pubs' deep association with the gallows. It was also customary for the cart bringing the condemned man from his prison cell to stop at every single pub along the way. Whenever the wagon pulled up outside another pub, the condemned man and all his guards would dismount, go in the pub, have a few drinks and then stumble back out to move on to the next one. The only people who could not join them were the two men who still had a job to do, namely the executioner and the chaplain. If you ever offer to buy someone a drink and they reply, 'Not for me, thanks. I'm on the wagon,' now you know the tradition they're referencing.

Pretty incredible, isn't it? The amount of language still in use today that originates from the gallows is amazing.

On its journey, the wagon transporting the condemned man used to start and stop so often that the lunging motion of the horses' jerking the wheels into rotation earned the nickname 'the lurch'. So, when the executioner and chaplain remained on the cart, while everyone else went into a pub, they were 'left in the lurch'.

There are even suggestions that the term 'pub crawl' refers to the pace of the cart moving along the streets. Meanwhile, having 'one for the road' is another, self-explanatory reference.

If a member of your family was condemned to be hanged, it was traditional to help them die as quick a death as possible. Friends and relatives would grab hold of the condemned individual's legs, hanging from them with all their weight, to make the rope pull tighter. Sometimes, however, the condemned might not have friends and family where he was due to be executed. If that was the case, he could pay a guard at the prison to do the job instead. If you've ever wondered why freeloaders around a celebrity might be described as 'hangers-on', there you have it. It refers to those who are not your true friends, but who might help you out for money.

Sometimes you might choose an unscrupulous guard who would agree to hang on to your legs but in reality would simply go through the motions. In other words, he would just 'pull your leg', paying lip service to his responsibilities, messing around and not being serious.

It was traditional for the condemned individual to wear a black covering over his head. This was partly to spare the crowds the sight of his eyes popping out of their sockets, and partly to save him seeing what was coming. It meant that, when the cart pulled the floor away from under their feet, the condemned took 'a leap into the dark'.

If not claimed by a relative, the property of the condemned man became the property of the hangman. It was one of many ways the executioner could cash in on his grisly profession. Another was to take advantage of the regulation that a hangman's rope could only be used once, to guarantee it had the integrity to hold fast throughout the execution. This meant that, after an execution, the hangman could retrieve the ropes he had used and sell them on the market. Given that he was not responsible for providing the rope himself, any money from the sale was pure profit. This gave us the expression 'money for old rope'.

I am sure at some point or another you have heard a man well blessed in the trouser department referred to as 'well-hung'. Apparently, the act of strangulation has the incongruous side effect of making the male organ engorged – something that was very apparent to the crowds at public hangings.

You may also have heard a failed project described as having 'gone west'. This refers to the route taken from the jails of London to Tyburn's famous gallows, which was located on the other side of the city's west gate.

Of course, executions did not always run smoothly. One of the most famous of all time was the execution of a man called Goodale. When he was hung, and the rope tightened around his neck, due to a freak set of circumstances it jerked his head clean off his shoulders, like a champagne cork popping from the bottle, sending showers of blood and gore spouting all over the gathered crowd. The whole nation was transfixed with the story, which appeared in newspapers everywhere for a number of weeks. It turned so many stomachs that questions were asked in parliament, and a full enquiry was launched by hangmen and other government officials. The incident was nicknamed 'The Goodale Mess', and undoubtedly this is the origin of the expression 'God awful mess', used to this day to describe any scene of particular carnage.

Who would have thought that such a grisly feature of our history would have contributed so richly to our modern language?

The Morning Star is a Grade II listed building, built about 1639 and claimed to be the oldest pub in the town. In 2010 a cluster of old documents was discovered in the roof, a series of accounts and letters that give incredible insight into the everyday life of an inn keeper in Wales in the early nineteenth century.

Another lovely old inn in Ruthin (or just outside it) is the Cross Keys, which dates back to the sixteenth century.

5.7

THE HORSE AND JOCKEY, WREXHAM

As I mentioned in the introduction to this section, up until the Middle Ages, Wrexham was a very significant town. Its population was greater than any Welsh town other than possibly Carmarthen, although it is difficult to be precise about such things, as records were not so good then as they are now. Either way, its long prominence gave it a rich history that I cannot really do justice to in a few paragraphs.

Wrexham has its own UNESCO world heritage site: the Pontcysyllte Aqueduct and Canal, a stone and cast-iron aqueduct designed by two great pioneers of the industrial revolution, Thomas Telford and William Jessop. It opened in 1805 and it carries the Llangollen Canal 126 foot over the Dee River valley. It is quite spectacular from any angle, but the view when traveling across is not one for the fainthearted. The bridge has no sides, so when you float across it in your barge, there appears to be nothing preventing you from plummeting the thirty-eight meters to the ground below. The aqueduct was planned as part of a bigger ambition to create a waterway linking the ports of the Severn and Bristol Channel in the south with the Port of Liverpool in the north. That vision never really materialised, but nonetheless the canal and aqueduct saw a lot of use, transporting coal from the pits of the northeast Wales coal fields to markets all over the world.

Also, in an earlier time, it was from just outside Wrexham that Owain Glyndŵr began his rebellion for Welsh independence from the English crown, which spanned the late fourteenth and early fifteenth centuries.

The Horse and Jockey is located in a thatched building in the town centre that is said to date back to the sixteenth century. Like most old pubs in Wales, it once had another function. It started out as a 'hall house', which means that it centred on a large room with no ceiling. It was then divided up into three cottages, one of which became an ale house called the Colliers. The buildings were then once again combined, becoming a single pub in 1868, and you can still see glimpses of its original timber-frame construction inside. The pub was renamed the Horse and Jockey in honour of Fred Archer (1857-1886). The Cheltenham-born jockey rode at nearby Bangor-on-Dee, and at many other racecourses. The picture on the pub sign was painted in 1938, copying an original painting of Fred Archer.

It survived attempts to demolish it in the 1950s as part of the town's redevelopment, as well as a fire in the 1980s.

There are tales of a ghost called George, who not only haunts the place but unusually also does the odd good turn. He is reported to have once saved a cleaner from injury, by grabbing hold of her leg as she began to topple off the chair on which she was standing. All in all, much more considerate than the kind of behaviour usually attributed to a pub ghost; good for you, George.

5.8

THE GROES INN,
TY'N-Y-GROES

Many times, in these pages, I have wimped out of naming the oldest pub in Wales. But it just might be the Groes Inn. As if that were not exciting enough, it is possibly also the birthplace of making pancakes on Shrove Tuesday! 'What?!' I hear you say. I know. It's a lot to take in.

Let's start with that 'oldest pub in Wales' claim. Until now, we have assessed the credibility of such claims against the age of the building the pub currently resides in. The Groes is believed to have been built in the fifteenth century as a small two-storey house: in other words, the building is old, very old, but not quite as old as the Priory in Milford Haven, the Cross Keys in Swansea, or a few others we have already mentioned. However, you will recall that these establishments have only been trading as licensed premises for a comparatively short time. Not so the Groes Inn: it has been trading as a licensed inn since 1573, and at the time of writing, I am not aware of another pub in Wales with that kind of provenance.

Like many of our old inns, this one doubled up as an administrative centre for local affairs, a court for local elders and noblemen to settle disputes and try criminals. That is possibly why it was originally called the Commercial Inn. It flourished in the sixteenth and seventeenth centuries owing to its location on the main road, which lead to one of the few crossing points of the river Conwy at Tal-Y-Cafn. Since 1897

269

there has been a bridge, but prior to that, travellers relied on a ferry. It was a simple affair: a floating platform pulled across the river by ropes which spanned it.

But back to the Groes. It was in the seventeenth century that most of the extensions and additions you see today were made, although it was also re-roofed in the eighteenth century. The interior is very traditional, and there is a lovely big fireplace in the north wall. It also has some really interesting sixteenth-century timbers in the walls and ceilings. Do you think they might have been recycled from an Elizabethan warship's masts? To be honest, I didn't ask.

Another nice quirk is the set of title deeds displayed at the top of the stairs. When the inn changed hands in 1889 the signing of the deeds was witnessed by the fourth Duke of Wellington (the grandson of the 'Iron Duke' himself). There is a room upstairs now named after him.

'All well and good,' I hear you cry, 'but what about the pancake day thing?' Well, I'm glad you asked. Perhaps I should begin by explaining what pancake day is, as it is not a global tradition. In fact, it is pretty much only observed in the UK and Ireland, with pockets in places where British people emigrated, such as the Antipodes and the Americas. We are talking about the tradition of eating pancakes on the religious festival known as Shrove Tuesday, the day before Ash Wednesday and the start of Lent. One day, in the car on the way home from school, I remember my children piping up, 'It's pancake day today, they said in school!' So being the guilt-ridden, sorry excuse for a parent I am, I replied, 'I know,' before dashing into the house and whipping up some batter – only to discover that my children had simply fancied pancakes that day, and knew they could bank on their crap dad not knowing the date. Then, when it really *was* pancake day, I ended up guilted into doing it all over again because they had friends over.

It's only fitting really: guilt is a big part of Shrove Tuesday. The word 'shrove' comes from an old Saxon word '*shriven*', which means 'absolved of sins'. Early Saxon Christians would make sure that they had confessed to all their sins on Shrove Tuesday so they could enter the holy fast of Lent free from the burden of guilt.

There is a theory that the flat bell chimed to draw people to confession on Shrove Tuesday was nicknamed 'the pancake bell', and many think this is the origin of the pancake day tradition.

A local historian called Stan Wicklen, however, has a different explanation. Shrove Tuesday is known in Welsh as *'Dydd Mawrth Ynyd'*, which means 'the day of the martyr Ynyd', a sixth-century Welsh saint. The name this pub goes by, the 'Groes', is actually an abbreviation of its proper name *'Groesynyd'*, which translates as 'Ynyd's cross'. In other words, the inn had the patronage of the saint whose festival day was Shrove Tuesday. This meant that the inn had a special tradition and celebration of their own, to mark their namesake's day. It involved playing tricks and practical jokes on visitors and passers-by, as well as the eating of Welsh cakes and other pan cakes and pastries. And that, in Stan Wicklen's opinion, is where the tradition of eating pancakes on Shrove Tuesday started.

These days the Groes is run by an independent Manchester-based brewery called JW Lees. They have a great reputation for ales, craft beers and food and the views from their beer garden are to die for. They are previous winners of the Good Pub Guide's 'Inn of the Year' award. But for some reason they don't have pancakes on their pudding menu. Not even on the children's menu. It's a bit like going to a pub in Melton Mowbray and finding they don't do pork pies.

5.9

THE HARP,
ABERGELE

Down the centuries Abergele has generally been quite a quiet place. It started off in the sixth century rather humbly, as a small village growing around an abbey. Then in 1294, it had a moment of fleeting excitement, as Edward I camped his army there during his invasion of Gwynedd; then it was pretty quiet again until the nineteenth century, when there was an invasion of a different kind, as English aristocrats poured into the area on their staycation alternatives to the grand tour of Europe.

With so little going on in the area, it's surprising that the Harp Inn has as much history as it does. It doesn't even have true antiquity on its side: the half-timber walls and multi-paned timber windows are an attempt to make it look older than its eighteenth-century origins. To be fair, though, it is believed to be built on the site of the old medieval prison, which was one of the town's few stone buildings in that period; that is how the site is described in a document dated 1344. If this is true, there are quite likely to be remnants of the old gaol in the cellars.

In the latter part of the eighteenth century, the inn caught the wave of a small boom in Abergele, when the Chester to Holyhead mail coaches and stagecoaches started to follow a new route, taking them through Abergele instead of a route further inland. Inns sprang up like a rash in the town, catering for the visitors this traffic created, and by 1862 there were sixteen of them, thirteen of which, like the Harp, were on the main road (which in town was called Market Street and Bridge Street).

There had been a livestock market in Abergele for hundreds of years, but at the turn of the twentieth century, the arrival of motorised vehicles meant that the old practice of holding these markets on the main road had to be brought to an end. Instead, an enterprising auctioneer called Frank Lloyd held livestock auctions at the Harp. They were known as the 'Smithfield at the Harp', and they were very successful. There is a 1914 record of a sale of sheep where more than £1,000 changed hands; that could have bought you a Rolls Royce motorcar at the time. Soon other similar auctions sprung up in other nearby inns, the Bee Hotel, on the other side of the street, among them. This association with agriculture saw the Harp flourish, and it was cemented by the Clwyd Cooperative Agricultural Society opening its branch there in 1917.

Of the sixteen inns that used to vie for trade on the streets of Abergele, only a handful now remain. Besides the Harp, there is also the Bull Hotel, which was built in the same era, originally as a tavern, before expanding to absorb the buildings around it until it became a sizable coaching inn.

In the nineteenth century, despite their aversion to drink, it became synonymous with Baptists and Mormons. A chap called Daniel Jones, from Llandulais, emigrated to the USA and went into business running a shipping company with a man called Joseph Smith. Smith was the founder of Mormonism and seen by its followers as a prophet. Smith and Jones hatched a plan to spread the faith in Wales, by bringing a boat load of Mormon missionaries to Abergele and using the Bull as a base. Their masterplan was foiled when they were imprisoned. There was a lot of suspicion about the religion in Britain at the time, so much so that, while the two men were incarcerated, a mob gathered outside and stormed it. The mob managed to get in and murdered Smith, with Jones only saved as he was visiting his lawyer at the time. Unperturbed, Jones had the idea of translating Mormon texts into

Welsh and distributing them, through the co-operation of friends in Carmarthen and Merthyr. It worked like a charm, and when he returned to the States in 1849, he took 249 Mormon coverts from Wales with him. He returned again in 1856, staying at the Bull, before returning to his home state of Utah with another 703.

While the holy ghost of Joseph Smith has not been spotted, the Bull is supposedly haunted by the ghost of a biker in leathers, who died in a motorcycle accident while staying at the inn.

These days Abergele has had a new lease of life, with the nearby Gwrych Castle having been used as the location for the TV show *I'm a Celebrity… Get Me Out of Here!* The castle is reputedly a hot spot of hauntings and paranormal activity, in particular the ghosts of several ladies. The first is the lady in white, who is believed by some to be the restless spirit of a woman buried on unconsecrated ground. Another is the ghost of the former owner of the castle, Winifred Cochrane, countess of Dundonald. She is believed to haunt the castle after her embittered husband (who she had written out of her will) bought the castle anyway, just so he could destroy it to show his contempt for her. There is also a lady in red who is believed to have died while on a fox hunt. Surely these tortured souls have suffered enough, and don't need to watch soap actors eating kangaroo anuses in the name of entertainment.

5.10 TAFARN PENLLAN / THE WHITE HORSE, CAPEL GARMON

C apel Garmon is a small village located high above the Conwy valley, not far from Bettws-y-Coed. The road leading up to it is very pretty, winding through a steep wood with streams and waterfalls cascading along its side. The village itself has some breathtaking views across the Snowdonia National Park and is best known for an ancient burial chamber with stone walls and a huge cap stone, which dates back more than 2,000 years BC. As you might imagine it is quite remote, so not the easiest sort of place for an old inn to survive.

In fact, the only reason we are still able to talk about this pretty little 400-year-old pub in the present tense is down to a large family and their labour of love. The Horse had been empty for more than five years when the current owner, Eryl Roberts, bought the place back in 2015.

Eryl is a farmer in the community and knew how important the pub was to his fellow villagers. A problem that scuppers many a would-be landlord in such a rural location is getting staff. This, however, is no problem for Eryl, who has ten children who all muck in and help out. That's not a typo by the way. He really does have ten children.

The inn itself is two former cottages that have been absorbed into one, and inside it has all the trappings of a traditional cosy inn, with plenty of beams and a log burner. It is run with a strong emphasis on the community, and it is in a part of Wales which is very proud to keep the Welsh language alive. While researching this book I came across an article in, of all places, *the Los Angeles Times*, where a journalist from said newspaper had stayed at the White Horse on a holiday tour of the UK. Not knowing much about Welsh culture, he was surprised to hear everyone at the pub speaking a language that was strange to him. In fact, up to that point he was unaware that Wales even had a language.

The preservation of the Welsh language at the White Horse may have changed Britain's entire political landscape in the late 1990s. It was while staying at the inn that the former leader of the Conservative party, William Hague, learned to sing the Welsh national anthem. He may not have realised it at the time, but this was to become quite a big political coup for him. During the years of John Major' premiership in the early 1990s, there was a growing feeling in Wales that Westminster was overlooking the country – a sentiment only compounded when the then Secretary of State for Wales, John Redwood, was caught on camera at a formal event pretending (badly) to sing along to the national anthem. People went apoplectic, and not long after the incident he was removed from the post in a reshuffle. Suffice it to say that when he was replaced in the role by William Hague, everyone was watching very closely to see if he would take the nation any more seriously. When it became clear he did know the words, a massive political point was scored. It possibly even played a part when the two men went head-to-head in 1997, to run for the party leadership. Hague went on to become leader, Redwood got knocked out in the second ballot.

5.11

THE PLOUGH INN, ST ASPAH

S t Asaph is Britain's second smallest city after St Davids, with a population of just over 3,000. It is very similar to St Davids in many ways, not least as it has been a settlement since the earliest days of British history. An archaeological dig revealed a set of teeth that are believed to be neanderthal, Roman remains were discovered under the cathedral, and the cathedral itself is all that remains of a grand sixth-century monastery. During the Interregnum, after the English Civil War, the cathedral lost its status as a place of worship, and was used to house livestock like pigs, horses and cattle.

I know that Rhyl is not everybody's cup of tea, but here is a pub that has made a very good living out of not being anywhere near Rhyl. Allow me to explain.

In 1881, parliament passed a law that outlawed drinking alcohol at Welsh pubs on a Sunday. I mentioned it before in our chapter about the Church Inn in Llanishen. However, there was an exception written into this statute for people making a long journey on the sabbath. To get served, however, they would need to prove that they were more than ten miles from home. Some sharp-thinking entrepreneurs in Rhyl hit on the idea of driving coaches from the town every Sunday, to take the town's folk on a 'long journey' so they could stop at a suitable boozer just over the ten-mile mark, which just so happened to be the

Plough in St Asaph. Every Sunday evening, trade at the Plough was boosted by the arrival of what became known as the 'four-in-hand from Rhyl', referring the number of drinks each of the passengers would buy when they got to the bar. When the coach was turned around for the return leg, children from St Asaph cottoned on that, if they ran behind the coach singing Welsh folk songs, the nostalgic old soaks on board would throw penny coins out to them for their trouble.

The venture was so successful that pretty soon an entire fleet was needed to transport people back and fore. There are echoes of Michael Gove's 'substantial meal' caveat for people wanting a drink down the pub during the coronavirus pandemic's regional tiers system, seen during 2020. It just goes to show, where drink is involved, people will find a way.

The Plough is clearly a bit of a magnet for people who like to run a gauntlet with the law: it was also a regular haunt of an early twentieth-century society fraudster called Violet Charlesworth. There is quite a well-known photograph of her taken in 1908, posing outside the Plough, with her new-fangled motor car, probably one of the first ever seen in St Asaph. Both she and this car became the stuff of scandal when she decided to fake her own death by driving it over a cliff in Conwy. She had hoped that it would be the perfect crime, not realising that in these early days of motoring, such an incident would be hot news, sensationalised across every newspaper in Europe. Suffice it to say that, having tried to disappear without trace, she was soon spotted by someone who had seen her photograph in the papers, and her ruse was over.

The Plough Inn dates back to the nineteenth century.

5.12
THE WHITE LION, BALA

B ala is an ancient town steeped in religion. A Calvinist theological college was established here in 1712, and one of the town's better-known stories is about a fifteen-year-old girl called Mary Jones. She saved up for six years to buy a Bible translated into Welsh, walking the twenty-five miles to Bala in order to buy it.

Maybe not a big party town then?

It was from Bala that Michael Jones, a Welsh congregational minister, missionary and principal of the theological college, departed for Argentina to found a Welsh settlement. He was one of the founding fathers of the Welsh nationalist movement, and the wellspring from which the tradition of Patagonia's Welsh-speaking population derives.

The town has two large historical coaching inns. The oldest of the two is the Bulls Head Hotel, which dates back to 1692. The exterior is stone built with five-roof apexes to the front, all painted black and white. A lot of what you can see on the outside has been extensively modernised and extended. Inside, it has a spacious L-shaped lounge with a large stone fireplace and pictures of old•Bala•on the walls. There is also a smaller bar and games room. It prides itself on its craft beers and is part of the Craft Union of pubs. I have read an item that says 'it is believed to be haunted' but sadly there were no further details about the form this haunting takes.

While the White Lion is not as old as the Bulls Head, it certainly looks older: the exterior is replete with black and white timber details, but sadly it is all part of a renovation. Having said that, the building was constructed in 1752, so it is no spring chicken. Today it is the bar part of the White Lion Royal Hotel, but historically it was the town-centre's main coaching inn, and inside are lots of architectural details that reveal its former life, not least the lovely gnarled walls either side of the fireplace.

The White Lion is also believed to be haunted. From the fragments I have been able to piece together it appears that, at the turn of the nineteenth century, there was a fire that claimed the lives of some people who got trapped in a corner of the bar. Their bodies were retrieved, but ever since this corner has frequently been a cold spot, where no degree of heating seems to be effective. There have also been reports of glasses being knocked off tables without anyone nearby.

The White Lion is part of the SA Brains Brewery chain.

5.13
THE GEORGE AND DRAGON, BEAUMARIS

B eaumaris on the Isle of Anglesey (or *Ynys Mon* in Welsh) was originally a Viking settlement. In 1295 it was chosen by Edward I as the site of one of his most impressive defensive castles, which is now a World Heritage Site. The area was at one time very marshy but commands quite the view over the straits of Anglesey; creatively, the French and Norman construction workers building the castle called it *beaux marais*, which means beautiful marsh.

When the town was given a Royal Charter by Edward I, it decreed that all trade on Anglesey was to be conducted in Beaumaris. This led to the blossoming of a very healthy shipbuilding industry. Less positively, however, the charter only provided English and Norman-French residents with any civic rights. Native Welsh residents of Beaumaris were disqualified from holding any civic office. They were also prohibited from carrying weapons, holding assemblies, or from buying houses or land within the borough. The charter also specifically prohibited Jews from living there at all. He knew a good spot for a castle, but Edward I was not the most inclusive of kings.

The website of the George and Dragon goes into a lot more historical detail than most, claiming that the establishment was built in 1410. This would make it one of the oldest pubs in Wales, but as is usually the case, it's probably not that simple. The building you see today is largely seventeenth century, although there are undoubtedly bits that once belonged to an older building that used to stand on this site. Margret Dunn, whose expertise in this field far outstrips mine, wrote that there was a house built on this site in 1541, and that it has been absorbed into the much-extended shell of the building that is there today.

The original building was a merchant's house and it used to have an upper floor that overhung the lower one on the street-facing side. This feature was lost when the building was substantially altered in the seventeenth and twentieth centuries.

On the inside, however, there are some wonderful features that survive from the original house: the beams, for example, and the wood panelling, are all pre-seventeenth century. Perhaps the most interesting original feature is a roof truss, but sadly it is not on public display as it forms part of the private living quarters. There are pictures on the back of the menus though, where you can also see its engraving of the Sacred Heart, a very Catholic image. It suggests that the George, much like the Robin Hood in Monmouth, was used by Catholics for secret masses or meetings, after their worship was outlawed during the Reformation.

The Catholics of the George, however, were altogether more defiant than those in Monmouth, as is evidenced by a Latin inscription accompanying the image. It reads, '*Pax deus vobis requie defuge deus providebit nosce te ipsum.*' This translates roughly as, 'The peace of God will provide you rest. Fight on [or evade]. Know yourself.' In my opinion this is a really rousing rallying cry.

In later history, the George and Dragon played host to a scandal, when a lady called Elizabeth Owen, who lived here in the late nineteenth century, successfully brought a claim against a former employer called Thomas Horricks, a gentleman of Liverpool. The claim was for the 'act of adultery' committed upon her in 1890 when she was twenty and he was seventy. The court ordered him to pay her two shillings a week.

These days the George is run by the family-owned Robinsons Brewery, and specialises in ales of their output. Any heavy metal fans will be delighted to learn that this includes 'Trooper', the ale endorsed by Iron Maiden. They always have five Cask Marque ales to choose from, with two guest ales that rotate. They do simple home pub food and are also listed in the AA Good Pub Guide.

No more than 100 yards away from the George and Dragon, as you walk towards the castle, is another Georgian coaching inn, Ye Olde Bulls Head Inn. Distinguished guests there have included Dr Johnson and Charles Dickens.

5.14

THE BULL INN, LLANGEFNI

There has been an inn on this site for hundreds of years. The original inn was referred to on a map drawn up by John Ogilby, dated 1675, as the Pen-y-Bont Inn. However, with the growth of traffic passing through Llangefni, it soon became inadequate for its needs. Eventually, in 1817, its then owner, Sir Richard Buckley, commissioned the pub that stands here now. Generally, the Victorians thought they knew best, demolishing everything they could to create something uniquely Victorian. Sir Richard, however, was unusually sympathetic for his time, and here we have a Victorian attempt to build a seventeenth-century vernacular property, albeit one a little bigger than that which it replaced.

As such, this construction is itself of some historic merit, and the building is now Grade II listed. The listing describes it as 'a good, substantially complete example of a Victorian coaching Inn and courtyard range. The Inn is an ambitiously scaled and particularly well-detailed example of neo-vernacular design, prominently sited in the centre of the town, it also forms a group with the adjacent town hall·and clock.'

The name change to 'the Bull' can also be dated to the new building, as Buckley's coat of arms had three bulls' heads on it. Buckley owned a vast estate in the area, and the Bull also served as the estate's administration office, where local farmers came to pay their rent.

These days the main part of the building is given over to a hotel. It is a double-depth, three-storey structure with a full-height gabled wing that forms an L shape. To the rear there are outbuildings that include tack rooms for storing harnesses, saddles and reigns; servant's quarters; and on the opposite side of the yard, lofted stables, connected to the tack rooms by a single-storey row of coach-houses. The yard and these buildings had their own access from Glanhwrfa Road, where you can still see the coachman's entrance, wide enough to drive horses and carriages through.

This place is absolutely riddled with ghosts, although it is unclear whether they derived from the earlier inn or the later ones. There have been many reports of ghostly laughter emanating from the cellar, but when more closely investigated, there is nobody there. There is also an apparition of an old lady in Victorian costume, who sits in a rocking chair on one of the upper floors.

These days the inn and pub are run by the SA Brains chain.

5.15
THE BLACK BOY,
CAERNARFON

It is fair to say that nineteenth-century Caernarfon was a town of contradictions. Evangelical and abstemious Methodists lived cheek by jowl with reprobates and drunkards in a small town that once boasted over fifty pubs. A journalist from *the Manchester Evening Post* wrote, 'I have travelled through many towns in England, but I have never seen so many drunkards in proportion to the number of the population, as in Caernarvon.' The burgesses of the town tried everything they could to curb the overindulgences of its citizens, and as late as 1848 drunks could still be sentenced to a spell in the stocks, a punishment more associated with the Middle Ages than the Victorian era.

But when the Reverend Bingley visited, it was not so much the drunks that bothered him as the over ebullient Methodists. He thought that they had 'more the appearance of heathen orgies than of the rational spirit of Christian devotion.' Now, I've met a few Methodists in my time, and I have to say I have never noticed much in the way of 'heathen orgies' about them. I'm wondering if Bingley might have got the Methodists and the drunks mixed up? Easy to do it you're a bit worse for wear yourself.

The street plan of Caernarfon is quite unchanged from the thirteenth century, and the centre of town still has defensive walls defining its outline. In English the street the Black Boy stands in is known as Northgate Street, in Welsh *Stryd Pedwar a chwech*, the street of four and six. This is believed to be a reference to the times sailors would dock in the town and look for lodgings, paying 4d for a hammock or 6d for a bed, usually with some female company.

The name of this inn throws up a lot of questions, and I am sure it makes some people uncomfortable, thinking it in some way a reference to slavery. There are a range of local considerations that suggest it is not, but in truth nobody knows for sure.

Many believe that the boy in question is Edward the Black Prince, the first Prince of Wales. Edward had a connection with the town: his grandfather Edward II, before he became king, was known as Edward of Caernarfon. During his lifetime, and the decades following, the Black Prince gained almost mythical status in the eyes of his adoring followers, who saw him as the paragon of chivalry. There are pubs named after him in places with nothing like the connections of Caernarfon, bolstering the credibility of this theory.

Others draw attention to the fact that the entrance to Caernarfon's harbour was once marked by a black buoy. Back in the days before most ordinary people could read, the name of an inn would have been represented solely through the picture on its sign, and it is plausible that originally a different sort of boy/buoy was represented here. There is an old sign with a picture of a black buoy at the rear of the inn, which would add weight to this.

Yet another theory draws on the old story that when Charles II was born, his skin was so dark that his mother called him 'the black boy'. Caernarfon was heavily Royalist during the English Civil War, and in centuries past the pub was known as the King's Arms, so this is more credible than it might initially seem.

Taking local considerations out of the equation, around Britain there are undoubtedly quite a few inns called the Black Boy, and often their name did derive from the picture of a black boy on the sign outside. This was to tell people that the inn sold produce from the Caribbean, for example rum. In other words, a fairly direct reference to the slave trade, which sadly must be considered as a possibility.

As far as the current owners are concerned, the name is a homage to a local man called John Ystumllyn, who the locals nicknamed 'Jac du', Welsh for 'Jack Black'. John was the first person of colour recorded as living in the area. It is known that he died in 1786, but very little about his early life is recorded. Given the timeframe, however, it is very likely that he had been a slave. However, when he lived and worked in the gardens of the Wynn family on their family estate, Ystumllyn, he did so as a free man. He took the name of the estate as his surname and was well liked and respected by all, especially for his phenomenal talent as a horticulturalist and gardener. He married a local girl and they lived together in a cottage owned by his employers.

My own personal feeling is that the pub was once the Black Buoy, becoming the Black Boy in the nineteenth century.

The inn itself is another old building that has been built in stages, absorbing everything around it. Most of the work was done in the seventeenth century, but the oldest part, the bar and lounge of the hotel wing, is believed to have been started around 1522. It certainly looks its age, with its beamed ceiling and inglenook fireplace. In places, the exterior walls are up to one-and-a-half metres thick. A passage to the rear leads to the dining room and kitchens, and there is a legend that this passage is built over a path that once led to a convent behind. A ghost of a nun frequently appears, walking hurriedly along the passage, disappearing into a wall where the entrance to the old nunnery would once have been.

These days the Black Boy has a great reputation for its ales, craft beers and simple homecooked food.

5.16
THE STAG,
DOLGELLAU

Dolgellau was the scene of the Welsh gold rush in the 1850s and 60s. Prospectors poured in, racing to establish the main lode, and by 1884 a commercial-scale operation had been established. Mining continued in the area right up until 1998. As recently as 2020 a viable new seam has been discovered, so there is every likelihood that it will resume in the area in the future. There has been a tradition of using Welsh gold for Royal wedding rings since 1923, started by the Queen Mother.

But long before there was the sniff of gold in the air, the town was already thriving, as is evidenced by the literally dozens of pubs in Dolgellau. The industry driving the commerce was cloth and fabric production, supplemented by travellers passing through. Even now the town is buzzing with ramblers heading to climb Cadair Idris, and holidaymakers crossing Snowdonia or heading towards the coast.

Today, the Stag is the oldest pub in the town, standing where the twisting roads converge on the seventeenth-century bridge. The building dates from around 1770. It has served the people of the area for centuries – including, fatefully, a gold miner called William Foulkes in 1904.

At the time, William Edward Smith and his sixteen-year-old daughter Edith both worked behind the bar of the Stag. One night Foulkes and a bunch of miners were drinking heavily in the parlour.

As young Edith served them, Smith was alerted by the sound of her crying out, 'Keep your hands off me!' On investigating he found Foulkes with his hands up the girl's skirt. In a fit of rage Smith lunged at Foulkes and set about him, raining down blow after blow until Foulkes fell to the ground. Smith dragged him out the back of the pub, but his body was already limp and lifeless. Smith was arrested and sent to the Assizes at the County Hall, only a stone's throw from the Stag. In passing judgement, Mr Justice Wills took into account Smith's previous good character and bound him over in the sum of £50 to keep the peace.

The Stag is now part of a terrace of buildings, but when it was built it would have stood alone. Most of its original stone masonry has been covered over with rendering, but from the beer garden you can still see the massive boulders used as masonry in Dolgellau in the eighteenth-century.

The inn used to have a yard with access via a narrow lane, which became an issue in the early twentieth century, with the introduction of licencing laws. It became clear to local law enforcement that the front door being bolted shut was no indication that the Stag was not open: all the regulars knew there was a rear entrance off the yard. Fortunately, the police were sufficiently reassured by the landlord to look no further into it.

There used to be a coaching inn just a few miles outside the town, called the Hywel Dda Inn, of a similar age to the Stag. It is no longer an inn or pub but an Airbnb, but it retains a lot more of its original features than the Stag, which is why I mention it.

5.17
PENLAN FAWR,
PWLLHELI

Pwllheli has changed substantially over the centuries. It was originally a medieval town, though there are few traces of that left. In fact, the Penlan Fawr is Pwllheli's oldest surviving building.

It was originally built in the sixteenth century, as a house, and a letter from a man called William Vaughan, in 1622, roughly dates its conversion. In this letter, Vaughan asks Sir William Maurice, one of the chief Crown administrators in Caernarfonshire, for a licence to sell wine in a Pwllheli building. There is evidence to suggest that the building in question was the Penlan Fawr, as in 2009, during some building works, the letters 'RV' were found carved into a porch column at the entrance to the building. This suggests that this building belonged to the estate of Richard Vaughan, William's father, the owner of the Corsygedol Estate between 1606 and 1636.

The reason so little of Pwllheli's medieval origins remain is that, like a few other places we have visited, the town was sacked and burned to the ground by Owain Glyndŵr. It was slow to recover, but over time locals recycled the ruins of the town, and by the seventeenth century, they had built up a thriving port and centre of shipbuilding.

Let's hope any pride they had in themselves was not dented when Dr Samuel Johnson visited in 1774. He described Pwlheli as a 'mean old town'. Rude!

To be fair, the town would have looked quite different in Johnson's day. As hard as it is to picture it now, the Penlan Fawr used to stand on the water's edge. Today, just to get down to the port on the Afon Erch is a good three-minute walk, and it is over half a mile to the sea.

This dramatic change in topography is due to a natural phenomenon that had a devastating effect on the town's main source of industry. As the river, which provided the town with its port, started to silt up, the shipbuilding industry dried up with it; the last ship was built here in 1878. In its heyday, round about the time of Johnson's visit, the Penlan Fawr (which back then was called the Red Lion) would have been crammed to the rafters with rowdy sailors, shipbuilders and smugglers, swigging their tankards of ale, trying to catch the eye of passing ladies of the night. This part of town, like so many old dockyards, was the red-light district, and trade was brisk. In the eighteenth century there were nine inns, taverns and ale houses (including the Penlan Fawr) in the area. By 1830 that number had risen to thirty-two. To remain competitive, the Penlan Fawr had a gaming room, which had a tradition that gave rise to an old ditty:

> *'Dancing ball yn Mhenlan Fawr,*
> *Crwc o ddwfr ar ganol llawr.'*

Which translates as:

> 'A dancing ball in Penlan Fawr,
> A pail of water in the middle of the floor.'

In 1892, when a local magistrate was looking for excuses to cull some of the town's many inns, this old rhyme was cited as evidence of its unique history.

All of which makes one particular chapter in the history of the Penlan pretty odd. In 1802 it opened its doors to the Rev John Hughes (from Brecon), who was the first Wesleyan preacher to visit the town. Despite his message of abstinence, the pub became the regular meeting place of the Wesleyans from then on. You need to bear in mind that, before the Industrial Revolution, towns did not generally have public buildings other than churches, which were strictly for the use of their denomination of worship. The only 'public houses' of the day were inns. They were commonly used as meeting rooms, courts, administrative centres and tribunals. The Penlan Fawr, not content with simply being a meeting place for Wesleyan Methodists, also had a faith school in one of its back rooms – yet another example of that uncomfortable but nonetheless inextricable link between pubs and churches in Wales.

The Penlan today is quite loyal to its origins, but with some minor modifications from the nineteenth century. The small windows have been opened out and a large entrance cut through the front of the imposing porch. Back in the 1990s, it still had fake half-timber fixed to the upper walls, an attempt by someone to make the oldest building in the town conform to their idea of what an old house should look like. Thankfully that has now been removed, a more recent and sympathetic restoration revealing the beautiful old masonry underneath. The interior is genuine and has remained quite unchanged over the last 300 years. The bar and lounge has a flagstone floor, a beamed ceiling and an inglenook fireplace.

5.18
THE GLYN ARMS,
HAWARDEN

Now I'm sure we've all met some know-it-all pub landlords in our lives: the kind of people who are always happy to put the world to rights, tell you how the country should be run, or wade into arguments with opening gambits like, 'Actually, I think you'll find...'

Should we be surprised, then, when we hear the tale of a former pub landlord who actually did go on to run the country? In fact, to be prime minister of the UK four times?

Only one paragraph in and I can almost hear the proper historians straining to correct me. Let me explain and expand.

The Glyn Arms is and always has been part of the Howarden estate. It is named after the Glyn family, who were the custodians of the estate from 1650. Sir Stephen Glynne, the ninth Baronet, became a close friend to William Ewart Gladstone, the two of them meeting while studying at Eton College and Oxford University together. Gladstone spent a lot of time at Howarden Castle, where he met and fell in love with Stephen's sister Catherine. They married in 1839. When Sir Stephen died in 1874, he had no children, so the estate passed through his sister's line to the Gladstones. That is how the pub landlord became William Gladstone.

So, by landlord, we mean the man who owned the inn and the land it stood on, rather than the man who stood behind the bar pouring pints and ending sentences with statement like, 'If you ask me, hanging is too good for 'em.'

If you really want to split hairs, the estate actually passed to William Gladstone the younger, the eldest son of the prime minister. Apparently, he was a very good organist. But he is rather seriously lacking in good story value, I'm sure you'll agree.

Prime Minister Gladstone did have some genuine connections with the pub. He and his wife lived for many years at the castle, taking an active interest in the running of the estate. Each year the estate's rents were audited at the Glyn Arms, and the event often included a formal dinner, at which William Ewart Gladstone frequently made speeches.

The Glyn Arms and the buildings adjoining it have a few features of interest. The pub was built around 1812 and was subsequently extended to the back to include a two-storey Victorian coach house, which is still there now. Next to the pub are the arched remains of what was known as 'the shambles'. Before the days of refrigeration, butchers' shops could not store meat, so the back entrance to the building was an area where animal carcasses could be butchered. The cut meat could then be passed to the stalls at the front of the building, to be sold, fresh, on what was the north side of the town marketplace. If you look closely at the arches on the side of the building facing the Glyn Arms, you can still see two hooks on each side of one of the openings, once used to hang the meat from.

Even as late as the early twentieth century, livestock auctions used to take place at the shambles. Today you can see a plaque presented by Erskine William Gladstone in 1953 to mark the coronation of Queen Elizabeth II. Benches of Hawarden oak had been installed below the plaque for waiting bus passengers.

5.19
THE WHITE LION,
LLANELIAN-YN-RHOS

A s we bring our travels around the ancient and historic pubs of
Wales to a close, I thought it would be fitting to save something
of a gem for last. It's got everything. A claim to be the oldest pub in
Wales (which I will dismiss with my usual candour), a link with the
church, gun fights, ghosts... The lot. And, of course, it is a truly great
pub – one of the best our nation has to offer.

It also has a connection to one of the most bizarre holy well legends
I have ever heard. We have come across quite a few ancient wells by
now. Some cure the sick, some heal the lame, some bestow long life,
one bestowed potency on a childless king and queen. But the spring
in the small hamlet of Llanelian-yn-Rhos is unique. If you really hate
somebody, and want something bad to happen to them, then this is
the place to wish for it.

The spring at Ffynon Elian is behind the church, which is itself
right next to the White Lion. It is called 'the Cursing Well of St Elian'
and successive vicars of St Elian's church would allow ill-wishers to
etch onto a stone the name of the person they wished to curse, before
dropping it into the well. Then all there was to do was to sit back,
knowing that something awful would happen to their nemesis soon.

How this legend ever came about is a mystery. Often, when a well
takes the name of a saint, then something of the essence of that saint
is said to transfer through its waters. For example, the waters at the

well of St Winfried are meant to bestow long life, springing as they do from the spot where she was brought back to life after being decapitated. But there is nothing in the story of St Elian that suggests he is a good conduit for cursing. Unless you are a greyhound. He had a real issue with greyhounds (Google it).

Now, far be it from me to suggest that successive unscrupulous men of the cloth might have been cashing in on the gullible, but there are records that suggest that, on more than one occasion, someone came to the well full of rage and scorn, only to return wracked with remorse (or even forgiveness) enquiring how to break the curse. They would then be told that, for a higher fee, it would be possible to retrieve the stone they had dropped in the well and the curse would be lifted.

Genius.

Eventually, in 1829, a man of stiff moral fibre was appointed as priest to the parish and he ended the practice, ordering that the well be filled in to prevent others from profiting from this scam in the future.

The inn and the fifteenth-century church have been inextricably linked for centuries. Quite apart from anything else, the path to the church crosses through the cobbled yard in front of the pub. There is a hint that there might have been an inn on this site, or very near it, for even longer. The pub's website quotes a document from the eighth century that mentions there was an ale house next door to the original church of St Elian. The only trouble is that there is nothing to say that the original church and the current church are on the same site. But it is possible.

Even if it does not have eighth-century roots, it's still a lovely old inn. If, before entering its door, you look across the road to Llan Cottage, you will get an idea of how it would once have looked: low and thatched, with small windows and a lateral chimney, all of which were altered in more recent history. The current owners have done a great job of restoring the old place to its former glory, with polished slate flagstone floors, under which there is reputed to be a well, and a huge inglenook with a curving lintel. Outhouses and an old barn have been absorbed into the building, and materials salvaged from an old, demolished chapel have been used to maintain integrity with the rest of the building.

One further feature you may notice is the pellet marks on a window frame, visible from outside the building. There is another lodged into a roof timber inside. Apparently, a local farmer got into a row with the then landlord, and in the absence of a handy well at which to lay a quick curse, he instead chose to fire a shotgun at the pub. No one was hurt, but the farmer found himself having an uncomfortable chat with the local constabulary.

As you would expect from a pub with such a long history as the White Lion, there is the obligatory peppering of ghosts. All the usual suspects: cold spots, glasses flying across the bar lots of inanimate objects moving for no discernible reason; even ghost cats occasionally scuttling across the bar. There is one story, however, which is rather unique.

This is a very old pub, with very old traditions, and there is a bench at one of the tables where the old men of the village always used to sit. Over time, sadly, they have all passed on, but it is still referred to as 'the elder's bench'. One evening after the pub was closed, the landlord (who is not from the village originally) was drinking with some friends in a house across the road. Noticing he was running low, he popped across the road to the pub to grab a bottle of wine. He unlocked the heavy door and flicked on the light, when he was startled to see an old man with a hood pulled up over his head, sitting on the elder's bench.

Startled, he called out, 'Who are you?'

The seated man replied, 'I am Elvin-the-hood.' The landlord scanned the room to see if anyone else was present, and when his eyes fell back on the bench, the old man had vanished.

A bit shaken up, he grabbed the bottle he had come to collect, locked up and went back to join his friends. 'You look like you've seen a ghost,' they joked as he entered the room.

He sat down, gathered himself, and told them what had just

happened. When he told them that the apparition's name was 'Elvin-the-hood', their jaws dropped to the floor. What the landlord could not possibly have known, not having grown up in the village, was that Elvin-the-hood was a real person. He was one of the old men who had once sat on that bench habitually, and he was a bit of a character, having taken to wearing a hood pulled up over his head to help avoid the many different people to whom he owed money. And if that wasn't creepy enough: Elvin-the-hood had once lived in the exact house they were all sitting in right that second...

But don't let Elvin-the-hood put you off. The White Lion is a wonderful old pub and well worth a visit. It is a free house, usually stocking Marstons and various guest ales. The pub is well known for its good food, having won the 'Best Gastropub in North Wales', along with various other hospitality awards down the years. It was once a favourite of the ex-Monty Python star Terry Jones, who used to drop in for a pint quite regularly, when visiting his mother's grave in the churchyard next door.

APPENDIX

M y late father used to love trivia, in particular lists. He kept a notebook about his person at all times, where he jotted them down. I remember one of them was 'Classical composers beginning with the letter "B"'. He started with the obvious ones – Beethoven, Bach and Brahms – and every time he encountered another, wherever he happened to be, at whatever the time or the occasion, he would pull out his book and add it to the list: Britten, Bartok, Berlioz...

It's no wonder I turned out like I did!

Another list was words that only exist in the negative: nonplussed, inscrutable, dishevelled, disappoint... As a small boy I asked him to let me read it once, and I was amused to discover he had missed one. I looked at him triumphantly and said, 'Listless?' He snatched the list off me and consulted it with a frown. Then he smiled kindly and looked up.

'Quite right,' he said. 'I am completely without list.' With a chortle at his own joke, he jotted it down.

He would have been eternally disappointed if I had written a book such as this without including a few lists. So, for you and for him, here are a few on subjects raised by this book. They are lists not leagues, so not in any order of merit.

Let us begin with the burning question:

Pub	Claimed Inauguration	Details
The White Lion, Llanelian-Yn-Rhos	Eighth century	Not the present building
Ty Mawr, Gwyddelwern	1081	Not the present building
The Skirrid Inn, Llanvihangel Crucorney	1110	Not the present building
The Old House, Llangynwyd	1147	Not the present building
The Priory Inn, Milford Haven	1200	Only a pub since the nineteenth century
The Llindir Inn, Henllan	1229	Not the present building
The Cross Keys, Swansea	1330	Only a pub since the eighteenth century
The Blue Anchor, Aberthaw	1380	Only a pub since the eighteenth century
The George and Dragon, Beaumaris	1410	Not the present building
The Groes Inn, Ty-n'y-Groes	1573	Trading in this building since 1573

So there you have it: the Groes Inn is probably the oldest pub in Wales.

The Hanbury Arms,
Caerleon

The Anchor,
Tintern

The Worms Head Hotel and Inn,
Rhossili

The Captain's Wife,
Sully

The Horse and Jockey,
Pontypool

The Old House,
Llangynwyd

The Boat Inn,
Chepstow

The Court House,
Caerphilly

The Bishops,
St Davids

The Harp Inn,
Old Radnor

The Three Cocks,
Three Cocks

The Groes Inn,
Ty'n-y-Groes

The Old Point House,
Angle

The Old Sailors,
Pwllgwaelod

The Ship Inn,
Tresaith

THE PRETTIEST PUBS IN WALES

The Bush Inn,
St Hilary

The Nantyffin Cider Mill,
Tretower

The Bell Inn,
Skenfrith

The White Hart,
Llangybi

The Blue Anchor,
Aberthaw

The Bear,
Crickhowell

The White Hart Inn,
Llanddarog

The Radnorshire Arms,
Presteigne

The Griffin Inn,
Llyswen

The Triangle,
Rhayader

The Llanthony Priory Inn,
Llanthony

The Cwmdu Inn,
Cwmdu

The Groes Inn,
Conwy

PUBS WITH FAMOUS PATRONS

Pub	*Alumni*
The Hanbury Arms, Caerleon	Alfred Lord Tennyson, Arthur Machen
The Robin Hood Inn, Monmouth	William Shakespeare
The King's Arms, Abergavenny	King Charles I
The King's Head, Monmouth	King Charles I
The Queen's Head, Monmouth	Oliver Cromwell, Horatio Lord Nelson

The White Hart, Llangybi	Jayne Seymour, Oliver Cromwell, T.S. Eliot
The Church Inn, Llanishen	David Lloyd George
The Blue Anchor, Aberthaw	Simon Cowell, the Belgian Royal Family
The Old Swan Inn, Llantwit Major	Charlie Chaplin, Errol Flynn, David Lloyd George, Winston Churchill, William Randolph Hearst, Marion Davis and Clark Gable
The Bush Inn, St Hilary	Benedict Cumberbatch, Martin Freeman
The Cross Keys, Swansea	Dylan Thomas, Baron Heycock
The Horse and Jockey, Pontypool	Lynn Davies
The King's Head, Llandovery	Twm Siôn Catti
The King's Arms, Pentyrch	Luke Goss, Tom Jones and Keanu Reeves
The Three Golden Cups, Southerndown	Bob Dylan

The Old House, Llangynwyd	Elizabeth Taylor, Richard Burton
The Harp Inn, Old Radnor	Charles I
The Buck Inn, Newtown	Charles I
Y Talbot, Tregaron	Jimmy Carter
The White Horse, Capel Garmon	William Hague
Ye Olde Bull Inn, Beaumaris	Charles Dickens and Doctor Johnson
The Glyn Arms, Hawarden	William Gladstone (landlord)
The Skirrid Inn, Llanvihangel Crucorney	Owain Glyndŵr, Judge Jeffries, the Devil

THE MOST HAUNTED PUBS IN WALES

Pub	Scariness
The Skirrid Inn Llanvihangel Crucorney	Mega scary
The Prince of Wales Kenfig	Really scary
The Talacre Arms Holywell	Really scary
Llanthony Abbey Llanthony	Pretty scary
The Queen's Head Monmouth	Pretty scary
The Welcome to Town Llanrhidian	A bit scary
The Bull Inn Llangefni	Quite scary
The Hundred House Bleddfa	Scary for pets
The Llindir Inn Henllan	Sort of scary

Pub	Significance
The Mermaid Tavern St Clears	Where the Rebecca Riots started
The Cow and Snuffers Cardiff	Popular with Lord Nelson
The Old Swan Inn Rhayader	One of the oldest pubs in Powys
The Serjeants Inn Eglwyswrw	Celebrated for hundreds of years
The Mermaid Inn Welshpool	Half-timber sixteenth-century pub, now a house
Hen Dafarn and Lletty Hotel Mostyn	Unusual sign from 1699 above the door
The Golden Grove Rossett	Thirteenth-century inn
The Talacre Arms Holywell	Lots of supernatural phenomena
Ye Olde Castle Inn Caergwrle	Seventeenth-century thatched pub

In the Middle Ages, beer was consumed more than water as the alcohol made it safer to drink

The oldest known recipe for beer is 4,000 years old, from Samaria

Residue discovered on stone mortars found in Raqefet Cave, northern Israel, are from·13,000 years ago,·suggesting that before agriculture the Natufian civilization had developed the production of beer

In the 1600s midwives created super strong beer to ease labour pain

Beer was not considered an alcoholic beverage in Russia until 2013

In the UK alone, 93,000 litres of beer are rumoured to be lost in facial hair every year

Germany is the largest hop producer in the world

Cenosillicaphobia is the fear of an empty glass

The Norwegian word for hangover directly translates as 'carpenters in the head'

The first beer cans were produced in 1935

Zythology is the study of beer

The moon has a crater called 'beer'

The first professional brewers were all women

At any given time, 0.7% of the world population is drunk

Belgium has over 4,000 brands of beer

A beer expert is called a Cerevisaphile

The first beer bottle was sold in 1850

The strongest beer in world is 67.5% proof

At the wife carrying championships in Finland, first prize is your wife's
weight in beer

The Czech Republic consumes more beer per capita than anywhere
in the world

Beer was only legalised in Iceland on 1st March 1989

In 1215 the Magna Carta made it law that British nobles could only
be sold beer in pints

Until the nineteenth century it was quite common for pubs to be used
as public spaces, such as courts, meeting places, chapels, morgues
and mortuaries

I must confess that in this book I have prioritised pubs by story value. Or occasionally where you have two or three pubs of a similar age in a similar vicinity I may have focussed on the oldest or most famous and passed the others by.

As such, there are quite a few ancient and historic pubs that I did not really include that can hold their own historically with any of the ones I did mention. I would of course recommend a visit to any of the following if you are in search of antiquity, quaintness and thunderingly good ales and craft beers:

Pub	Age	Location
The Three Salmons	17th C	Usk
The Royal Oak	16th C	Llantrisant (mon)
The Bell Inn	17th C	Skenfrith
The Beaufort Arms	18th C	Monmouth
The Golden Lion	17th C	Magor
The Star	16th C	Dinas Powys
The Lamb & Flag	18th C	Wick
The Fox & Hounds	18th C	Llancarfan
The Vale of Glamorgan	16th C	Cowbridge
The Duke of Wellington	17th C	Cowbridge

The Bear	15th C	Cowbridge
The White Hart	16th C	Llantwit Major
The Tudor Tavern	17th C	Llantwit Major
The Carne Arms	17th C	Llysworney
The Angel	18th C	Neath
The White Hart	18th C	Cenarth
The Ship Inn	18th C	Fishguard
The Sailor's Rest	18th C	Fishguard
The Ship and Anchor	18th C	Fishguard
The Farmer's Arms	18th C	Fishguard
The Dolfor Inn	17th C	Dolfor
The Oak Inn	17th C	Guidfield
The Red Lion	17th C	Llanafan Fawr
The Plas-yn-Dinas Inn	16th C	Llanfechain
The Blue Bell Inn	18th C	Llancurig
The Whistling Badger	16th C	Llanidloes
The Black Boy Inn	16th C	Newtown

The Cwmdeuddwr	17th C	Rhayader
The Raven	18th C	Llanarmon-Yn-Ial
Gawain and the Green Knight	19th C	Connah's Quay
Ye Olde Bull Inn	17th C	Beaumaris

In preparation for the publication of this book, I took it upon myself to visit all of the pubs herein, as soon as lockdown restrictions permitted. It was quite an undertaking. There are eighty-nine of them, and they are spread right the way across our beautiful country. So, with military precision, I mapped them all out in the most time-efficient order to get around them all.

Having gone to that trouble, I figured I might as well share all my research with you. I've even included their telephone numbers so you can call ahead.

In total, there are more than thirty hours of driving between these pubs, so this is not an undertaking you will be able to rush. But as so many of these great hostelries offer rooms, it is one you can take very much at your own pace. It also makes it easier to divvy up days between you and your companions, so one of you can be 'des' while the others are able to fully immerse themselves in the experience.

Pub	Postcode	Approx Mins Drive	Contact Details
The Prince of Wales, Cardiff	CF10 1FA	Ground zero	029 2064 4449
The City Arms, Cardiff	CF10 1EA	1	029 2064 1913
The Goat Major, Cardiff	CF10 1PU	1	029 2033 7161
The Rummer Tavern, Cardiff	CF10 1AY	1	0121 272 5499
The Plymouth Arms, St Fagans	CF5 6DU	17	029 2056 9173
The King's Arms, Pentyrch	CF15 9QF	6	029 2089 0202
The Courthouse, Caerphilly	CF83 1FN	17	029 2088 8120
The Travellers Rest, Thornhill	CF83 1LY	6	029 2085 9021
The Church Inn, Llanishen	CF14 5EH	7	029 2076 3601
The Murenger House, Newport	NP20 1GA	25	01633 263977
The Hanbury Arms, Caerleon	NP18 1AA	9	01633 420361

The Old Bull Inn, Caerleon	NP18 1AE	1	01633 420636
The White Hart, Llangybi	NP15 1NP	9	01633 450258
Cross Keys, Usk	NP15 1BG	6	01291 672 535
The Horse and Jockey, Pontymoel	NP4 0JB	10	01495 762723
Rose Inn, Redwick	NP26 3DU	31	01633 880501
The Mounton Brook Lodge, Pwllmeyric	NP16 6LF	21	01291 621490
The Boat Inn, Chepstow	NP16 5HH	7	01291 626548
The Anchor, Tintern	NP16 6TE	15	01291 689582
The Lion, Trellech	NP25 4PA	11	01600 860322
The Ship, Raglan	NP15 2DY	17	01291 691825
The Robin Hood Inn, Monmouth	NP25 3EQ	11	01600 713240

The King's Head, Monmouth	NP25 3DY	1	01600 713417
The Queen's Head, Monmouth	NP25 3DL	1	01600 712767
The Skirrid Inn, Llanvihangel Crucorney	NP7 8DH	27	01873 890258
The Llanthony Priory Hotel, Llanthony	NP7 7NN	14	01873 890487
The King's Arms, Abergavenny	NP7 5AA	25	01873 855074
The Bear Hotel, Crickhowell	NP8 1BW	13	01873 810408
The Bridge End Inn, Crickhowell	NP8 1AR	1	01873 810338
Nantyffin Cider Mill, Tretower	NP8 1SG	7	01873 810775
The Three Cocks, Three Cocks	LD3 0SL	25	01497 847215
The Griffin Inn, Llyswen	LD3 0UR	4	01874 754542

The Harp Inn, Old Radnor	LD8 2RH	35	01544 350655
The Radnorshire Arms, Presteigne	LD8 2BE	13	01544 267536
The George and Dragon, Knighton	LD7 1BL	13	01547 528532
The Hundred House Inn, Bleddfa	LD7 1PA	13	01547 550409
The Buck Inn, Newtown	SY16 2NP	42	01686 622699
The Green Inn, Llangedwyn	SY10 9JW	48	01691 828234
The White Lion, Bala	LL23 7AE	36	01678 520314
Ty Mawr, Gwdderlwen	LL21 9DH	29	Not available Summer 2021
The Horse and Jockey, Wrexham	LL11 1BG	38	01978 351083
The Glyn Arms, Hawarden	CH5 3NS	26	01244 569988

The Morning Star, Ruthin	LL15 1HH	30	01824 703017
The King's Head, Llanrhaeadr	LL16 4NL	8	01745 890278
The Guildhall Tavern, Denbigh	LL16 3NU	7	01745 816533
The Llindir Inn, Henllan	LL16 5BH	7	01745 812188
The Plough Inn, St Aspah	LL17 0LU	10	01745 585080
The Old Tavern Inn, Llanerch-Y-Mor, Holywell	CH8 9DX	19	01745 563588
The Harp, Abergele	LL22 7AA	31	01745 799721
The White Lion, Llanelian-Yn-Rhos	LL29 8YA	14	01492 515807
The Groes Inn, Ty'n-y-Groes	LL32 8TN	19	01492 650545
Tafarn Penlan The White Horse, Capel Garmon	LL26 0RW	24	01690 710721

The George and Dragon, Beaumaris	LL58 8AA	57	01248 810491
The Bull Inn, Llangefni	LL77 7LR	21	01248 722119
The Black Boy, Caernarvon	LL55 1RW	28	01286 673604
Penlan Fawr, Pwllheli	LL53 5DE	39	01758 613834
The Stag, Dollellau	LL40 1AU	60	07846 202522
The Aleppo Merchant, Carno	SY17 5LL	41	01686 420210
The Triangle Inn, Rhayader	LD6 5AR	43	01597 810537
Y Talbot, Tregaron	SY25 6JL	60	01974 298208
The King's Head, Llandovery	SA20 0AB	49	01550 720393
Bunch of Grapes, Newcastle Emlyn	SA38 9DU	63	01239 711185

The Three Horseshoes, Cenarth	SA38 9JL	7	01239 710119
The Pendre Inn, Cilgerran	SA43 2SL	12	01239 614223
The Golden Lion, Newport	SA42 0SY	18	01239 820321
The Royal Oak, Fishguard	SA65 9HA	13	01348 218632
The Bishops, St Davids	SA62 6SL	24	01437 720422
The Priory Inn, Milford Haven	SA73 3JB	43	01646 695231
New Inn, Amroth	SA67 8NW	40	01834 812368
The Black Lion, St Clears	SA33 4AA	19	01994 231700
The Angel Vaults, Carmarthen	SA31 1PQ	13	07989 001000
The White Hart, Llanddarog	SA32 8NS	11	01267 275395

The Old Moathouse, Kidwelly	SA17 5AX	24	01554 891874
The Welcome to Town, Llanrhidian	SA3 1EH	86	01792 390281
The Worms Head, Rhossili	SA3 1PP	22	01792 390512
The White Rose, Mumbles	SA3 4AR	34	01792 368426
The Cross Keys, Swansea	SA1 3LH	16	01792 630921
The Old House, Llangynwyd	CF34 9SB	37	01656 336033
The Prince of Wales, Kenfig	CF33 4PR	20	01656 740356
The Jolly Sailor, Newton	CF36 5PD	10	01656 782403
The Laleston Inn, Laleston	CF32 0HS	8	01656 652946
The Three Golden Cups, Southerndown	CF32 0RW	13	01656 880432

The Plough & Harrow, Monknash	CF71 7QQ	10	01656 890209
The Old Swan, Llantwit Major	CF61 1SB	11	01446 792230
The Blue Anchor, Aberthaw	CF62 3DD	12	01446 750329
The Bush, St Hilary	CF71 7DP	16	01446 776888
The Market Place, Cowbridge	CF71 7AH	5	01446 774800
The Captain's Wife, Sully	CF64 5UG	30	029 2053 0066
The Baron's Court, Penarth	CF64 1ND	14	029 2000 3197

BIBLIOGRAPHY, SOURCES AND REFERENCES

I am in debt to the following reference sources, which made the compilation of this book possible:

Legends and folklore of Bridgend and the Vale by Graham Loveluck-Edwards (2020)

Hidden Inns of Wales by Peter Long (2003)

Hidden Inns of Wales Edited by Barbara Vesey (2000)

Historic Inns and Taverns of Wales and the Marches by Paul R Davis (1993)

CAMRA's Good Beer Guide (2019)

The Michelin Eating Out in Pubs Guide (2019)

hauntedhappenings.co.uk

historypoints.org

theparanormaldatabase.com

Cardiff the Biography by Dic Mortimer (2014)

An enquiry into the truth of the tradition concerning the Discovery of America, By Prince Madog ab Owen Gwynedd, about the year, 1170 by John Williams (1771)

Traditional Buildings of Britain by RW Brunskill (1981)

Houses of the Welsh Countryside by P Smith (1988)

The Buildings of Britain (Clwyd) by E Hubbard (1986)

The Buildings of Britain (Powys) by R Haslam (1979)

Royal Commission on Ancient and Historic Monuments (Wales) by HMSO

hisdoryan.co.uk

Lettres et Voyages, 1725-1729, by César de Saussure

The Old Villages of Denbighshire and Flintshire by Dewi Morris (2007)

Discovering the Historic Houses of Snowdonia by Margret Dunn (2014)

A historical tour through Monmouthshire, illustrated with views by Sir R. C. Hoare, bart., and other engravings: by William Coxe (1904)

A catalogue of books relating to the history and topography of England, Wales, Scotland, Ireland, by Sir Richard Colt Hoare, Bart (1815)

The Itinerary in Wales of John Leland in or About the Years 1536-1539, by John Leland and Lucy Toulmin Smith (2017)

Local history societies the length and breadth of Wales

The archives of: *South Wales Argus, South Wales Echo, Western Mail, Bristol Mercury, Milford Mercury* and *the Daily Post.*

ACKNOWLEDGEMENTS

I am deeply grateful to the owners, managers, staff and regulars of all the pubs I have visited over the years, for taking the time to regale me with the amazing stories that made it into this book. You are what made this book possible, but more importantly, you are what make the Great British pub such an amazing institution, one which we must all preserve.

OTHER BOOKS BY THE AUTHOR:
Legends and Folklore of Bridgend and the Vale
Available from Amazon (UK)

For more information on any of these books, to buy further copies,
or for more information on the author, please visit
www.grahamloveluckedwards.co.uk